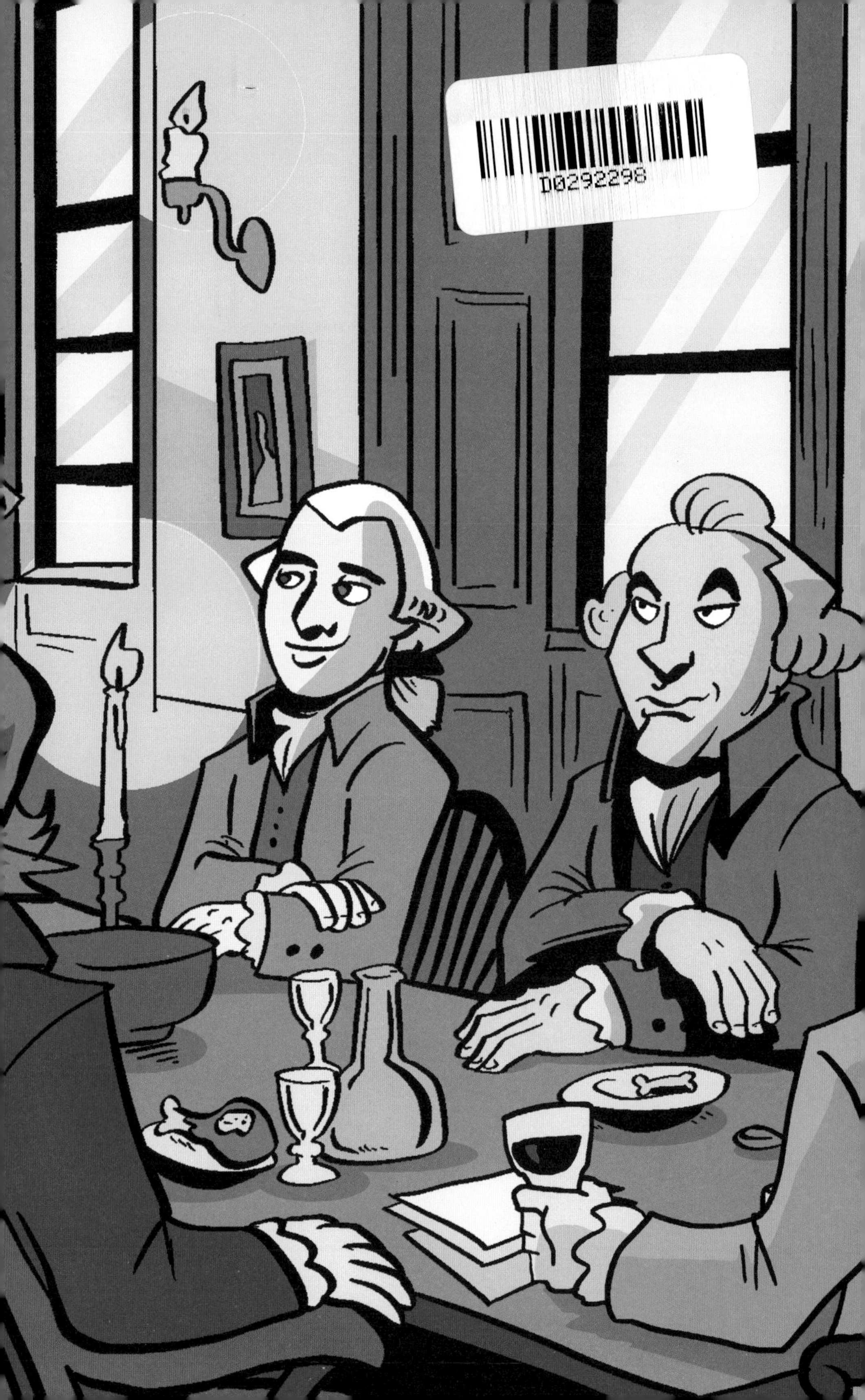

SHOW ME HISTORY!™

GEORGE WASHINGTON

SOLDIER and STATESMAN!

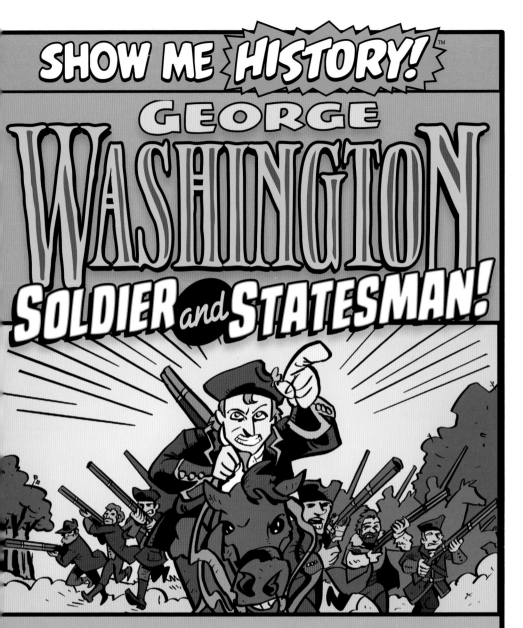

BY
MARK SHULMAN

ILLUSTRATED BY
KELLY TINDALL

LETTERING & DESIGN BY
SWELL TYPE

COVER ART BY
IAN CHURCHILL

PORTABLE
PRESS

SAN DIEGO, CALIFORNIA

Portable Press
An imprint of Printers Row Publishing Group
10350 Barnes Canyon Road, Suite 100, San Diego, CA 92121
www.portablepress.com • mail@portablepress.com

Copyright © 2020 Portable Press

Printers Row Publishing Group is a division of Readerlink Distribution Services, LLC. Portable Press is a registered trademark of Readerlink Distribution Services, LLC.

Correspondence regarding the content of this book should be sent to Portable Press, Editorial Department, at the above address. Author and illustrator inquiries should be sent to Oomf, Inc., www.oomf.com.

Portable Press
Publisher: Peter Norton • Associate Publisher: Ana Parker
Senior Developmental Editor: April Graham Farr
Developmental Editor: Vicki Jaeger
Production Team: Julie Greene, Rusty von Dyl

O•MF Produced by Oomf, Inc., www.Oomf.com
Director: Mark Shulman
Producer: James Buckley Jr.

Author: Mark Shulman
Illustrator: Kelly Tindall
Inks for pages 26-27 by Scott Chantler
Colorist: Shane Corn
Assistant Editor: Michael Centore
Research: Christine Fulton
Lettering & design by Swell Type: John Roshell, Forest Dempsey,
    Sarah Jacobs, Drewes McFarling
Cover illustrator: Ian Churchill

Library of Congress Control Number: 2020941741

ISBN: 978-1-64517-410-3

Printed in China

24 23 22 21 20   1 2 3 4 5

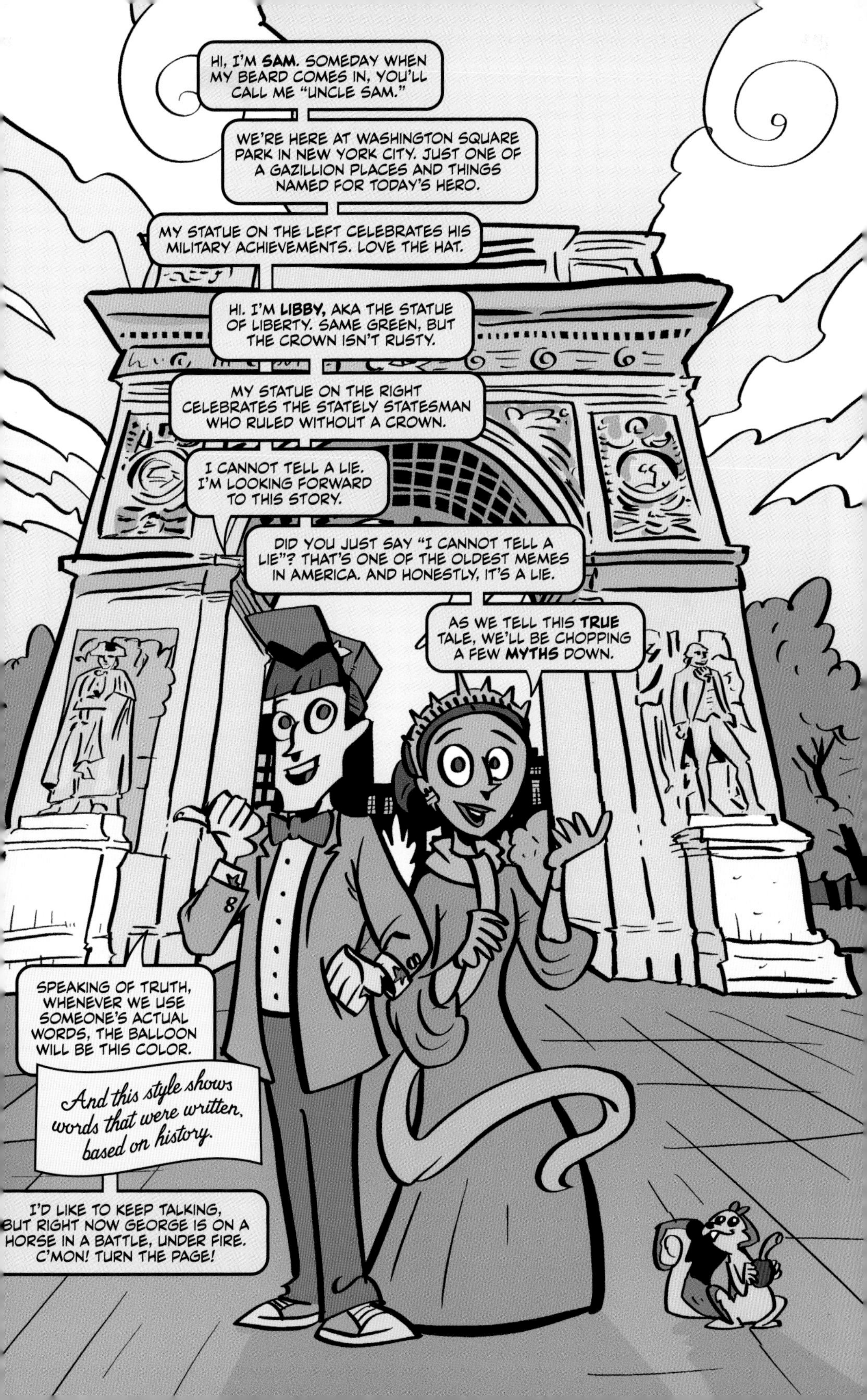
HI, I'M SAM. SOMEDAY WHEN MY BEARD COMES IN, YOU'LL CALL ME "UNCLE SAM."
WE'RE HERE AT WASHINGTON SQUARE PARK IN NEW YORK CITY. JUST ONE OF A GAZILLION PLACES AND THINGS NAMED FOR TODAY'S HERO.
MY STATUE ON THE LEFT CELEBRATES HIS MILITARY ACHIEVEMENTS. LOVE THE HAT.
HI. I'M LIBBY, AKA THE STATUE OF LIBERTY. SAME GREEN, BUT THE CROWN ISN'T RUSTY.
MY STATUE ON THE RIGHT CELEBRATES THE STATELY STATESMAN WHO RULED WITHOUT A CROWN.
I CANNOT TELL A LIE. I'M LOOKING FORWARD TO THIS STORY.
DID YOU JUST SAY "I CANNOT TELL A LIE"? THAT'S ONE OF THE OLDEST MEMES IN AMERICA. AND HONESTLY, IT'S A LIE.
AS WE TELL THIS TRUE TALE, WE'LL BE CHOPPING A FEW MYTHS DOWN.
SPEAKING OF TRUTH, WHENEVER WE USE SOMEONE'S ACTUAL WORDS, THE BALLOON WILL BE THIS COLOR.
And this style shows words that were written, based on history.
I'D LIKE TO KEEP TALKING, BUT RIGHT NOW GEORGE IS ON A HORSE IN A BATTLE, UNDER FIRE. C'MON! TURN THE PAGE!
8

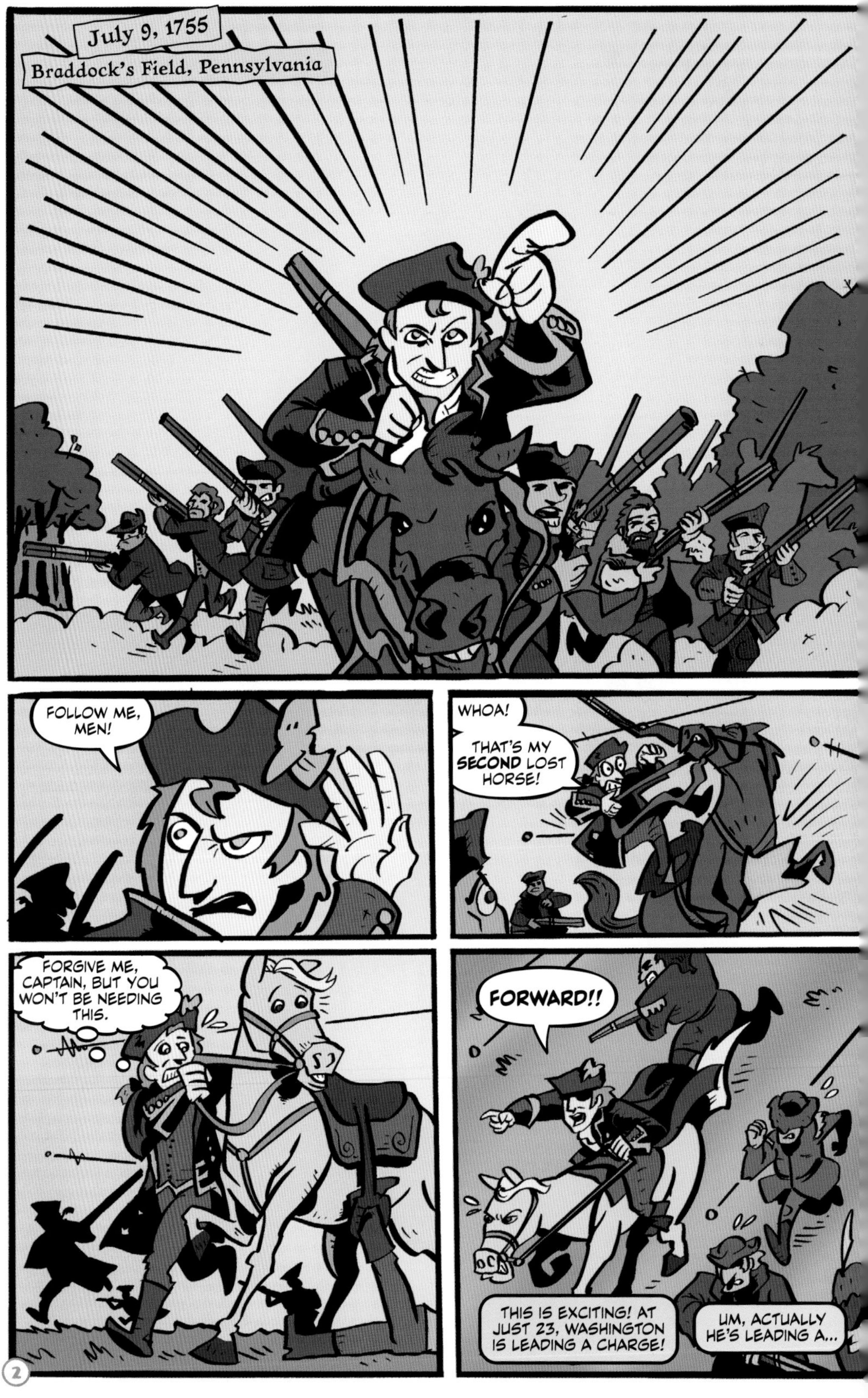
July 9, 1755
Braddock's Field, Pennsylvania
FOLLOW ME, MEN!
WHOA!
THAT'S MY SECOND LOST HORSE!
FORGIVE ME, CAPTAIN, BUT YOU WON'T BE NEEDING THIS.
FORWARD!!
THIS IS EXCITING! AT JUST 23, WASHINGTON IS LEADING A CHARGE!
UM, ACTUALLY HE'S LEADING A...

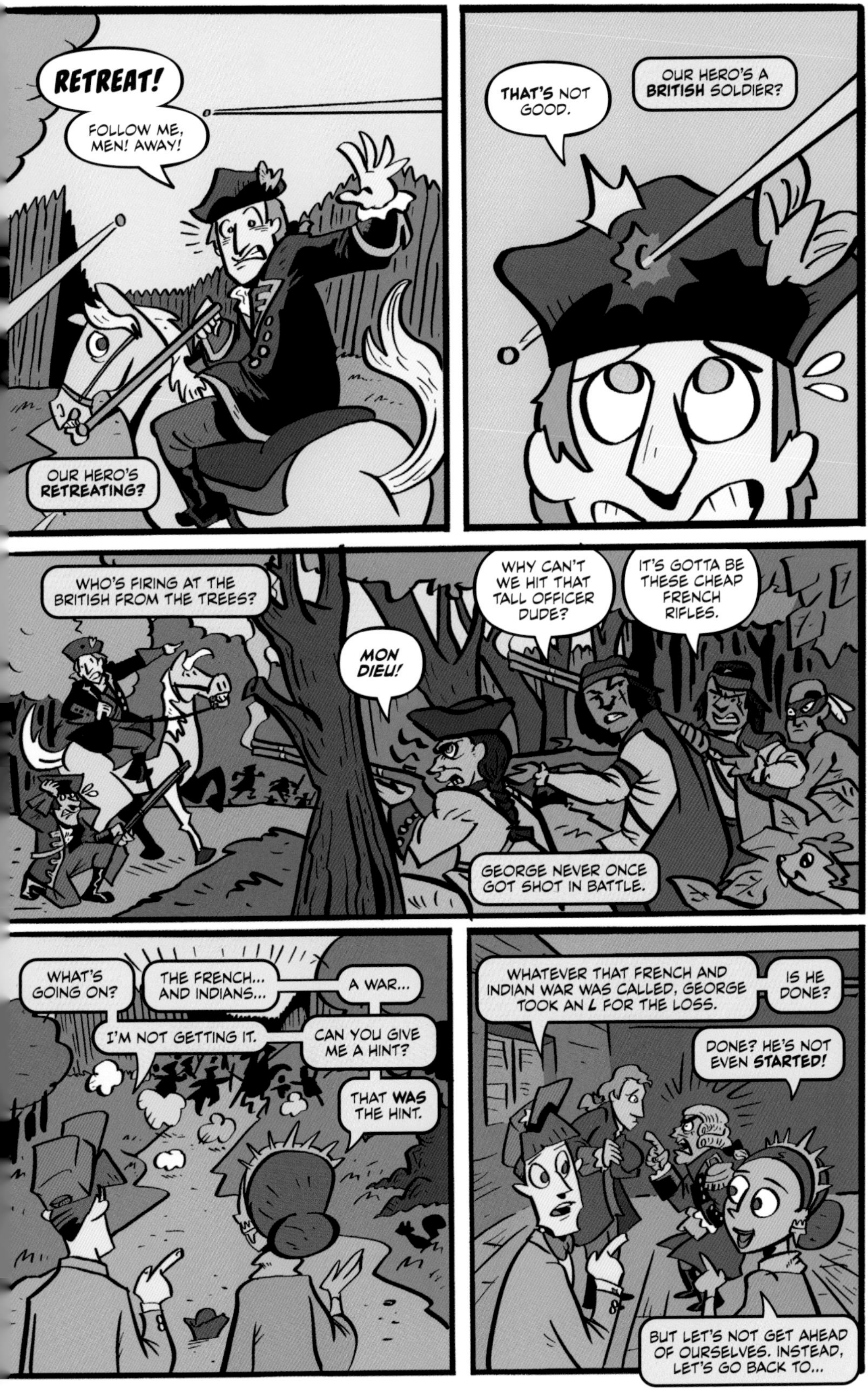
RETREAT!
FOLLOW ME, MEN! AWAY!
OUR HERO'S RETREATING?
THAT'S NOT GOOD.
OUR HERO'S A BRITISH SOLDIER?
WHO'S FIRING AT THE BRITISH FROM THE TREES?
MON DIEU!
WHY CAN'T WE HIT THAT TALL OFFICER DUDE?
IT'S GOTTA BE THESE CHEAP FRENCH RIFLES.
GEORGE NEVER ONCE GOT SHOT IN BATTLE.
WHAT'S GOING ON?
THE FRENCH... AND INDIANS...
A WAR...
I'M NOT GETTING IT.
CAN YOU GIVE ME A HINT?
THAT WAS THE HINT.
WHATEVER THAT FRENCH AND INDIAN WAR WAS CALLED, GEORGE TOOK AN L FOR THE LOSS.
IS HE DONE?
DONE? HE'S NOT EVEN STARTED!
BUT LET'S NOT GET AHEAD OF OURSELVES. INSTEAD, LET'S GO BACK TO...

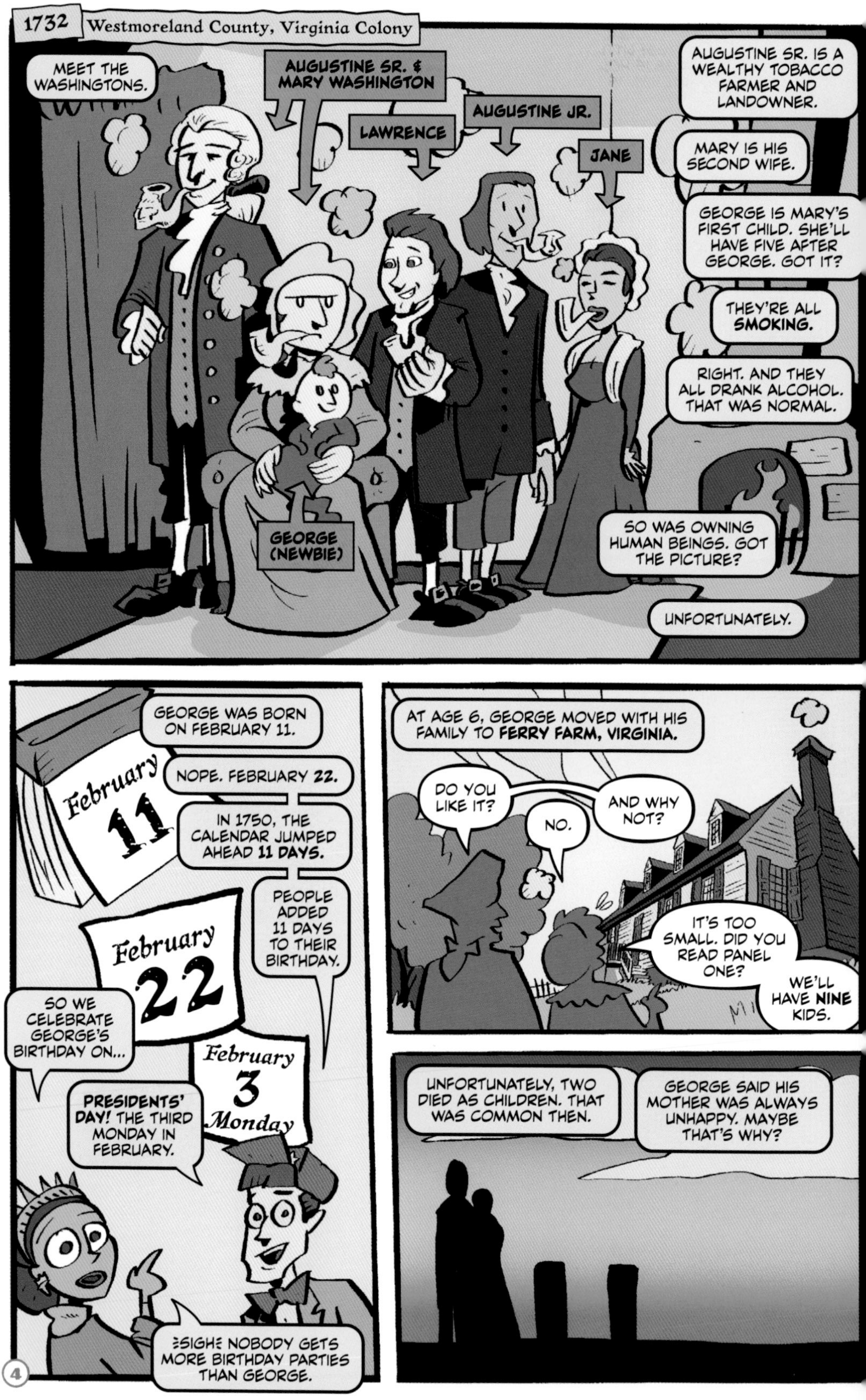

1732
Westmoreland County, Virginia Colony
MEET THE WASHINGTONS.
AUGUSTINE SR. & MARY WASHINGTON
LAWRENCE
AUGUSTINE JR.
JANE
GEORGE (NEWBIE)
AUGUSTINE SR. IS A WEALTHY TOBACCO FARMER AND LANDOWNER.
MARY IS HIS SECOND WIFE.
GEORGE IS MARY'S FIRST CHILD. SHE'LL HAVE FIVE AFTER GEORGE. GOT IT?
THEY'RE ALL **SMOKING.**
RIGHT. AND THEY ALL DRANK ALCOHOL. THAT WAS NORMAL.
SO WAS OWNING HUMAN BEINGS. GOT THE PICTURE?
UNFORTUNATELY.
GEORGE WAS BORN ON FEBRUARY 11.
February 11
NOPE. FEBRUARY **22.**
IN 1750, THE CALENDAR JUMPED AHEAD **11 DAYS.**
PEOPLE ADDED 11 DAYS TO THEIR BIRTHDAY.
February 22
SO WE CELEBRATE GEORGE'S BIRTHDAY ON...
February 3 Monday
PRESIDENTS' DAY! THE THIRD MONDAY IN FEBRUARY.
SIGH NOBODY GETS MORE BIRTHDAY PARTIES THAN GEORGE.
AT AGE 6, GEORGE MOVED WITH HIS FAMILY TO **FERRY FARM, VIRGINIA.**
DO YOU LIKE IT?
NO.
AND WHY NOT?
IT'S TOO SMALL. DID YOU READ PANEL ONE?
WE'LL HAVE **NINE** KIDS.
UNFORTUNATELY, TWO DIED AS CHILDREN. THAT WAS COMMON THEN.
GEORGE SAID HIS MOTHER WAS ALWAYS UNHAPPY. MAYBE THAT'S WHY?

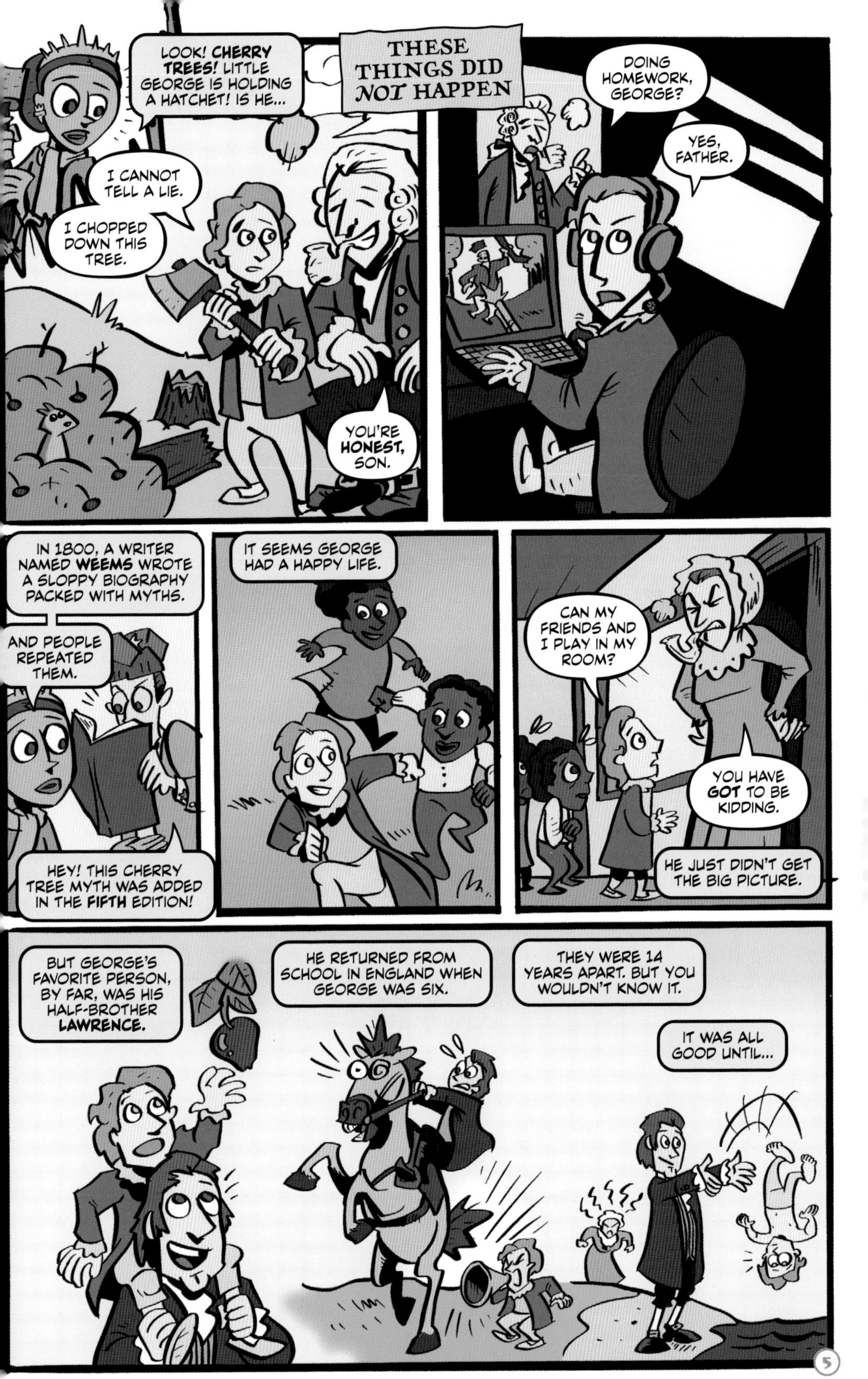
LOOK! CHERRY TREES! LITTLE GEORGE IS HOLDING A HATCHET! IS HE...
THESE THINGS DID NOT HAPPEN
I CANNOT TELL A LIE.
I CHOPPED DOWN THIS TREE.
YOU'RE HONEST, SON.
DOING HOMEWORK, GEORGE?
YES, FATHER.
IN 1800, A WRITER NAMED WEEMS WROTE A SLOPPY BIOGRAPHY PACKED WITH MYTHS.
AND PEOPLE REPEATED THEM.
HEY! THIS CHERRY TREE MYTH WAS ADDED IN THE FIFTH EDITION!
IT SEEMS GEORGE HAD A HAPPY LIFE.
CAN MY FRIENDS AND I PLAY IN MY ROOM?
YOU HAVE GOT TO BE KIDDING.
HE JUST DIDN'T GET THE BIG PICTURE.
BUT GEORGE'S FAVORITE PERSON, BY FAR, WAS HIS HALF-BROTHER LAWRENCE.
HE RETURNED FROM SCHOOL IN ENGLAND WHEN GEORGE WAS SIX.
THEY WERE 14 YEARS APART. BUT YOU WOULDN'T KNOW IT.
IT WAS ALL GOOD UNTIL...

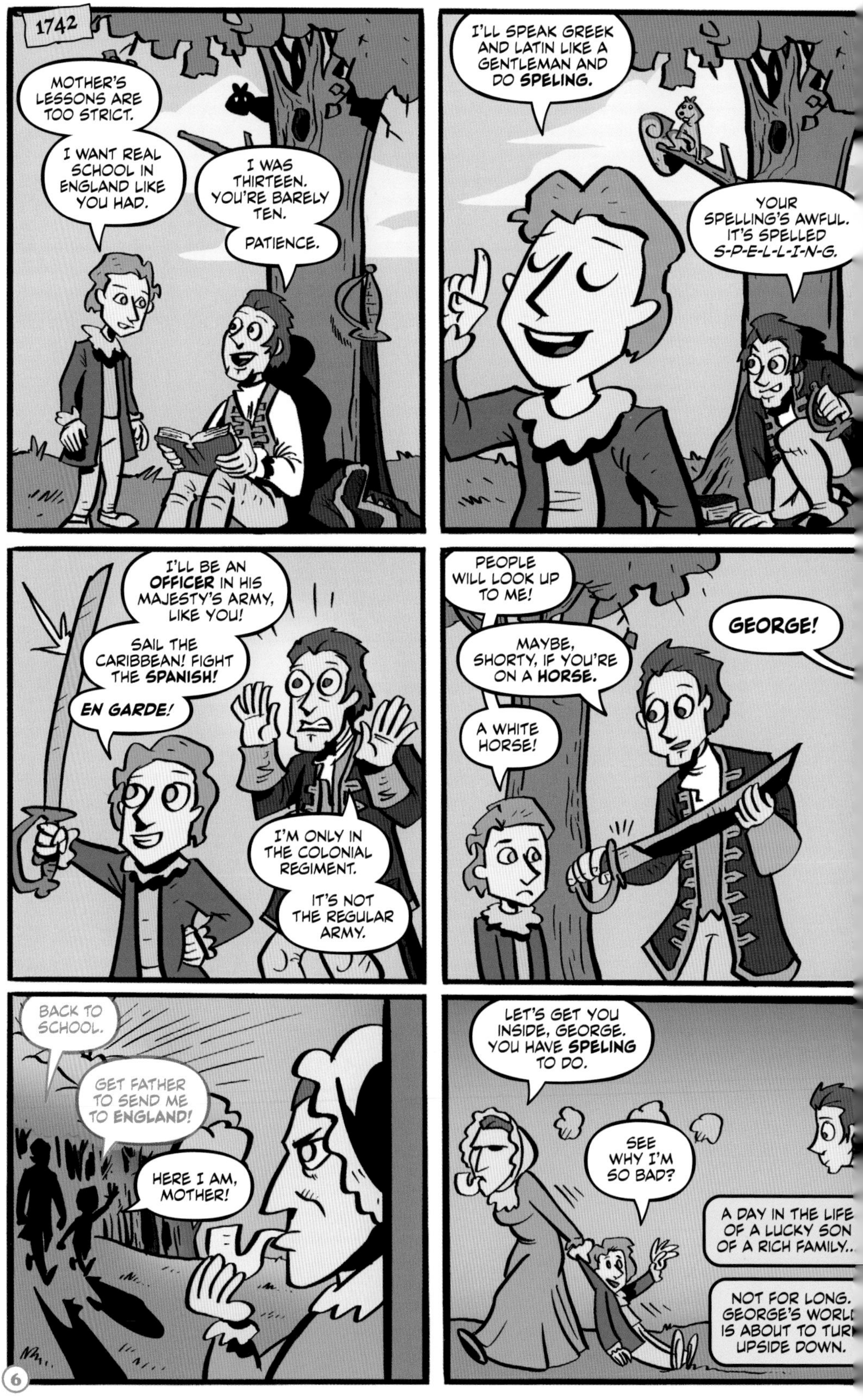

1742
MOTHER'S LESSONS ARE TOO STRICT.
I WANT REAL SCHOOL IN ENGLAND LIKE YOU HAD.
I WAS THIRTEEN. YOU'RE BARELY TEN.
PATIENCE.
I'LL SPEAK GREEK AND LATIN LIKE A GENTLEMAN AND DO **SPELING.**
YOUR SPELLING'S AWFUL. IT'S SPELLED *S-P-E-L-L-I-N-G.*
I'LL BE AN **OFFICER** IN HIS MAJESTY'S ARMY, LIKE YOU!
SAIL THE CARIBBEAN! FIGHT THE **SPANISH!**
EN GARDE!
I'M ONLY IN THE COLONIAL REGIMENT.
IT'S NOT THE REGULAR ARMY.
PEOPLE WILL LOOK UP TO ME!
MAYBE, SHORTY, IF YOU'RE ON A **HORSE.**
A WHITE HORSE!
GEORGE!
BACK TO SCHOOL.
GET FATHER TO SEND ME TO **ENGLAND!**
HERE I AM, MOTHER!
LET'S GET YOU INSIDE, GEORGE. YOU HAVE **SPELING** TO DO.
SEE WHY I'M SO BAD?
A DAY IN THE LIFE OF A LUCKY SON OF A RICH FAMILY...
NOT FOR LONG. GEORGE'S WORLD IS ABOUT TO TURN UPSIDE DOWN.

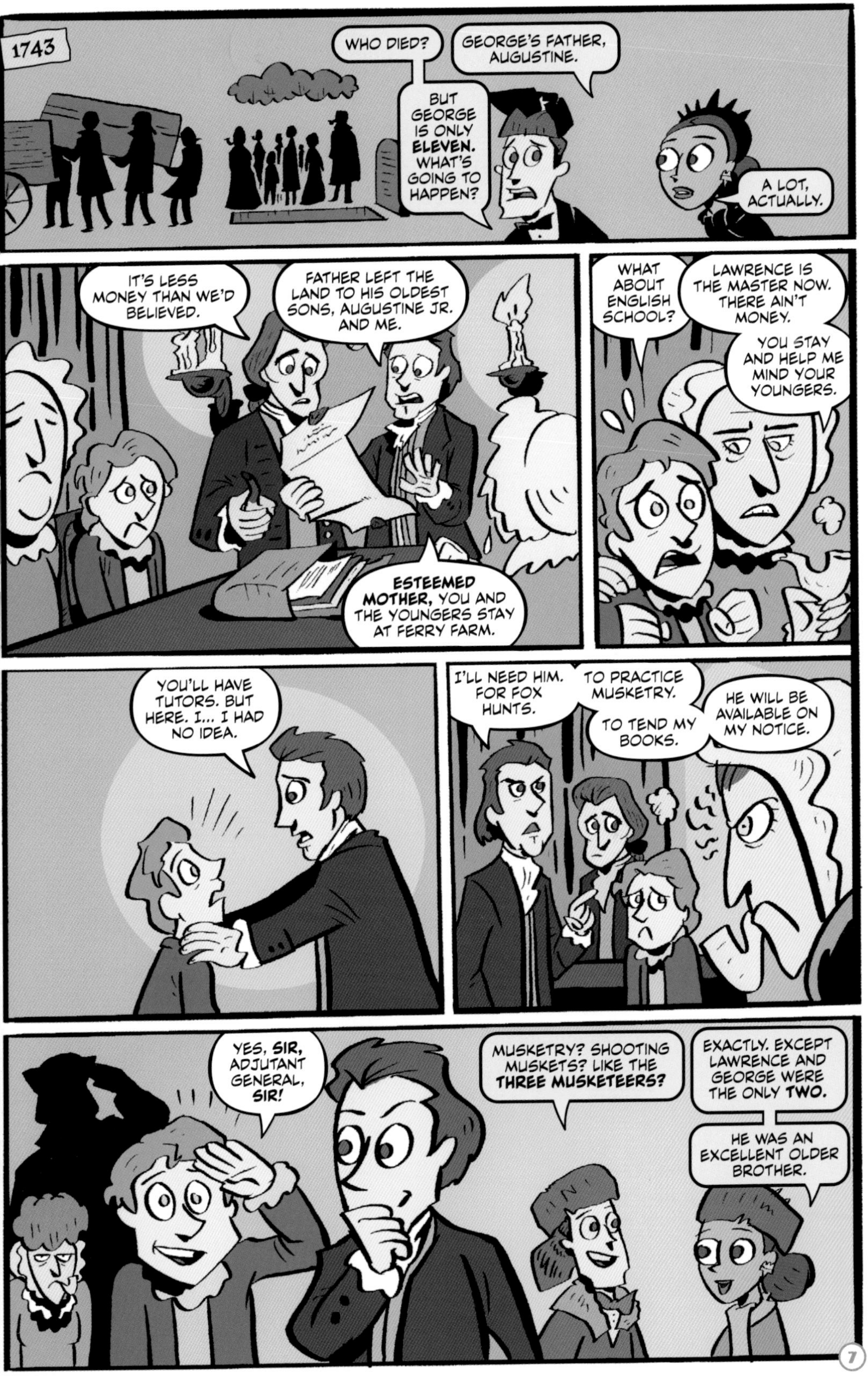
1743
WHO DIED?
GEORGE'S FATHER, AUGUSTINE.
BUT GEORGE IS ONLY **ELEVEN.** WHAT'S GOING TO HAPPEN?
A LOT, ACTUALLY.
IT'S LESS MONEY THAN WE'D BELIEVED.
FATHER LEFT THE LAND TO HIS OLDEST SONS, AUGUSTINE JR. AND ME.
ESTEEMED MOTHER, YOU AND THE YOUNGERS STAY AT FERRY FARM.
WHAT ABOUT ENGLISH SCHOOL?
LAWRENCE IS THE MASTER NOW. THERE AIN'T MONEY.
YOU STAY AND HELP ME MIND YOUR YOUNGERS.
YOU'LL HAVE TUTORS. BUT HERE. I... I HAD NO IDEA.
I'LL NEED HIM. FOR FOX HUNTS.
TO PRACTICE MUSKETRY.
TO TEND MY BOOKS.
HE WILL BE AVAILABLE ON MY NOTICE.
YES, **SIR,** ADJUTANT GENERAL, **SIR!**
MUSKETRY? SHOOTING MUSKETS? LIKE THE **THREE MUSKETEERS?**
EXACTLY. EXCEPT LAWRENCE AND GEORGE WERE THE ONLY **TWO.**
HE WAS AN EXCELLENT OLDER BROTHER.

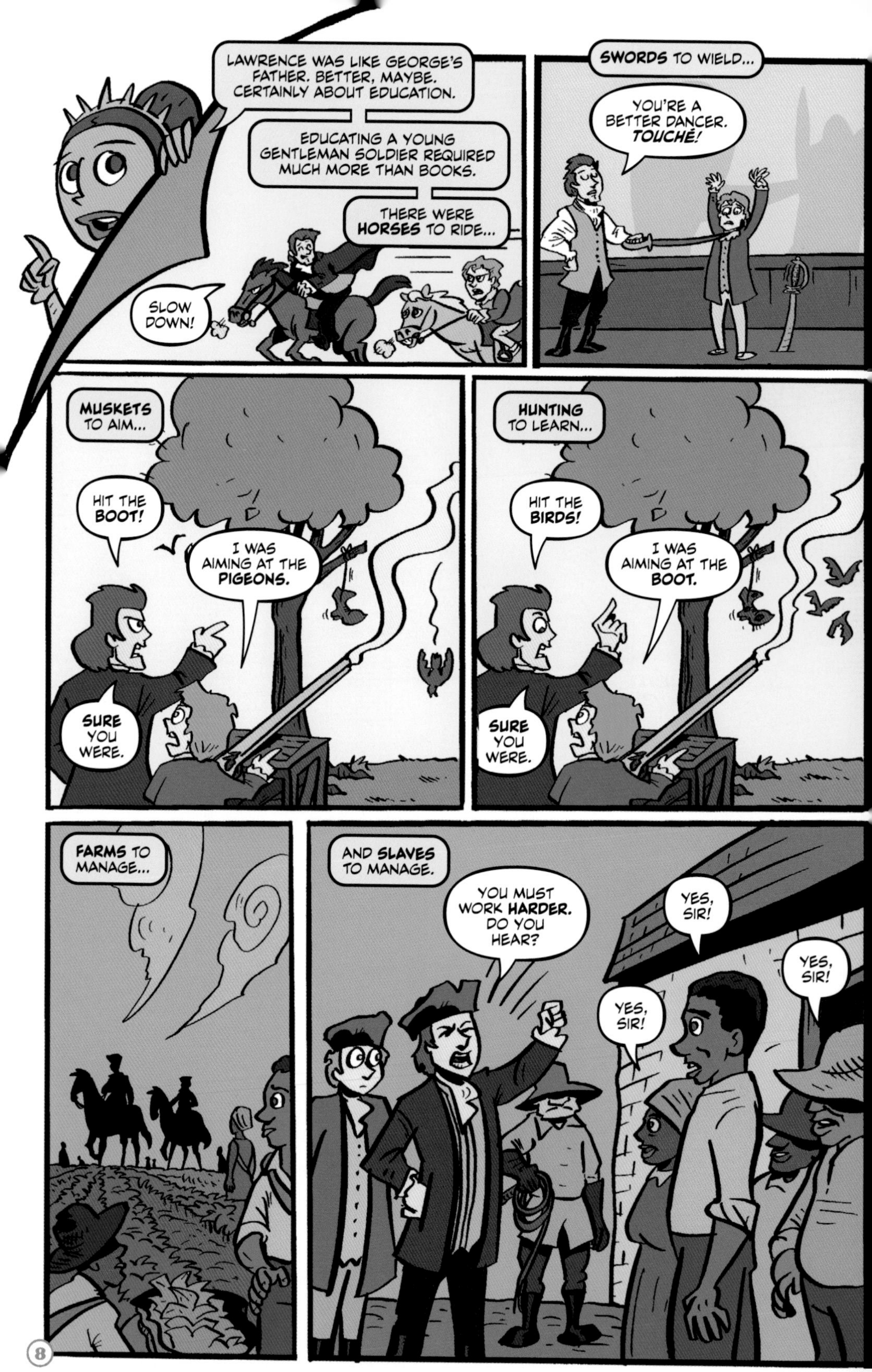
LAWRENCE WAS LIKE GEORGE'S FATHER. BETTER, MAYBE. CERTAINLY ABOUT EDUCATION.
EDUCATING A YOUNG GENTLEMAN SOLDIER REQUIRED MUCH MORE THAN BOOKS.
THERE WERE HORSES TO RIDE...
SLOW DOWN!
SWORDS TO WIELD...
YOU'RE A BETTER DANCER. TOUCHÉ!
MUSKETS TO AIM...
HIT THE BOOT!
I WAS AIMING AT THE PIGEONS.
SURE YOU WERE.
HUNTING TO LEARN...
HIT THE BIRDS!
I WAS AIMING AT THE BOOT.
SURE YOU WERE.
FARMS TO MANAGE...
AND SLAVES TO MANAGE.
YOU MUST WORK HARDER. DO YOU HEAR?
YES, SIR!
YES, SIR!
YES, SIR!

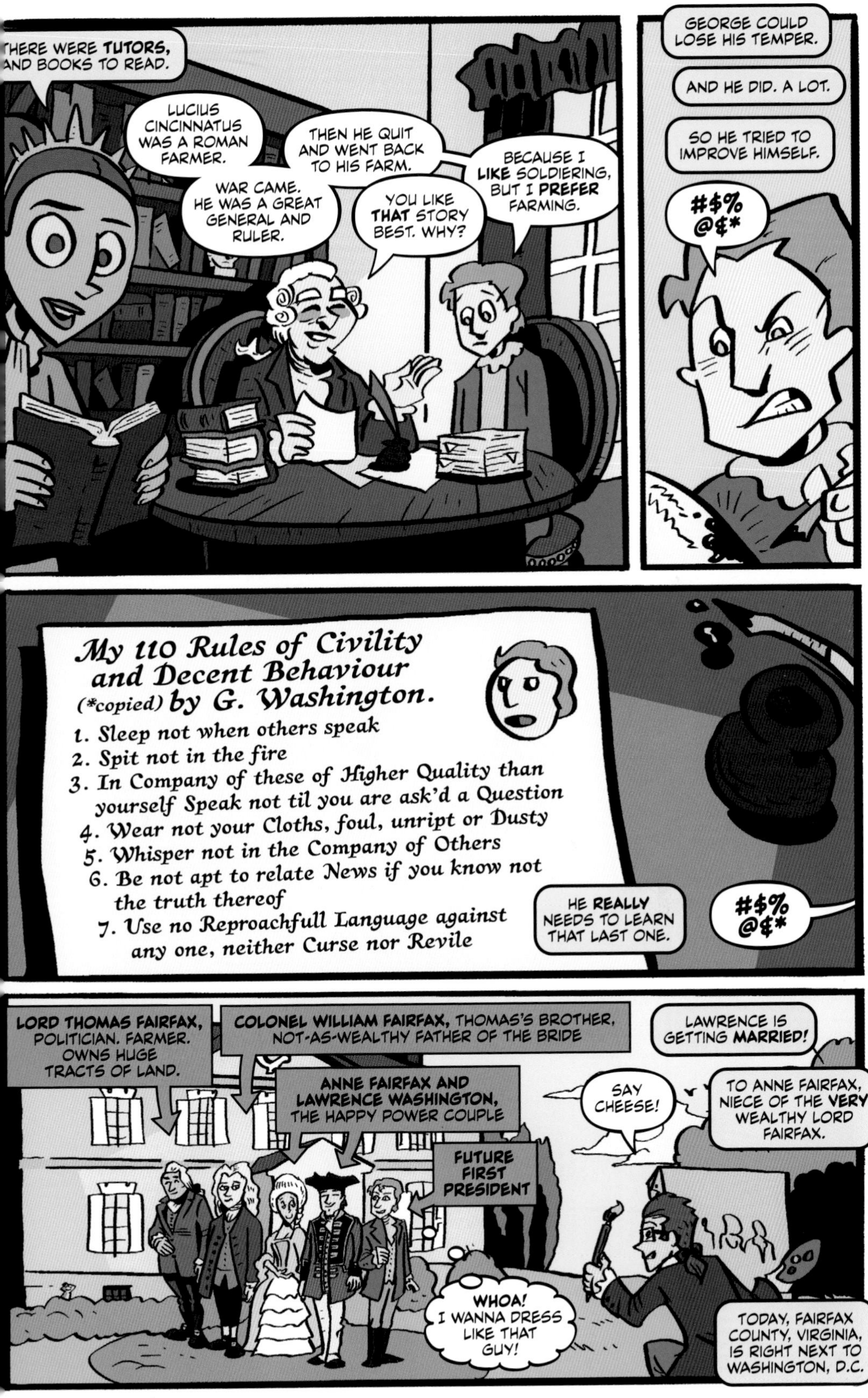

THERE WERE TUTORS, AND BOOKS TO READ.
LUCIUS CINCINNATUS WAS A ROMAN FARMER.
WAR CAME. HE WAS A GREAT GENERAL AND RULER.
THEN HE QUIT AND WENT BACK TO HIS FARM.
YOU LIKE THAT STORY BEST. WHY?
BECAUSE I LIKE SOLDIERING, BUT I PREFER FARMING.
GEORGE COULD LOSE HIS TEMPER.
AND HE DID. A LOT.
SO HE TRIED TO IMPROVE HIMSELF.
#$% @&*
My 110 Rules of Civility and Decent Behaviour (*copied) by G. Washington.
1. Sleep not when others speak
2. Spit not in the fire
3. In Company of these of Higher Quality than yourself Speak not til you are ask'd a Question
4. Wear not your Cloths, foul, unript or Dusty
5. Whisper not in the Company of Others
6. Be not apt to relate News if you know not the truth thereof
7. Use no Reproachfull Language against any one, neither Curse nor Revile
HE REALLY NEEDS TO LEARN THAT LAST ONE.
#$% @&*
LORD THOMAS FAIRFAX, POLITICIAN. FARMER. OWNS HUGE TRACTS OF LAND.
COLONEL WILLIAM FAIRFAX, THOMAS'S BROTHER, NOT-AS-WEALTHY FATHER OF THE BRIDE
LAWRENCE IS GETTING MARRIED!
ANNE FAIRFAX AND LAWRENCE WASHINGTON, THE HAPPY POWER COUPLE
SAY CHEESE!
TO ANNE FAIRFAX, NIECE OF THE VERY WEALTHY LORD FAIRFAX.
FUTURE FIRST PRESIDENT
WHOA! I WANNA DRESS LIKE THAT GUY!
TODAY, FAIRFAX COUNTY, VIRGINIA, IS RIGHT NEXT TO WASHINGTON, D.C.

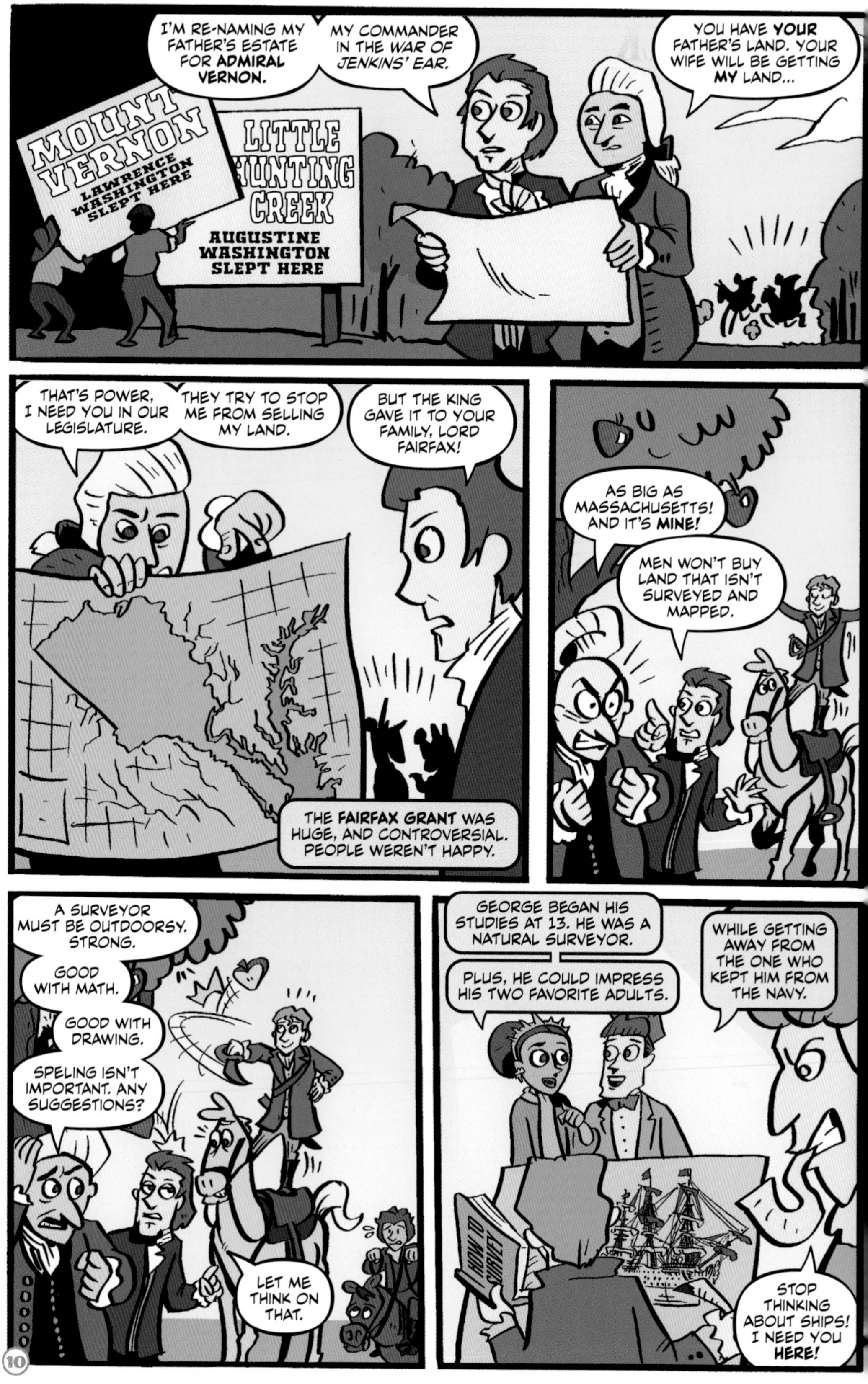
I'M RE-NAMING MY FATHER'S ESTATE FOR **ADMIRAL VERNON.**
MY COMMANDER IN THE *WAR OF JENKINS' EAR.*
MOUNT VERNON
LAWRENCE WASHINGTON SLEPT HERE
LITTLE HUNTING CREEK
AUGUSTINE WASHINGTON SLEPT HERE
YOU HAVE **YOUR** FATHER'S LAND. YOUR WIFE WILL BE GETTING **MY** LAND...
THAT'S POWER, I NEED YOU IN OUR LEGISLATURE.
THEY TRY TO STOP ME FROM SELLING MY LAND.
BUT THE KING GAVE IT TO YOUR FAMILY, LORD FAIRFAX!
THE **FAIRFAX GRANT** WAS HUGE, AND CONTROVERSIAL. PEOPLE WEREN'T HAPPY.
AS BIG AS MASSACHUSETTS! AND IT'S **MINE!**
MEN WON'T BUY LAND THAT ISN'T SURVEYED AND MAPPED.
A SURVEYOR MUST BE OUTDOORSY. STRONG.
GOOD WITH MATH.
GOOD WITH DRAWING.
SPELING ISN'T IMPORTANT. ANY SUGGESTIONS?
LET ME THINK ON THAT.
GEORGE BEGAN HIS STUDIES AT 13. HE WAS A NATURAL SURVEYOR.
PLUS, HE COULD IMPRESS HIS TWO FAVORITE ADULTS.
WHILE GETTING AWAY FROM THE ONE WHO KEPT HIM FROM THE NAVY.
HOW TO SURVEY
STOP THINKING ABOUT SHIPS! I NEED YOU **HERE!**

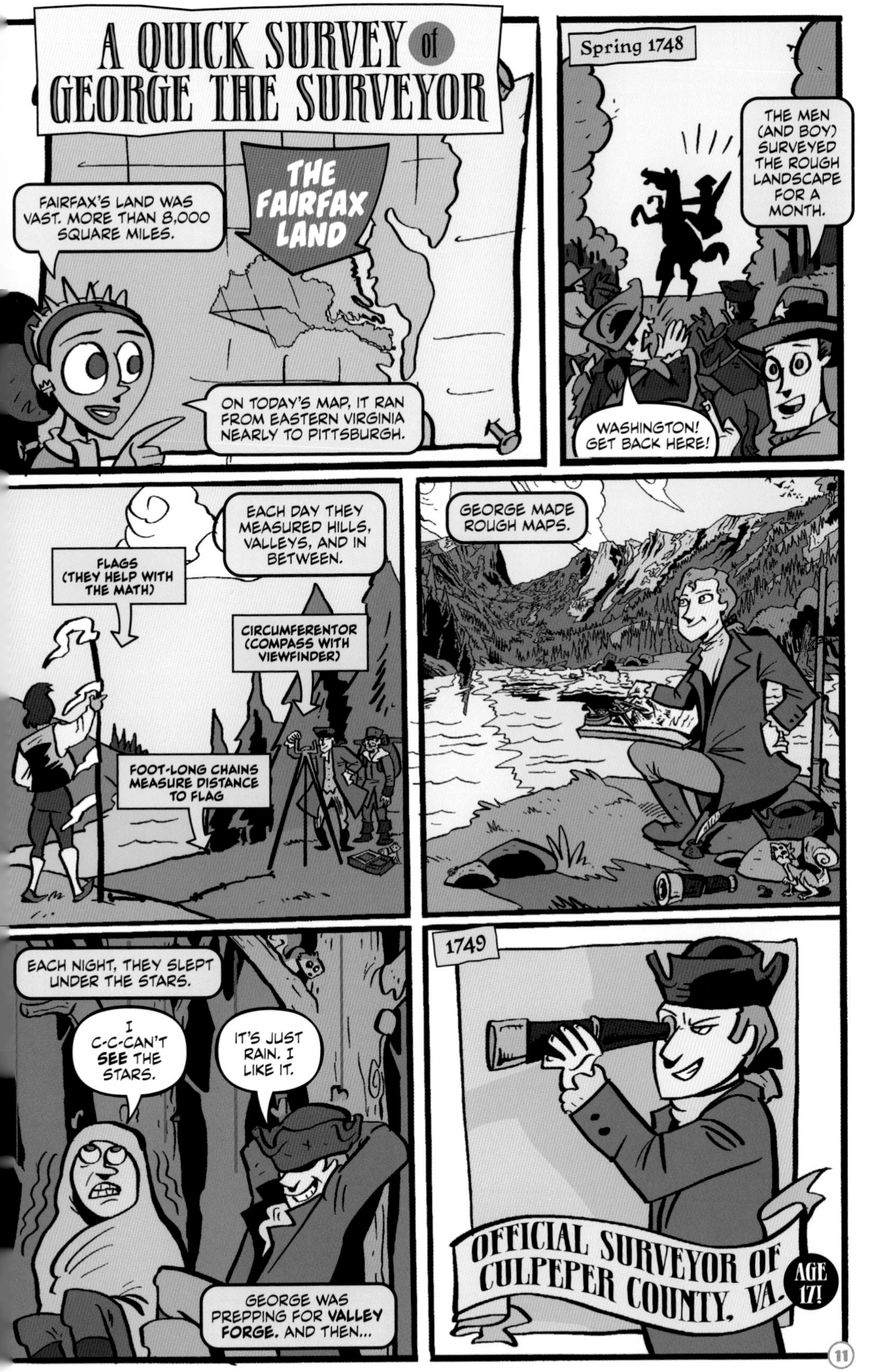
A QUICK SURVEY of GEORGE THE SURVEYOR
FAIRFAX'S LAND WAS VAST. MORE THAN 8,000 SQUARE MILES.
THE FAIRFAX LAND
ON TODAY'S MAP, IT RAN FROM EASTERN VIRGINIA NEARLY TO PITTSBURGH.
Spring 1748
THE MEN (AND BOY) SURVEYED THE ROUGH LANDSCAPE FOR A MONTH.
WASHINGTON! GET BACK HERE!
EACH DAY THEY MEASURED HILLS, VALLEYS, AND IN BETWEEN.
FLAGS (THEY HELP WITH THE MATH)
CIRCUMFERENTOR (COMPASS WITH VIEWFINDER)
FOOT-LONG CHAINS MEASURE DISTANCE TO FLAG
GEORGE MADE ROUGH MAPS.
EACH NIGHT, THEY SLEPT UNDER THE STARS.
I C-C-CAN'T SEE THE STARS.
IT'S JUST RAIN. I LIKE IT.
GEORGE WAS PREPPING FOR VALLEY FORGE. AND THEN...
1749
OFFICIAL SURVEYOR OF CULPEPER COUNTY, VA.
AGE 17!

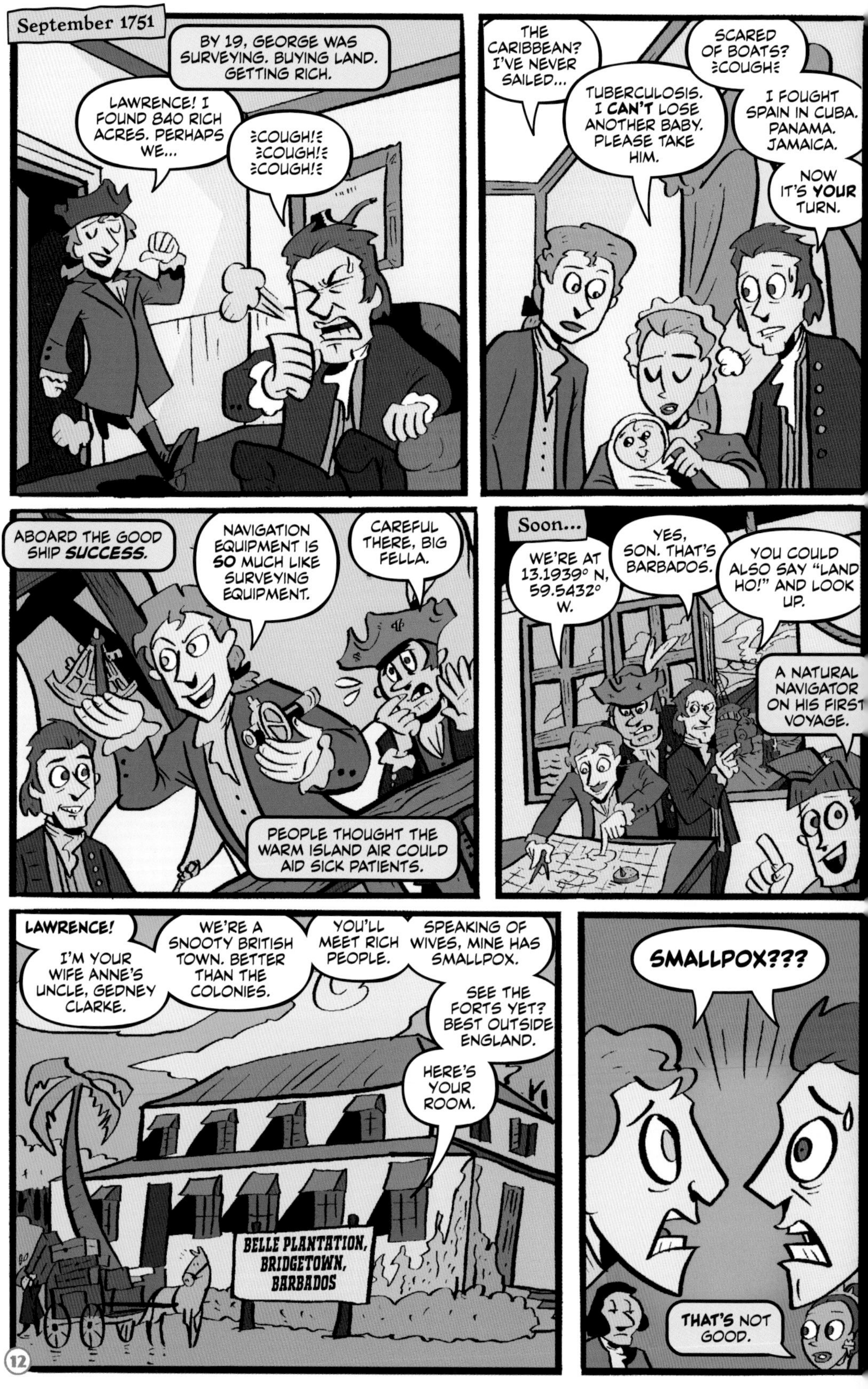
September 1751
BY 19, GEORGE WAS SURVEYING. BUYING LAND. GETTING RICH.
LAWRENCE! I FOUND 840 RICH ACRES. PERHAPS WE...
COUGH! COUGH! COUGH!
THE CARIBBEAN? I'VE NEVER SAILED...
TUBERCULOSIS. I **CAN'T** LOSE ANOTHER BABY. PLEASE TAKE HIM.
SCARED OF BOATS? COUGH
I FOUGHT SPAIN IN CUBA. PANAMA. JAMAICA.
NOW IT'S **YOUR** TURN.
ABOARD THE GOOD SHIP ***SUCCESS.***
NAVIGATION EQUIPMENT IS **SO** MUCH LIKE SURVEYING EQUIPMENT.
CAREFUL THERE, BIG FELLA.
PEOPLE THOUGHT THE WARM ISLAND AIR COULD AID SICK PATIENTS.
Soon...
WE'RE AT 13.1939° N, 59.5432° W.
YES, SON. THAT'S BARBADOS.
YOU COULD ALSO SAY "LAND HO!" AND LOOK UP.
A NATURAL NAVIGATOR ON HIS FIRST VOYAGE.
LAWRENCE!
I'M YOUR WIFE ANNE'S UNCLE, GEDNEY CLARKE.
WE'RE A SNOOTY BRITISH TOWN. BETTER THAN THE COLONIES.
YOU'LL MEET RICH PEOPLE.
SPEAKING OF WIVES, MINE HAS SMALLPOX.
SEE THE FORTS YET? BEST OUTSIDE ENGLAND.
HERE'S YOUR ROOM.
BELLE PLANTATION, BRIDGETOWN, BARBADOS
SMALLPOX???
THAT'S NOT GOOD.

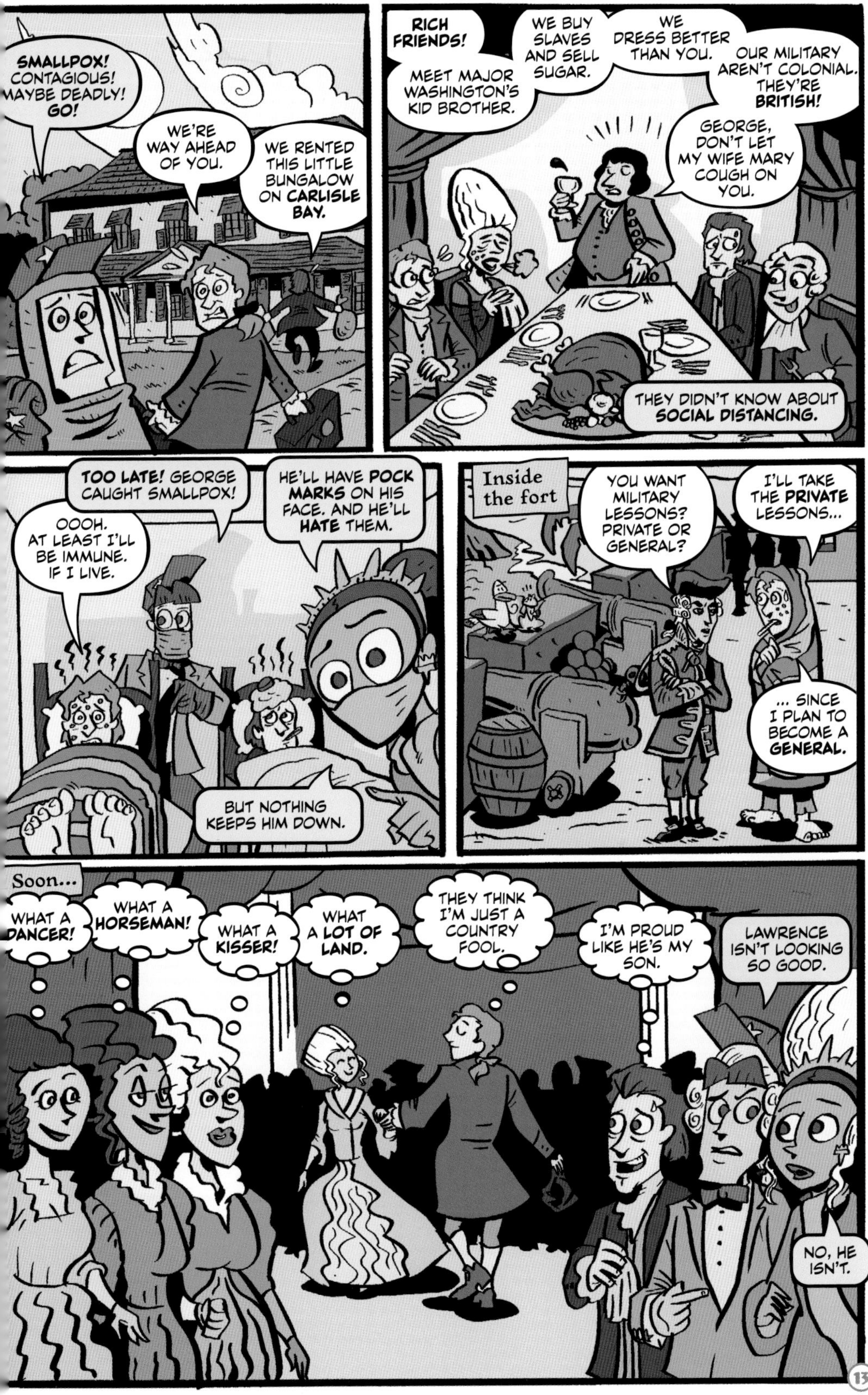
SMALLPOX! CONTAGIOUS! MAYBE DEADLY! GO!
WE'RE WAY AHEAD OF YOU.
WE RENTED THIS LITTLE BUNGALOW ON CARLISLE BAY.
RICH FRIENDS!
MEET MAJOR WASHINGTON'S KID BROTHER.
WE BUY SLAVES AND SELL SUGAR.
WE DRESS BETTER THAN YOU.
OUR MILITARY AREN'T COLONIAL. THEY'RE BRITISH!
GEORGE, DON'T LET MY WIFE MARY COUGH ON YOU.
THEY DIDN'T KNOW ABOUT SOCIAL DISTANCING.
TOO LATE! GEORGE CAUGHT SMALLPOX!
OOOH. AT LEAST I'LL BE IMMUNE. IF I LIVE.
HE'LL HAVE POCK MARKS ON HIS FACE. AND HE'LL HATE THEM.
BUT NOTHING KEEPS HIM DOWN.
Inside the fort
YOU WANT MILITARY LESSONS? PRIVATE OR GENERAL?
I'LL TAKE THE PRIVATE LESSONS...
... SINCE I PLAN TO BECOME A GENERAL.
Soon...
WHAT A DANCER!
WHAT A HORSEMAN!
WHAT A KISSER!
WHAT A LOT OF LAND.
THEY THINK I'M JUST A COUNTRY FOOL.
I'M PROUD LIKE HE'S MY SON.
LAWRENCE ISN'T LOOKING SO GOOD.
NO, HE ISN'T.

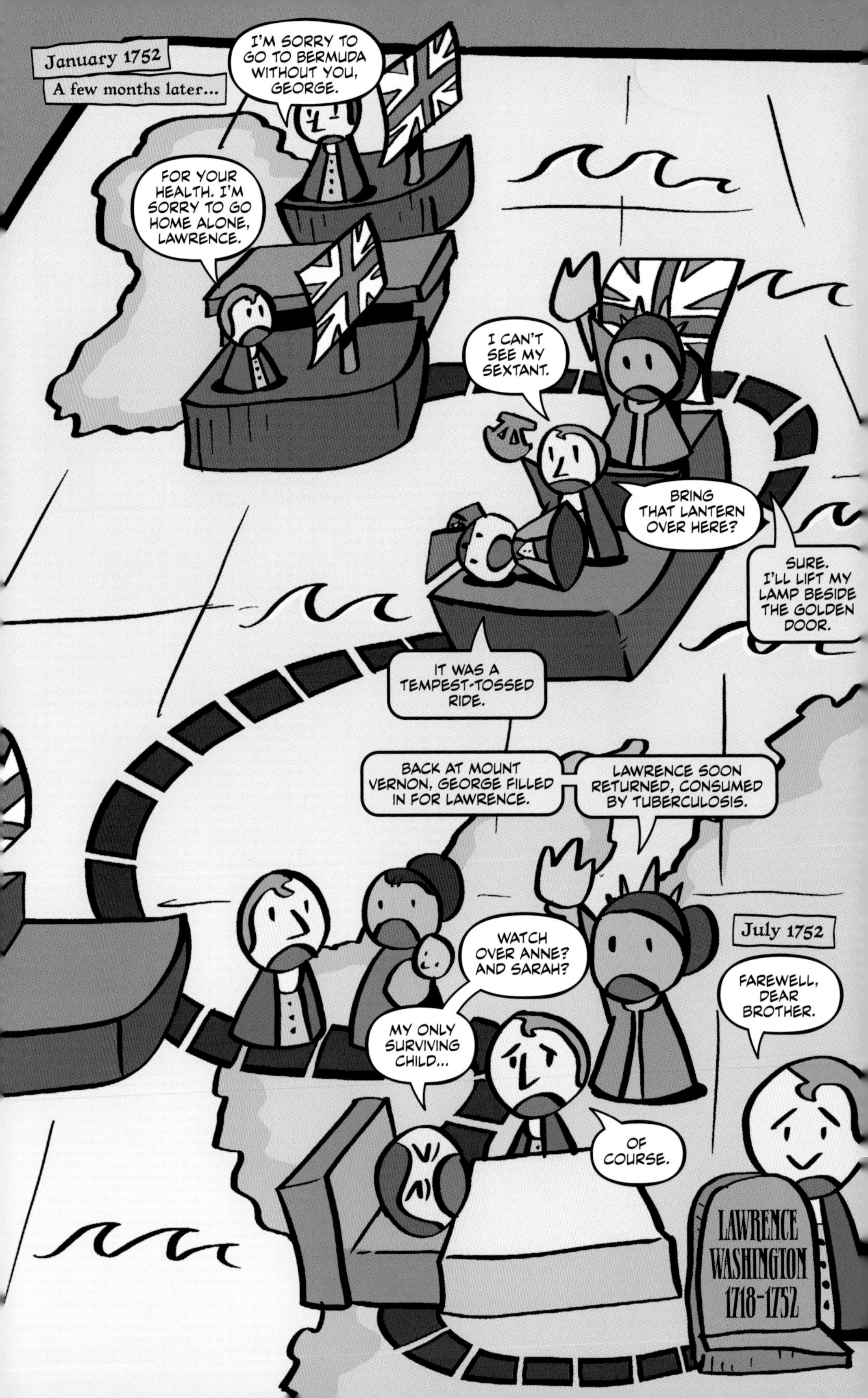
January 1752
A few months later...
I'M SORRY TO GO TO BERMUDA WITHOUT YOU, GEORGE.
FOR YOUR HEALTH. I'M SORRY TO GO HOME ALONE, LAWRENCE.
I CAN'T SEE MY SEXTANT.
BRING THAT LANTERN OVER HERE?
SURE. I'LL LIFT MY LAMP BESIDE THE GOLDEN DOOR.
IT WAS A TEMPEST-TOSSED RIDE.
BACK AT MOUNT VERNON, GEORGE FILLED IN FOR LAWRENCE.
LAWRENCE SOON RETURNED, CONSUMED BY TUBERCULOSIS.
July 1752
WATCH OVER ANNE? AND SARAH?
MY ONLY SURVIVING CHILD...
OF COURSE.
FAREWELL, DEAR BROTHER.
LAWRENCE WASHINGTON 1718-1752

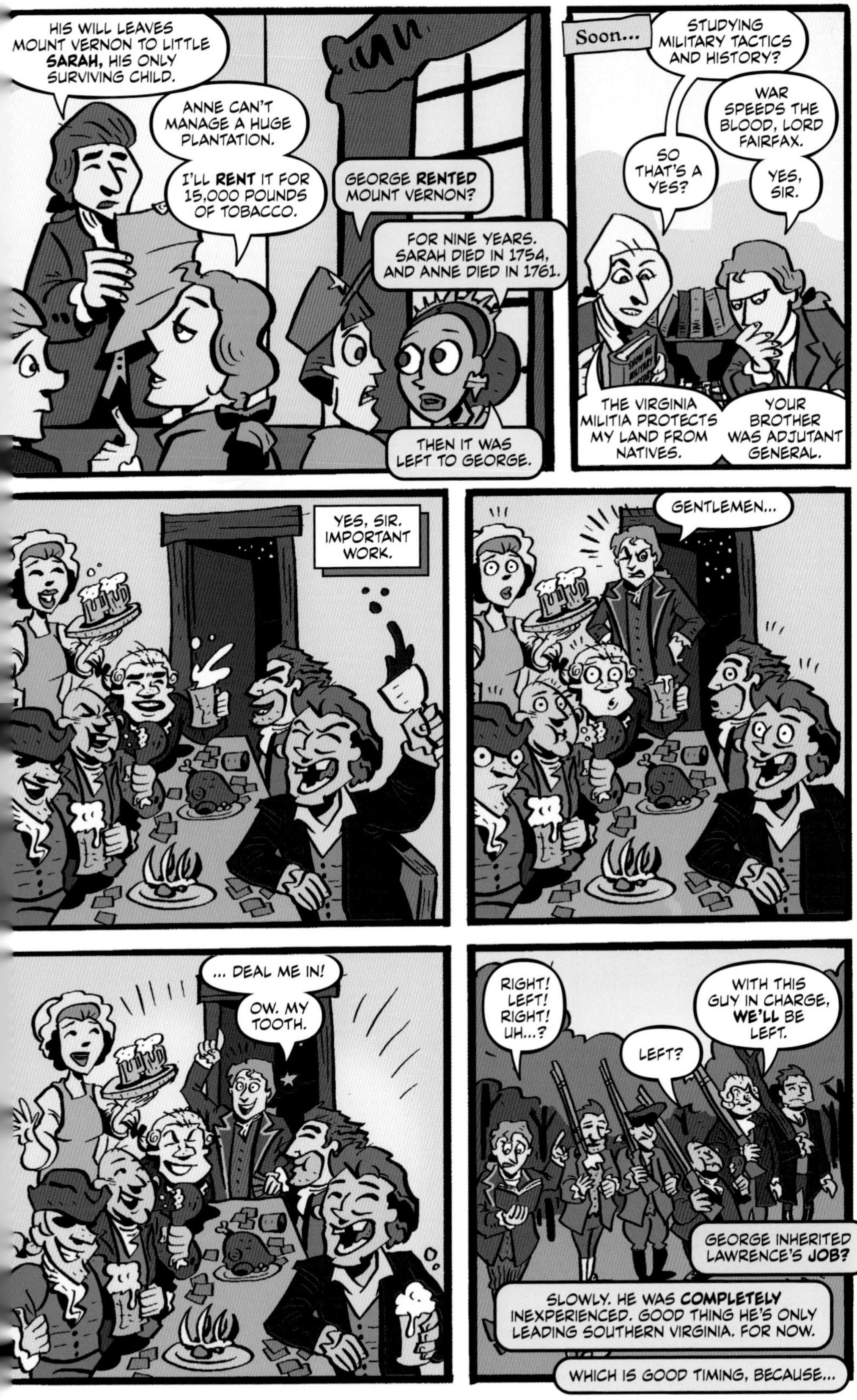
HIS WILL LEAVES MOUNT VERNON TO LITTLE **SARAH,** HIS ONLY SURVIVING CHILD.
ANNE CAN'T MANAGE A HUGE PLANTATION.
I'LL **RENT** IT FOR 15,000 POUNDS OF TOBACCO.
GEORGE **RENTED** MOUNT VERNON?
FOR NINE YEARS. SARAH DIED IN 1754, AND ANNE DIED IN 1761.
THEN IT WAS LEFT TO GEORGE.
Soon...
STUDYING MILITARY TACTICS AND HISTORY?
WAR SPEEDS THE BLOOD, LORD FAIRFAX.
SO THAT'S A YES?
YES, SIR.
THE VIRGINIA MILITIA PROTECTS MY LAND FROM NATIVES.
YOUR BROTHER WAS ADJUTANT GENERAL.
YES, SIR. IMPORTANT WORK.
GENTLEMEN...
... DEAL ME IN!
OW. MY TOOTH.
RIGHT! LEFT! RIGHT! UH...?
LEFT?
WITH THIS GUY IN CHARGE, **WE'LL** BE LEFT.
GEORGE INHERITED LAWRENCE'S **JOB?**
SLOWLY. HE WAS **COMPLETELY** INEXPERIENCED. GOOD THING HE'S ONLY LEADING SOUTHERN VIRGINIA. FOR NOW.
WHICH IS GOOD TIMING, BECAUSE...

The FRENCH & INDIAN WAR is ALL ABOUT GEORGE

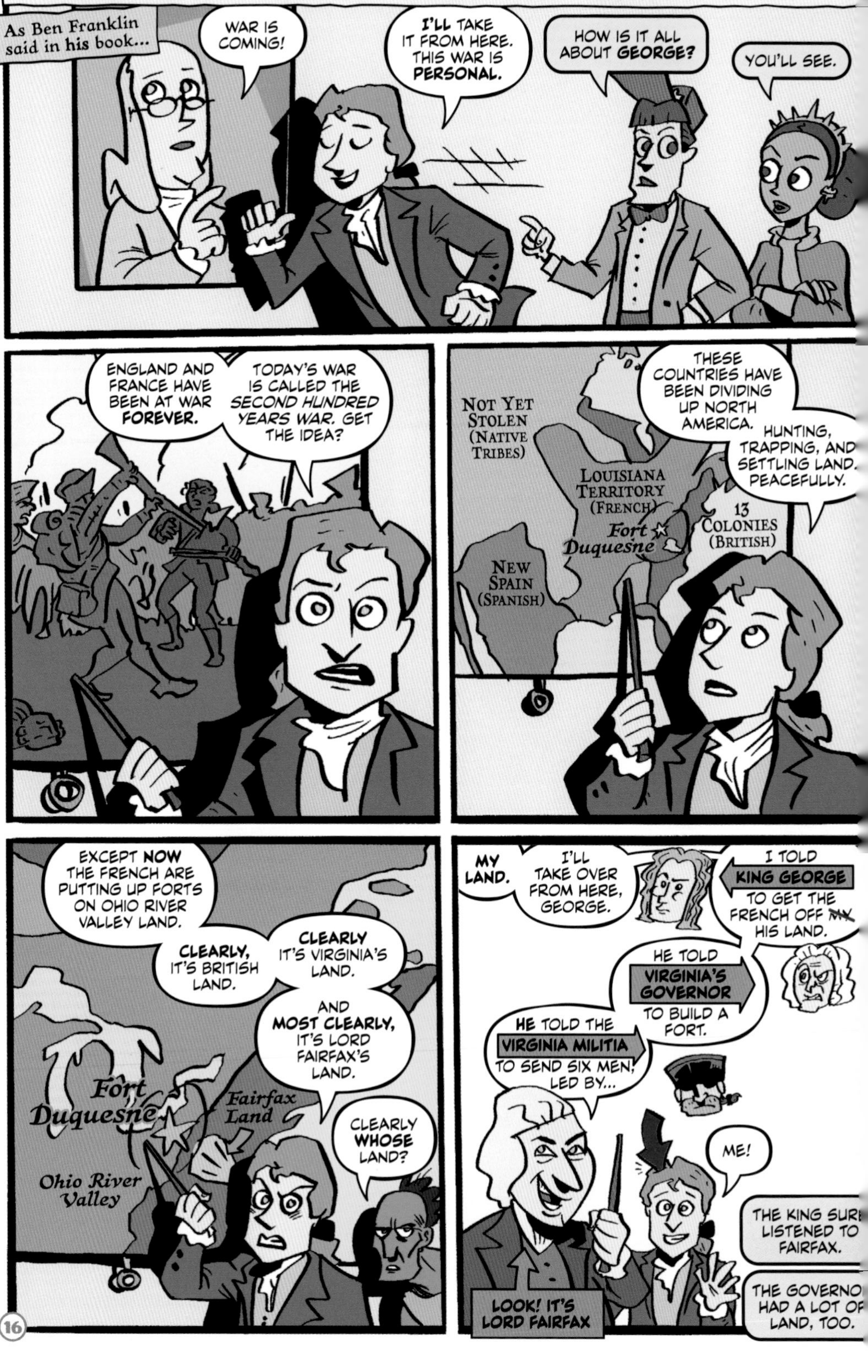

As Ben Franklin said in his book...
WAR IS COMING!
I'LL TAKE IT FROM HERE. THIS WAR IS PERSONAL.
HOW IS IT ALL ABOUT GEORGE?
YOU'LL SEE.
ENGLAND AND FRANCE HAVE BEEN AT WAR FOREVER.
TODAY'S WAR IS CALLED THE SECOND HUNDRED YEARS WAR. GET THE IDEA?
THESE COUNTRIES HAVE BEEN DIVIDING UP NORTH AMERICA.
HUNTING, TRAPPING, AND SETTLING LAND. PEACEFULLY.
NOT YET STOLEN (NATIVE TRIBES)
LOUISIANA TERRITORY (FRENCH)
Fort Duquesne
NEW SPAIN (SPANISH)
13 COLONIES (BRITISH)
EXCEPT NOW THE FRENCH ARE PUTTING UP FORTS ON OHIO RIVER VALLEY LAND.
CLEARLY, IT'S BRITISH LAND.
CLEARLY IT'S VIRGINIA'S LAND.
AND MOST CLEARLY, IT'S LORD FAIRFAX'S LAND.
Fort Duquesne
Fairfax Land
Ohio River Valley
CLEARLY WHOSE LAND?
MY LAND.
I'LL TAKE OVER FROM HERE, GEORGE.
I TOLD KING GEORGE TO GET THE FRENCH OFF ~~MY~~ HIS LAND.
HE TOLD VIRGINIA'S GOVERNOR TO BUILD A FORT.
HE TOLD THE VIRGINIA MILITIA TO SEND SIX MEN, LED BY...
ME!
THE KING SUR LISTENED TO FAIRFAX.
THE GOVERNO HAD A LOT OF LAND, TOO.
LOOK! IT'S LORD FAIRFAX

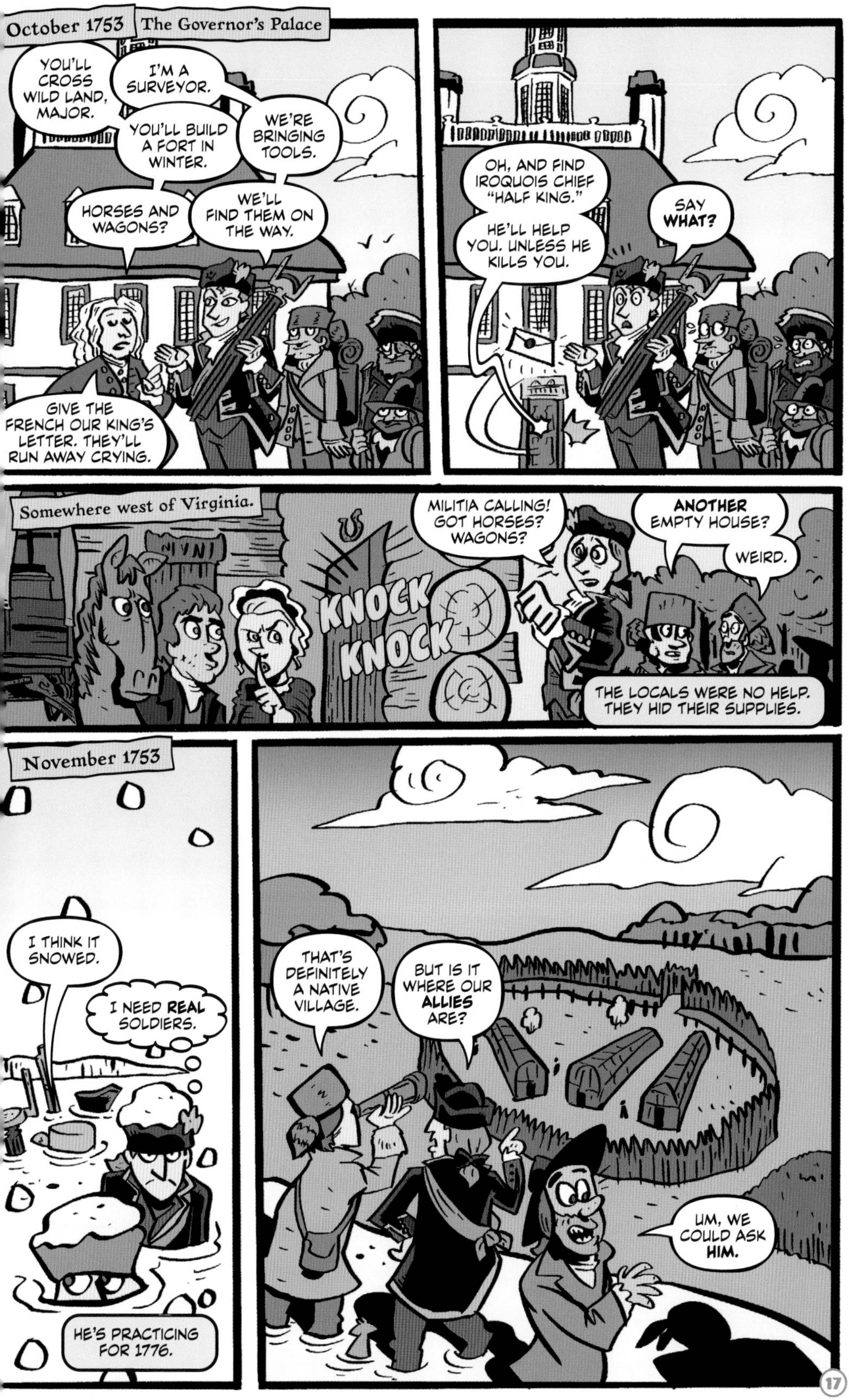
October 1753
The Governor's Palace
YOU'LL CROSS WILD LAND, MAJOR.
I'M A SURVEYOR.
YOU'LL BUILD A FORT IN WINTER.
WE'RE BRINGING TOOLS.
HORSES AND WAGONS?
WE'LL FIND THEM ON THE WAY.
GIVE THE FRENCH OUR KING'S LETTER. THEY'LL RUN AWAY CRYING.
OH, AND FIND IROQUOIS CHIEF "HALF KING."
HE'LL HELP YOU. UNLESS HE KILLS YOU.
SAY WHAT?
Somewhere west of Virginia.
KNOCK KNOCK
MILITIA CALLING! GOT HORSES? WAGONS?
ANOTHER EMPTY HOUSE?
WEIRD.
THE LOCALS WERE NO HELP. THEY HID THEIR SUPPLIES.
November 1753
I THINK IT SNOWED.
I NEED REAL SOLDIERS.
HE'S PRACTICING FOR 1776.
THAT'S DEFINITELY A NATIVE VILLAGE.
BUT IS IT WHERE OUR ALLIES ARE?
UM, WE COULD ASK HIM.

I'M CHIEF TANACHARISON. SOME CALL ME HALF KING.

I'M MAJOR WASHINGTON.

WASHINGTON? LONG AGO THERE WAS JOHN WASHINGTON.

WE CALLED HIM "DEVOURER OF VILLAGES."

HOW'D MY GREAT GRANDFATHER GET SUCH A GREAT NAME??

FIVE OF OUR CHIEFS SURRENDERED TO HIM. HE **KILLED** THEM.

OOPS...

DON'T SWEAT. WE HATE THE FRENCH! THEY KILLED MY DAD.

YEAH! LET'S HIT THAT FRENCH FORT!

WHEW!

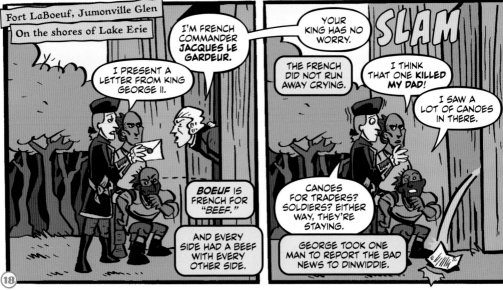

Fort LaBoeuf, Jumonville Glen
On the shores of Lake Erie

I'M FRENCH COMMANDER **JACQUES LE GARDEUR.**

I PRESENT A LETTER FROM KING GEORGE II.

BOEUF IS FRENCH FOR *"BEEF,"*

AND EVERY SIDE HAD A BEEF WITH EVERY OTHER SIDE.

YOUR KING HAS NO WORRY.

THE FRENCH DID NOT RUN AWAY CRYING.

SLAM

I THINK THAT ONE **KILLED MY DAD!**

I SAW A LOT OF CANOES IN THERE.

CANOES FOR TRADERS? SOLDIERS? EITHER WAY, THEY'RE STAYING.

GEORGE TOOK ONE MAN TO REPORT THE BAD NEWS TO DINWIDDIE.

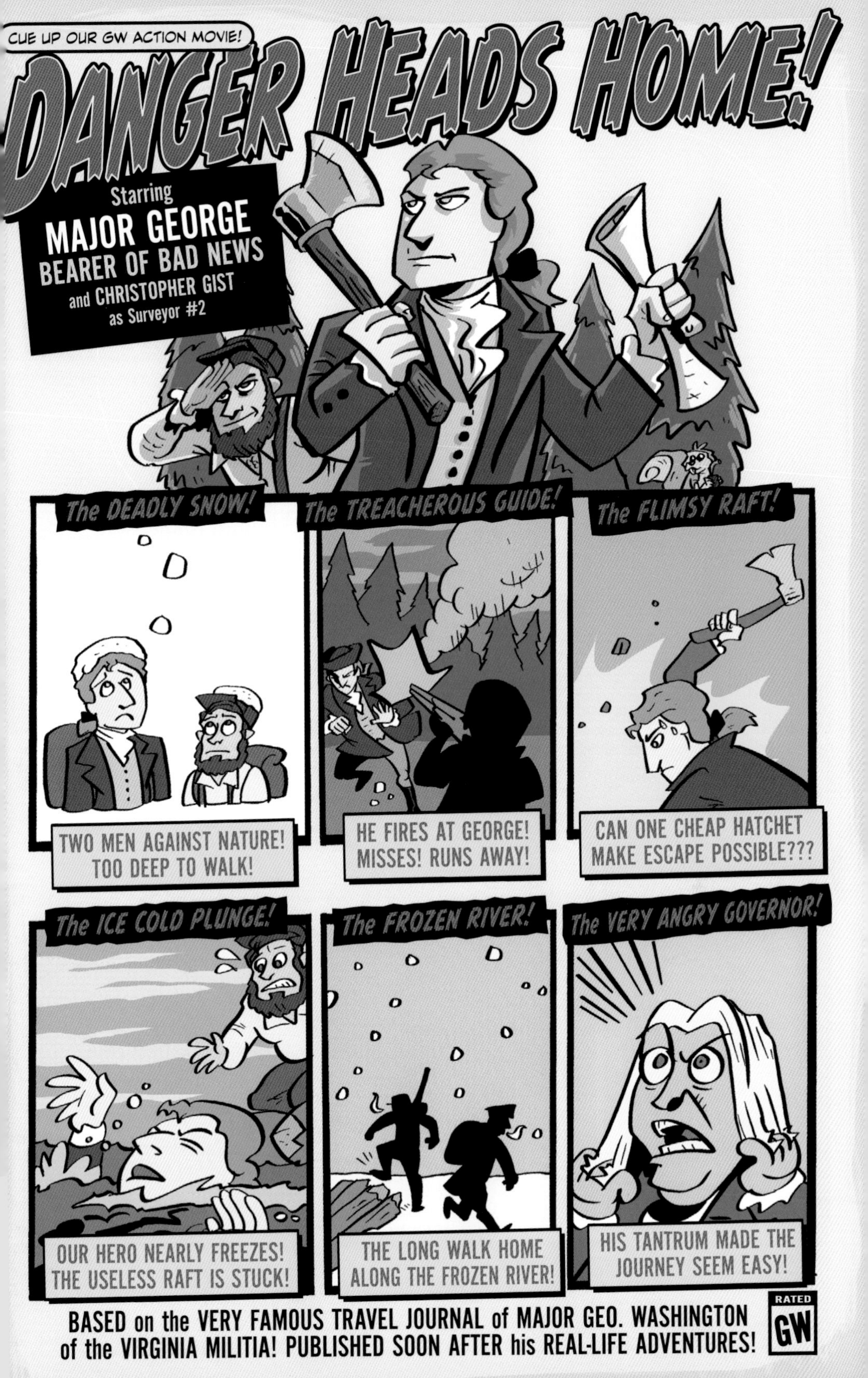
CUE UP OUR GW ACTION MOVIE!
DANGER HEADS HOME!
Starring
MAJOR GEORGE
BEARER OF BAD NEWS
and CHRISTOPHER GIST
as Surveyor #2
The DEADLY SNOW!
TWO MEN AGAINST NATURE! TOO DEEP TO WALK!
The TREACHEROUS GUIDE!
HE FIRES AT GEORGE! MISSES! RUNS AWAY!
The FLIMSY RAFT!
CAN ONE CHEAP HATCHET MAKE ESCAPE POSSIBLE???
The ICE COLD PLUNGE!
OUR HERO NEARLY FREEZES! THE USELESS RAFT IS STUCK!
The FROZEN RIVER!
THE LONG WALK HOME ALONG THE FROZEN RIVER!
The VERY ANGRY GOVERNOR!
HIS TANTRUM MADE THE JOURNEY SEEM EASY!
BASED on the VERY FAMOUS TRAVEL JOURNAL of MAJOR GEO. WASHINGTON of the VIRGINIA MILITIA! PUBLISHED SOON AFTER his REAL-LIFE ADVENTURES!
RATED
GW

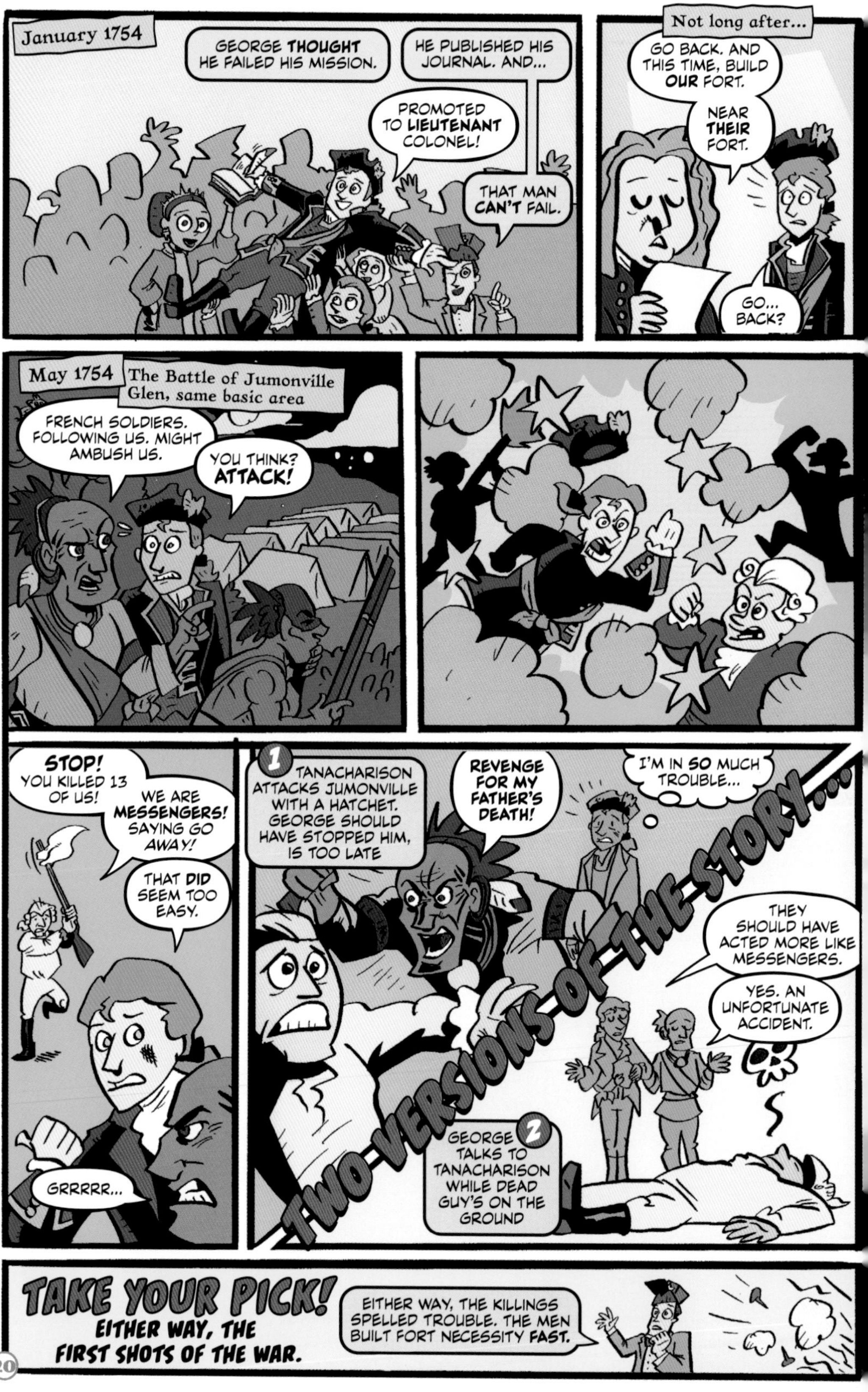
January 1754
GEORGE THOUGHT HE FAILED HIS MISSION.
HE PUBLISHED HIS JOURNAL. AND...
PROMOTED TO LIEUTENANT COLONEL!
THAT MAN CAN'T FAIL.
Not long after...
GO BACK. AND THIS TIME, BUILD OUR FORT.
NEAR THEIR FORT.
GO... BACK?
May 1754
The Battle of Jumonville Glen, same basic area
FRENCH SOLDIERS. FOLLOWING US. MIGHT AMBUSH US.
YOU THINK? ATTACK!
STOP! YOU KILLED 13 OF US!
WE ARE MESSENGERS! SAYING GO AWAY!
THAT DID SEEM TOO EASY.
GRRRRR...
TWO VERSIONS OF THE STORY...
1 TANACHARISON ATTACKS JUMONVILLE WITH A HATCHET. GEORGE SHOULD HAVE STOPPED HIM, IS TOO LATE
REVENGE FOR MY FATHER'S DEATH!
I'M IN SO MUCH TROUBLE...
THEY SHOULD HAVE ACTED MORE LIKE MESSENGERS.
YES. AN UNFORTUNATE ACCIDENT.
GEORGE 2 TALKS TO TANACHARISON WHILE DEAD GUY'S ON THE GROUND
TAKE YOUR PICK!
EITHER WAY, THE FIRST SHOTS OF THE WAR.
EITHER WAY, THE KILLINGS SPELLED TROUBLE. THE MEN BUILT FORT NECESSITY FAST.

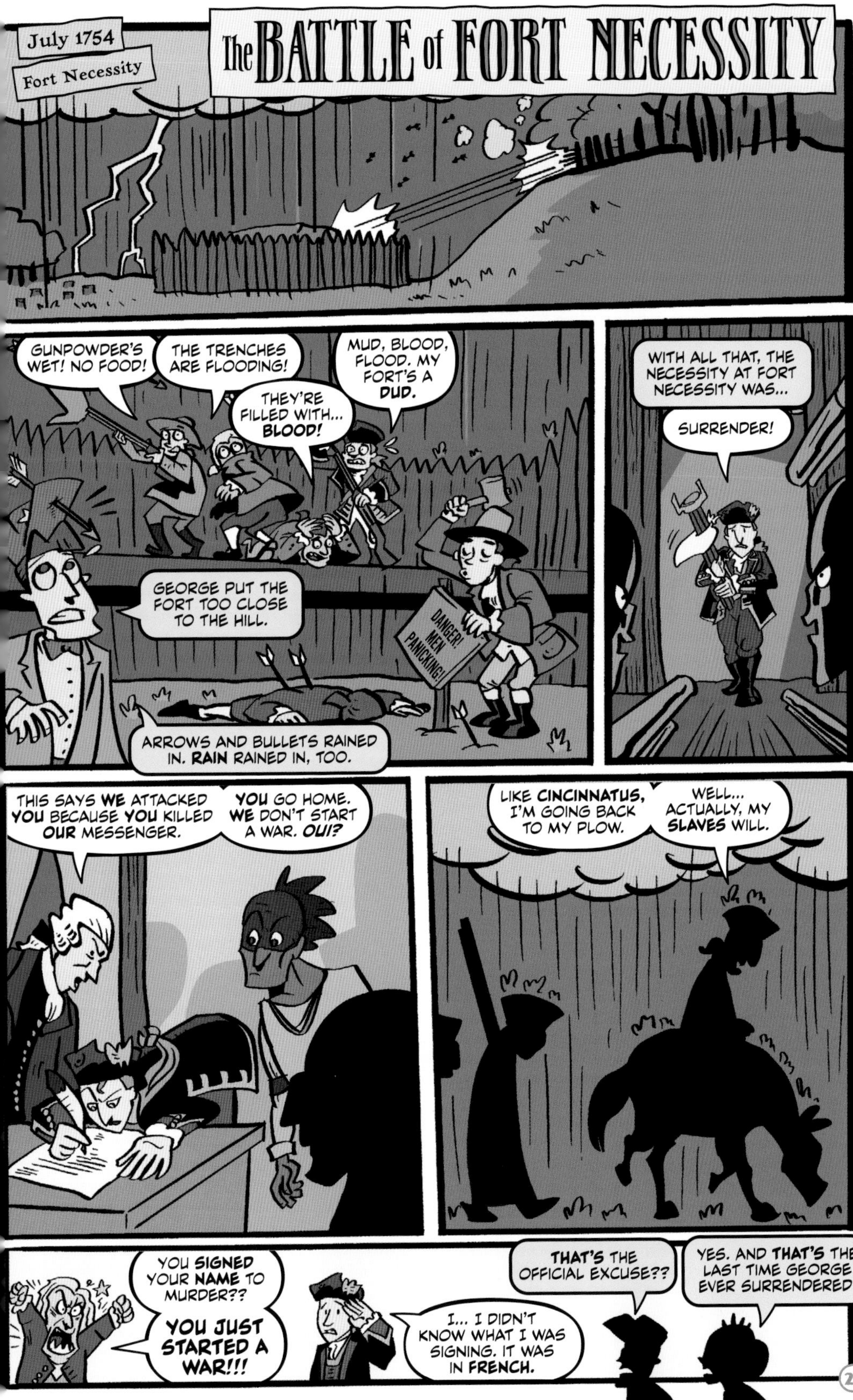

July 1754
Fort Necessity
The BATTLE of FORT NECESSITY
GUNPOWDER'S WET! NO FOOD!
THE TRENCHES ARE FLOODING!
THEY'RE FILLED WITH... BLOOD!
MUD, BLOOD, FLOOD. MY FORT'S A DUD.
GEORGE PUT THE FORT TOO CLOSE TO THE HILL.
DANGER! MEN PANICKING!
ARROWS AND BULLETS RAINED IN. RAIN RAINED IN, TOO.
WITH ALL THAT, THE NECESSITY AT FORT NECESSITY WAS...
SURRENDER!
THIS SAYS WE ATTACKED YOU BECAUSE YOU KILLED OUR MESSENGER.
YOU GO HOME. WE DON'T START A WAR. OUI?
LIKE CINCINNATUS, I'M GOING BACK TO MY PLOW.
WELL... ACTUALLY, MY SLAVES WILL.
YOU SIGNED YOUR NAME TO MURDER??
YOU JUST STARTED A WAR!!!
I... I DIDN'T KNOW WHAT I WAS SIGNING. IT WAS IN FRENCH.
THAT'S THE OFFICIAL EXCUSE??
YES. AND THAT'S THE LAST TIME GEORGE EVER SURRENDERED.

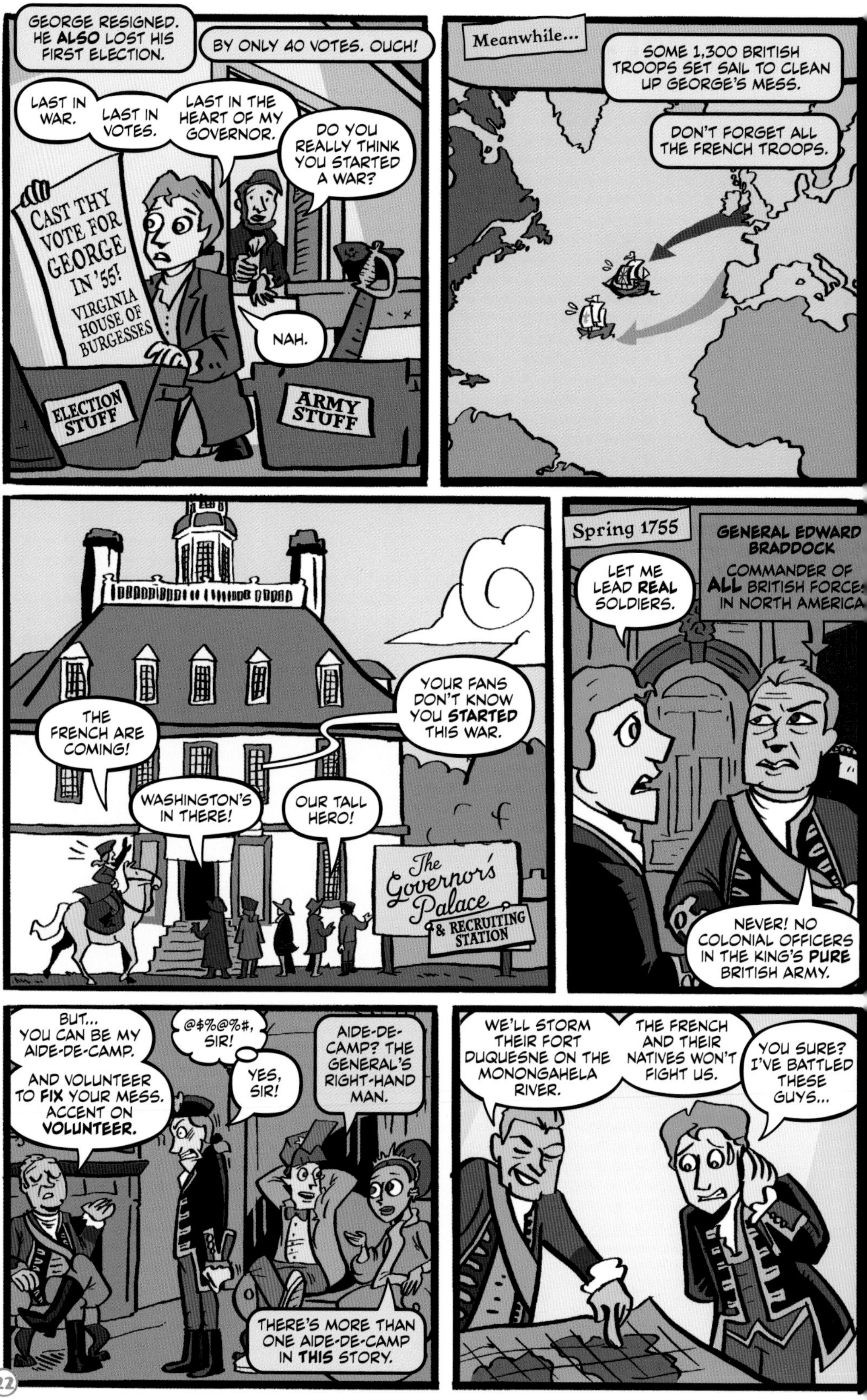

GEORGE RESIGNED. HE ALSO LOST HIS FIRST ELECTION.
BY ONLY 40 VOTES. OUCH!
LAST IN WAR.
LAST IN VOTES.
LAST IN THE HEART OF MY GOVERNOR.
DO YOU REALLY THINK YOU STARTED A WAR?
CAST THY VOTE FOR GEORGE IN '55! VIRGINIA HOUSE OF BURGESSES
NAH.
ELECTION STUFF
ARMY STUFF
Meanwhile...
SOME 1,300 BRITISH TROOPS SET SAIL TO CLEAN UP GEORGE'S MESS.
DON'T FORGET ALL THE FRENCH TROOPS.
THE FRENCH ARE COMING!
YOUR FANS DON'T KNOW YOU STARTED THIS WAR.
WASHINGTON'S IN THERE!
OUR TALL HERO!
The Governor's Palace & RECRUITING STATION
Spring 1755
GENERAL EDWARD BRADDOCK COMMANDER OF ALL BRITISH FORCES IN NORTH AMERICA
LET ME LEAD REAL SOLDIERS.
NEVER! NO COLONIAL OFFICERS IN THE KING'S PURE BRITISH ARMY.
BUT... YOU CAN BE MY AIDE-DE-CAMP.
AND VOLUNTEER TO FIX YOUR MESS. ACCENT ON VOLUNTEER.
@$%@%#, SIR!
YES, SIR!
AIDE-DE-CAMP? THE GENERAL'S RIGHT-HAND MAN.
THERE'S MORE THAN ONE AIDE-DE-CAMP IN THIS STORY.
WE'LL STORM THEIR FORT DUQUESNE ON THE MONONGAHELA RIVER.
THE FRENCH AND THEIR NATIVES WON'T FIGHT US.
YOU SURE? I'VE BATTLED THESE GUYS...

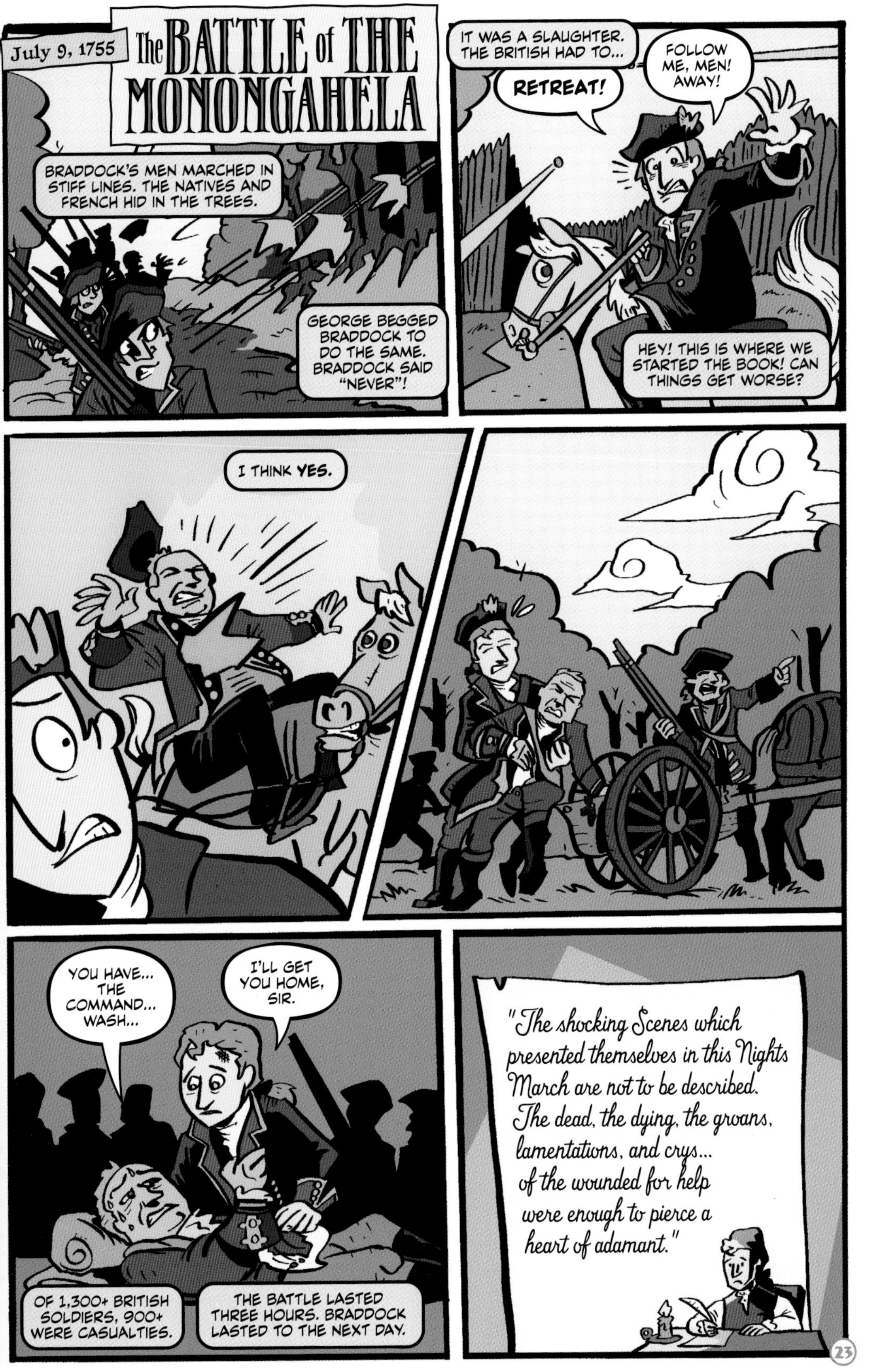

July 9, 1755
The BATTLE of THE MONONGAHELA
BRADDOCK'S MEN MARCHED IN STIFF LINES. THE NATIVES AND FRENCH HID IN THE TREES.
GEORGE BEGGED BRADDOCK TO DO THE SAME. BRADDOCK SAID "NEVER"!
IT WAS A SLAUGHTER. THE BRITISH HAD TO...
RETREAT!
FOLLOW ME, MEN! AWAY!
HEY! THIS IS WHERE WE STARTED THE BOOK! CAN THINGS GET WORSE?
I THINK **YES.**
YOU HAVE... THE COMMAND... WASH...
I'LL GET YOU HOME, SIR.
OF 1,300+ BRITISH SOLDIERS, 900+ WERE CASUALTIES.
THE BATTLE LASTED THREE HOURS. BRADDOCK LASTED TO THE NEXT DAY.
"The shocking Scenes which presented themselves in this Nights March are not to be described. The dead, the dying, the groans, lamentations, and crys... of the wounded for help were enough to pierce a heart of adamant."

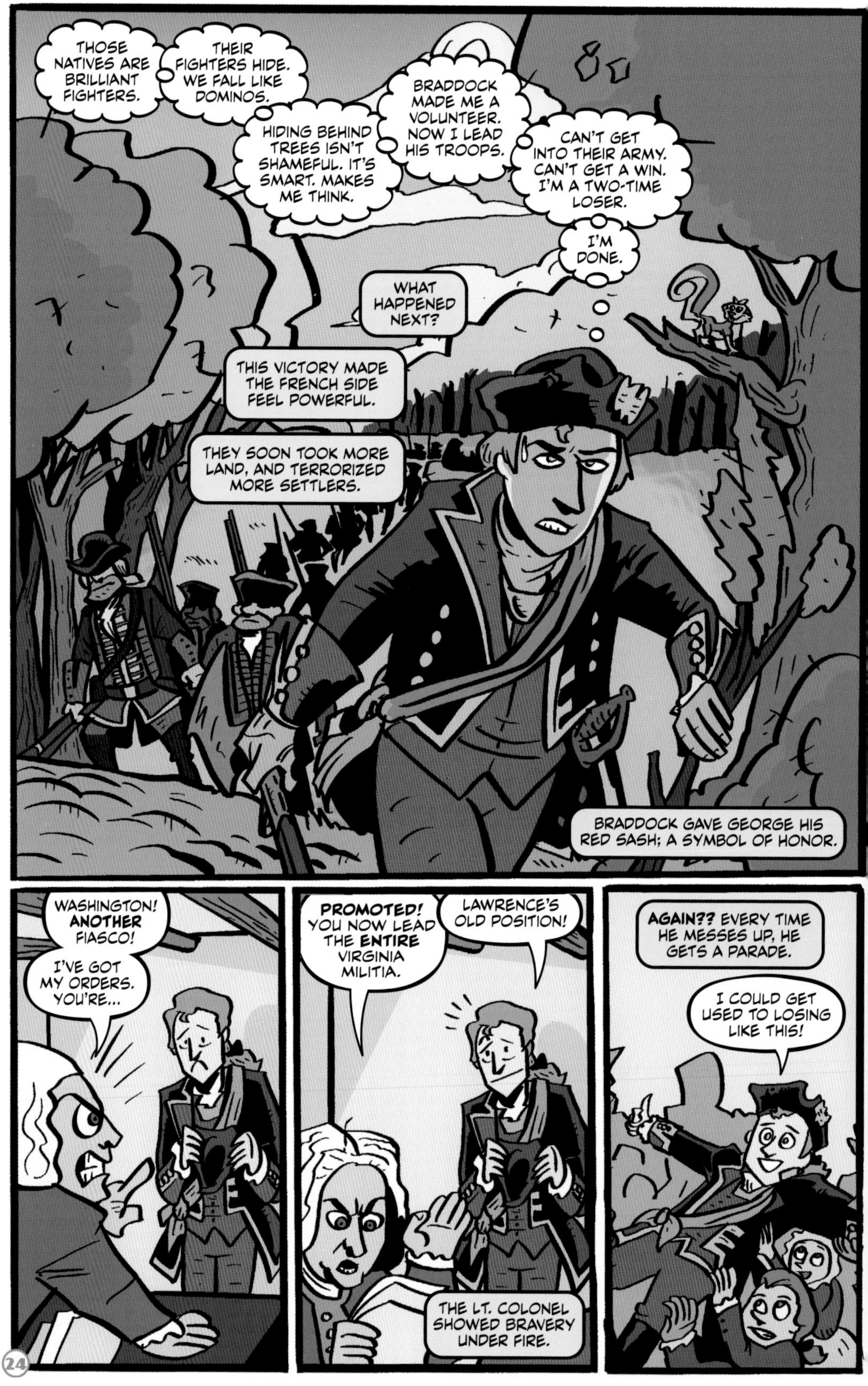
THOSE NATIVES ARE BRILLIANT FIGHTERS.
THEIR FIGHTERS HIDE. WE FALL LIKE DOMINOS.
HIDING BEHIND TREES ISN'T SHAMEFUL. IT'S SMART. MAKES ME THINK.
BRADDOCK MADE ME A VOLUNTEER. NOW I LEAD HIS TROOPS.
CAN'T GET INTO THEIR ARMY. CAN'T GET A WIN. I'M A TWO-TIME LOSER.
I'M DONE.
WHAT HAPPENED NEXT?
THIS VICTORY MADE THE FRENCH SIDE FEEL POWERFUL.
THEY SOON TOOK MORE LAND, AND TERRORIZED MORE SETTLERS.
BRADDOCK GAVE GEORGE HIS RED SASH; A SYMBOL OF HONOR.
WASHINGTON! **ANOTHER** FIASCO!
I'VE GOT MY ORDERS. YOU'RE...
PROMOTED! YOU NOW LEAD THE **ENTIRE** VIRGINIA MILITIA.
LAWRENCE'S OLD POSITION!
THE LT. COLONEL SHOWED BRAVERY UNDER FIRE.
AGAIN?? EVERY TIME HE MESSES UP, HE GETS A PARADE.
I COULD GET USED TO LOSING LIKE THIS!

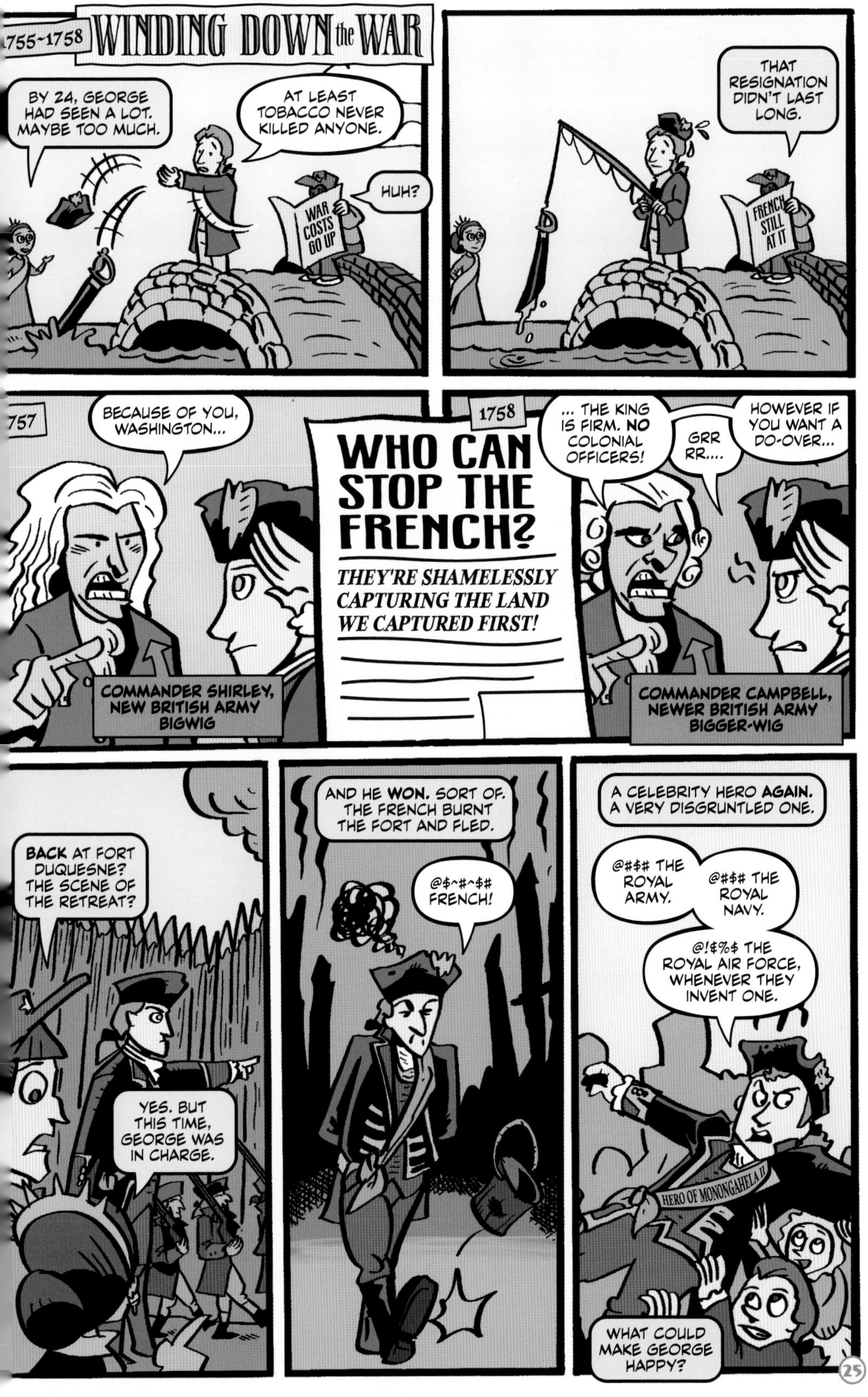
1755~1758
WINDING DOWN the WAR
BY 24, GEORGE HAD SEEN A LOT. MAYBE TOO MUCH.
AT LEAST TOBACCO NEVER KILLED ANYONE.
HUH?
WAR COSTS GO UP
THAT RESIGNATION DIDN'T LAST LONG.
FRENCH STILL AT IT
1757
BECAUSE OF YOU, WASHINGTON...
COMMANDER SHIRLEY, NEW BRITISH ARMY BIGWIG
1758
WHO CAN STOP THE FRENCH?
THEY'RE SHAMELESSLY CAPTURING THE LAND WE CAPTURED FIRST!
... THE KING IS FIRM. NO COLONIAL OFFICERS!
GRR RR....
HOWEVER IF YOU WANT A DO-OVER...
COMMANDER CAMPBELL, NEWER BRITISH ARMY BIGGER-WIG
BACK AT FORT DUQUESNE? THE SCENE OF THE RETREAT?
YES. BUT THIS TIME, GEORGE WAS IN CHARGE.
AND HE WON. SORT OF. THE FRENCH BURNT THE FORT AND FLED.
@$^#^$# FRENCH!
A CELEBRITY HERO AGAIN. A VERY DISGRUNTLED ONE.
@#$# THE ROYAL ARMY.
@#$# THE ROYAL NAVY.
@!$%$ THE ROYAL AIR FORCE, WHENEVER THEY INVENT ONE.
HERO OF MONONGAHELA II
WHAT COULD MAKE GEORGE HAPPY?

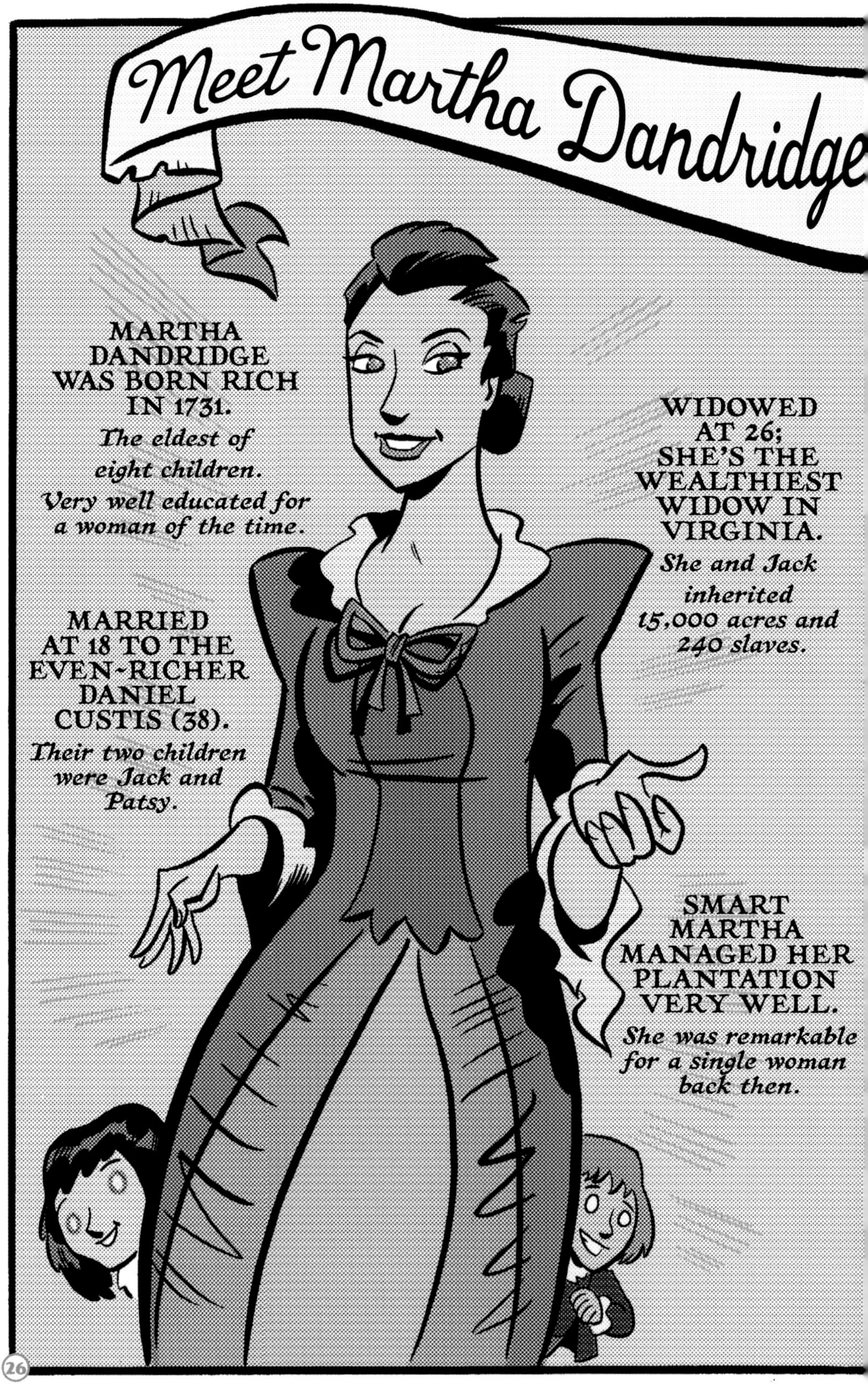
Meet Martha Dandridge
MARTHA DANDRIDGE WAS BORN RICH IN 1731.
The eldest of eight children.
Very well educated for a woman of the time.
MARRIED AT 18 TO THE EVEN-RICHER DANIEL CUSTIS (38).
Their two children were Jack and Patsy.
WIDOWED AT 26; SHE'S THE WEALTHIEST WIDOW IN VIRGINIA.
She and Jack inherited 15,000 acres and 240 slaves.
SMART MARTHA MANAGED HER PLANTATION VERY WELL.
She was remarkable for a single woman back then.

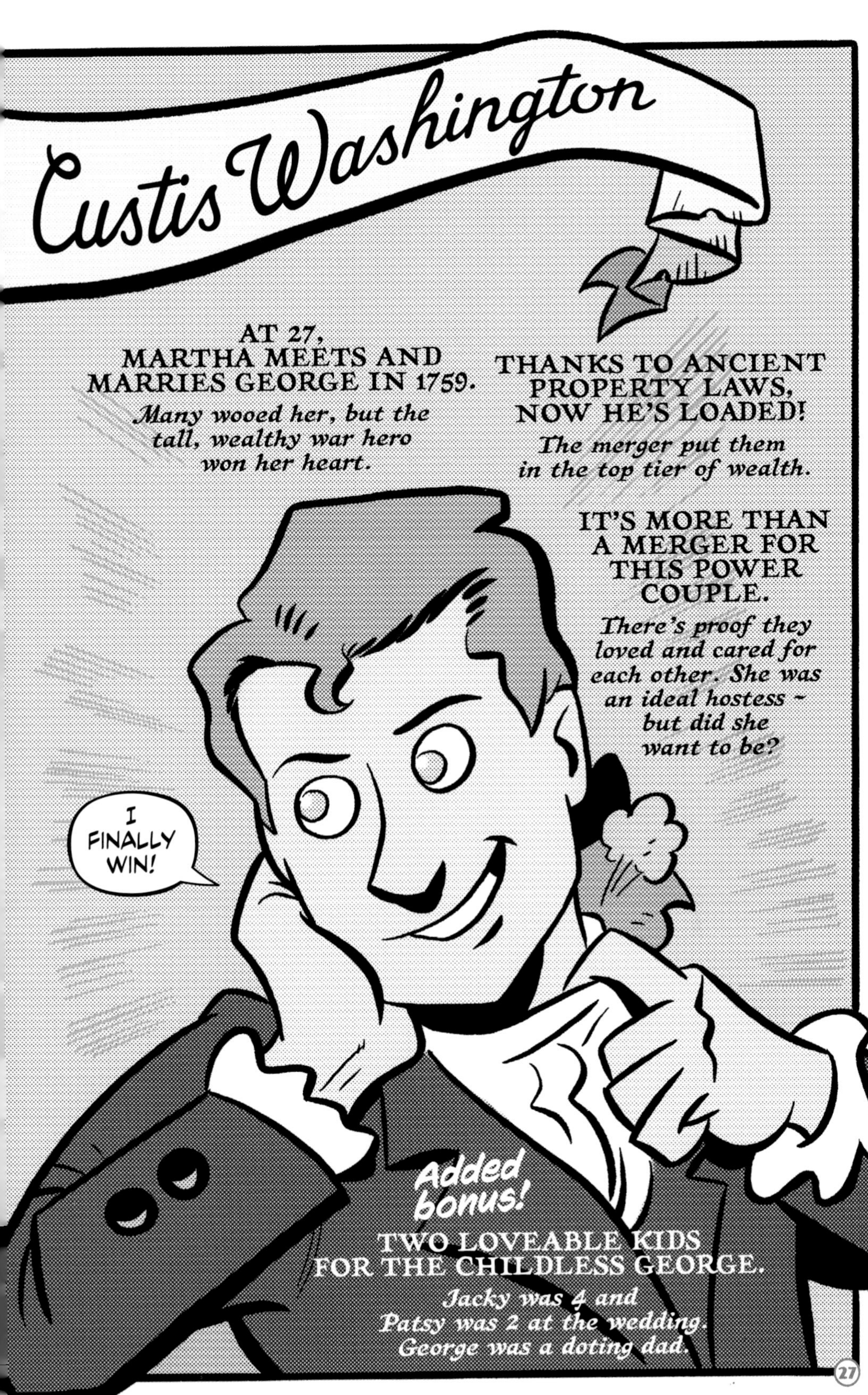

Custis Washington
AT 27, MARTHA MEETS AND MARRIES GEORGE IN 1759.
Many wooed her, but the tall, wealthy war hero won her heart.
THANKS TO ANCIENT PROPERTY LAWS, NOW HE'S LOADED!
The merger put them in the top tier of wealth.
IT'S MORE THAN A MERGER FOR THIS POWER COUPLE.
There's proof they loved and cared for each other. She was an ideal hostess ~ but did she want to be?
I FINALLY WIN!
Added bonus!
TWO LOVEABLE KIDS FOR THE CHILDLESS GEORGE.
Jacky was 4 and Patsy was 2 at the wedding. George was a doting dad.

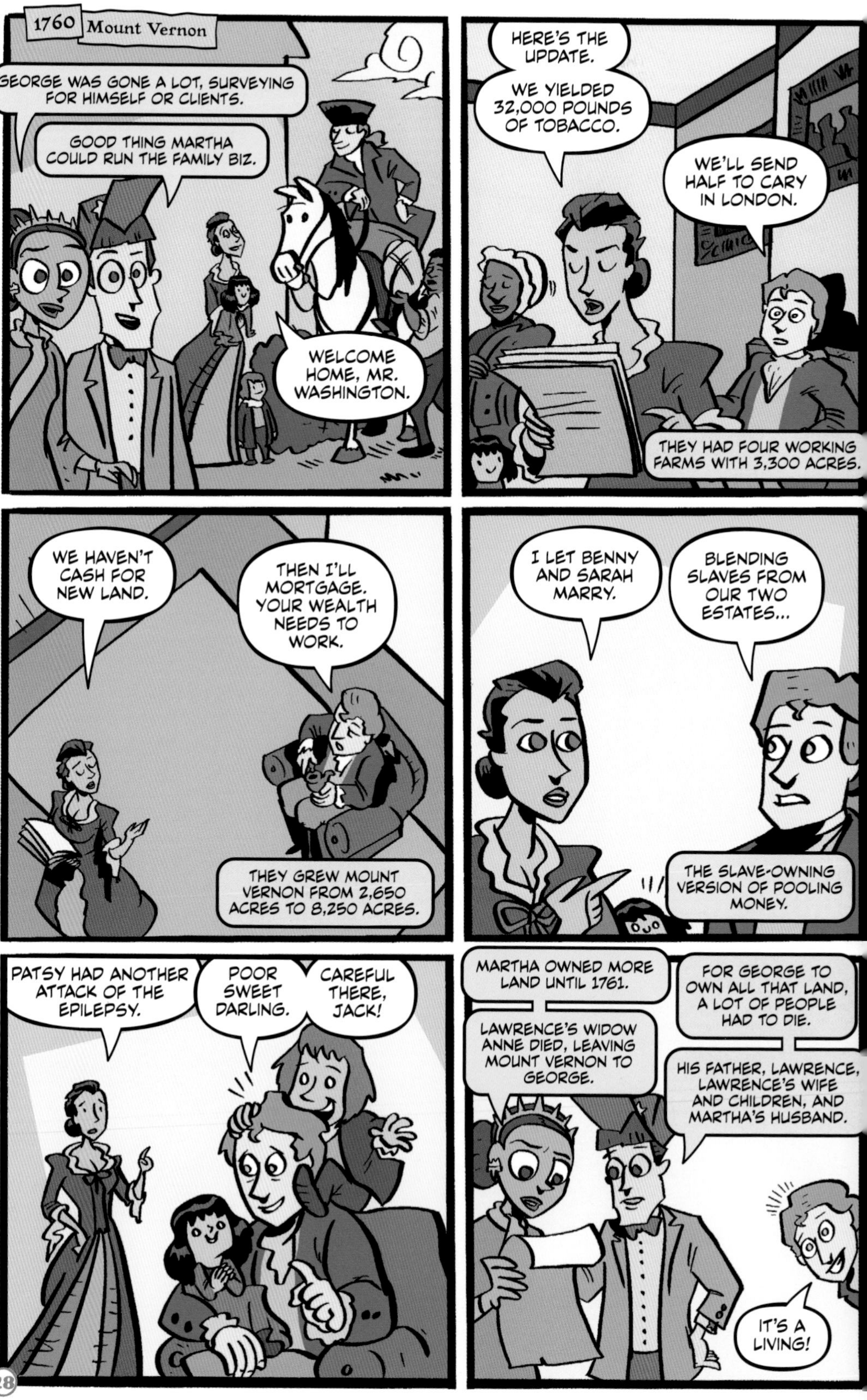
1760 Mount Vernon
GEORGE WAS GONE A LOT, SURVEYING FOR HIMSELF OR CLIENTS.
GOOD THING MARTHA COULD RUN THE FAMILY BIZ.
WELCOME HOME, MR. WASHINGTON.
HERE'S THE UPDATE.
WE YIELDED 32,000 POUNDS OF TOBACCO.
WE'LL SEND HALF TO CARY IN LONDON.
THEY HAD FOUR WORKING FARMS WITH 3,300 ACRES.
WE HAVEN'T CASH FOR NEW LAND.
THEN I'LL MORTGAGE. YOUR WEALTH NEEDS TO WORK.
THEY GREW MOUNT VERNON FROM 2,650 ACRES TO 8,250 ACRES.
I LET BENNY AND SARAH MARRY.
BLENDING SLAVES FROM OUR TWO ESTATES...
THE SLAVE-OWNING VERSION OF POOLING MONEY.
PATSY HAD ANOTHER ATTACK OF THE EPILEPSY.
POOR SWEET DARLING.
CAREFUL THERE, JACK!
MARTHA OWNED MORE LAND UNTIL 1761.
LAWRENCE'S WIDOW ANNE DIED, LEAVING MOUNT VERNON TO GEORGE.
FOR GEORGE TO OWN ALL THAT LAND, A LOT OF PEOPLE HAD TO DIE.
HIS FATHER, LAWRENCE, LAWRENCE'S WIFE AND CHILDREN, AND MARTHA'S HUSBAND.
IT'S A LIVING!

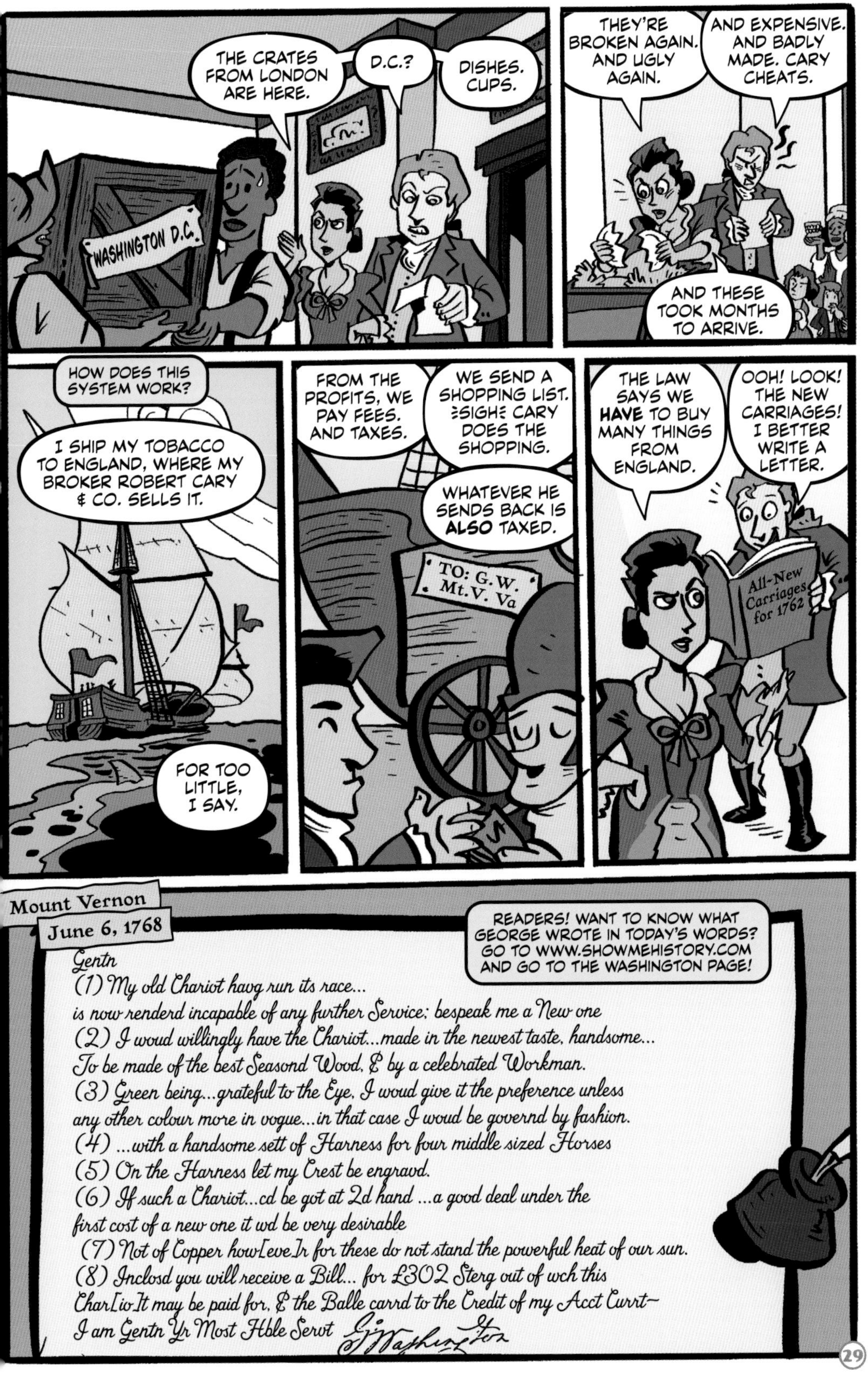
THE CRATES FROM LONDON ARE HERE.
D.C.?
DISHES. CUPS.
WASHINGTON D.C.
THEY'RE BROKEN AGAIN. AND UGLY AGAIN.
AND EXPENSIVE. AND BADLY MADE. CARY CHEATS.
AND THESE TOOK MONTHS TO ARRIVE.
HOW DOES THIS SYSTEM WORK?
I SHIP MY TOBACCO TO ENGLAND, WHERE MY BROKER ROBERT CARY & CO. SELLS IT.
FOR TOO LITTLE, I SAY.
FROM THE PROFITS, WE PAY FEES. AND TAXES.
WE SEND A SHOPPING LIST. *SIGH* CARY DOES THE SHOPPING.
WHATEVER HE SENDS BACK IS ALSO TAXED.
TO: G.W. Mt.V. Va
THE LAW SAYS WE HAVE TO BUY MANY THINGS FROM ENGLAND.
OOH! LOOK! THE NEW CARRIAGES! I BETTER WRITE A LETTER.
All-New Carriages for 1762
Mount Vernon
June 6, 1768
READERS! WANT TO KNOW WHAT GEORGE WROTE IN TODAY'S WORDS? GO TO WWW.SHOWMEHISTORY.COM AND GO TO THE WASHINGTON PAGE!
Gentn
(1) My old Chariot havg run its race...
is now renderd incapable of any further Service; bespeak me a New one
(2) I woud willingly have the Chariot...made in the newest taste, handsome...
To be made of the best Seasond Wood, & by a celebrated Workman.
(3) Green being...grateful to the Eye, I woud give it the preference unless
any other colour more in vogue...in that case I woud be governd by fashion.
(4) ...with a handsome sett of Harness for four middle sized Horses
(5) On the Harness let my Crest be engravd.
(6) If such a Chariot...cd be got at 2d hand ...a good deal under the
first cost of a new one it wd be very desirable
(7) Not of Copper how[eve]r for these do not stand the powerful heat of our sun.
(8) Inclosd you will receive a Bill... for £302 Sterg out of wch this
Char[io]t may be paid for, & the Balle carrd to the Credit of my Acct Currt—
I am Gentn Yr Most Hble Servt G Washington

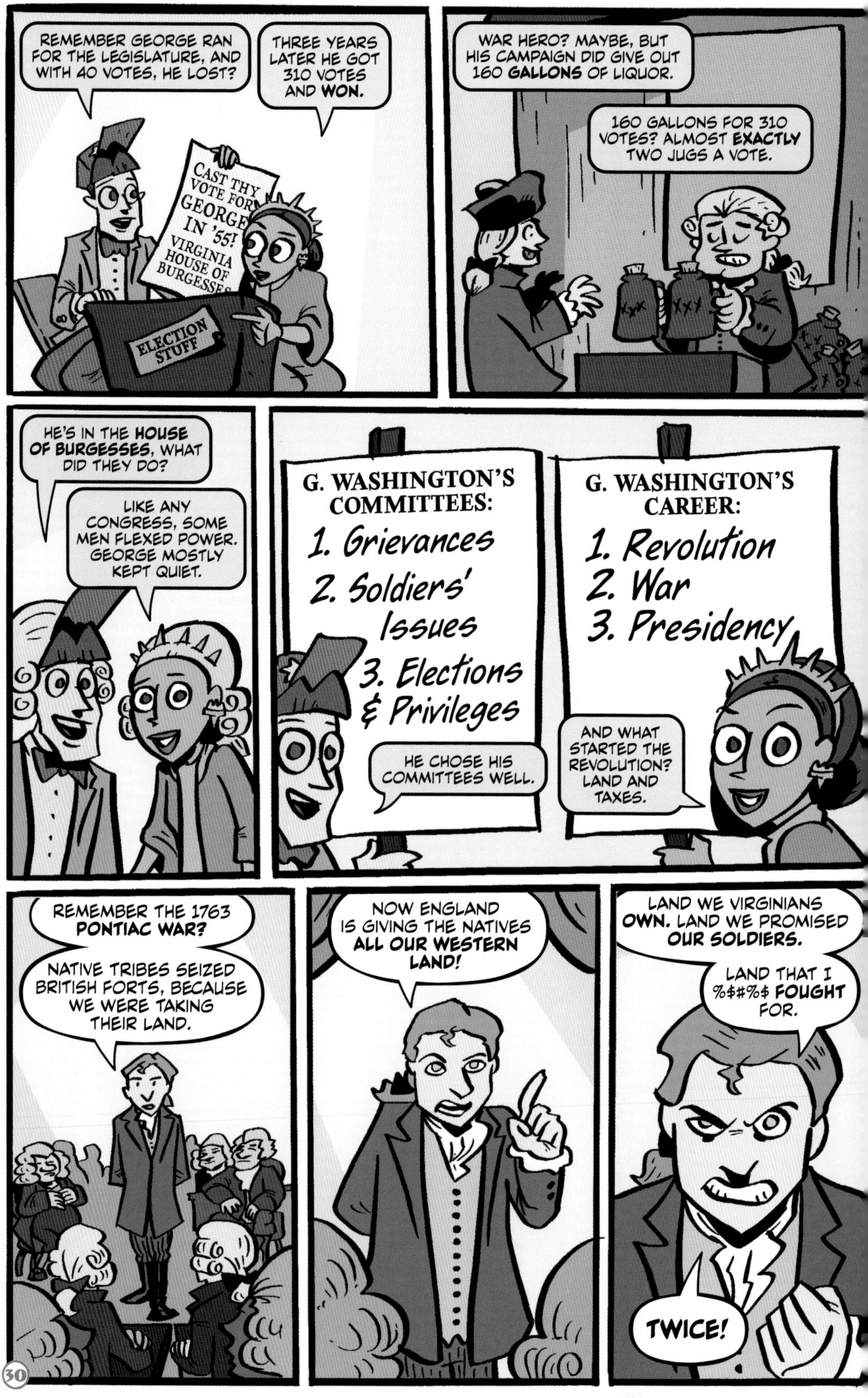
REMEMBER GEORGE RAN FOR THE LEGISLATURE, AND WITH 40 VOTES, HE LOST?
THREE YEARS LATER HE GOT 310 VOTES AND WON.
CAST THY VOTE FOR GEORGE IN '55! VIRGINIA HOUSE OF BURGESSES
ELECTION STUFF
WAR HERO? MAYBE, BUT HIS CAMPAIGN DID GIVE OUT 160 GALLONS OF LIQUOR.
160 GALLONS FOR 310 VOTES? ALMOST EXACTLY TWO JUGS A VOTE.
HE'S IN THE HOUSE OF BURGESSES, WHAT DID THEY DO?
LIKE ANY CONGRESS, SOME MEN FLEXED POWER. GEORGE MOSTLY KEPT QUIET.
G. WASHINGTON'S COMMITTEES:
1. Grievances
2. Soldiers' Issues
3. Elections & Privileges
HE CHOSE HIS COMMITTEES WELL.
G. WASHINGTON'S CAREER:
1. Revolution
2. War
3. Presidency
AND WHAT STARTED THE REVOLUTION? LAND AND TAXES.
REMEMBER THE 1763 PONTIAC WAR?
NATIVE TRIBES SEIZED BRITISH FORTS, BECAUSE WE WERE TAKING THEIR LAND.
NOW ENGLAND IS GIVING THE NATIVES ALL OUR WESTERN LAND!
LAND WE VIRGINIANS OWN. LAND WE PROMISED OUR SOLDIERS.
LAND THAT I %$#%$ FOUGHT FOR.
TWICE!

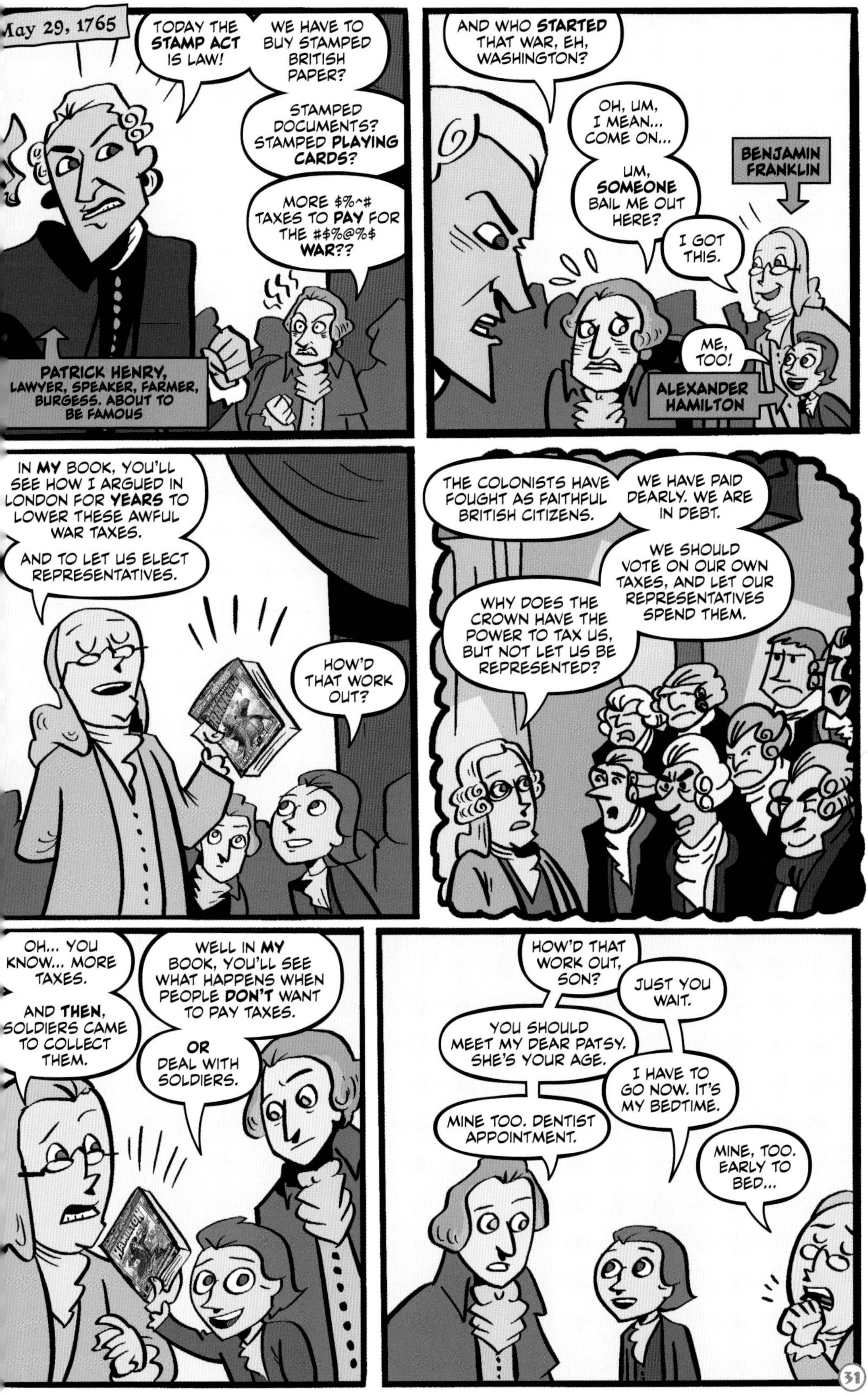
May 29, 1765
TODAY THE STAMP ACT IS LAW!
WE HAVE TO BUY STAMPED BRITISH PAPER?
STAMPED DOCUMENTS? STAMPED PLAYING CARDS?
MORE $%^# TAXES TO PAY FOR THE #$%@%$ WAR??
PATRICK HENRY, LAWYER, SPEAKER, FARMER, BURGESS. ABOUT TO BE FAMOUS
AND WHO STARTED THAT WAR, EH, WASHINGTON?
OH, UM, I MEAN... COME ON...
UM, SOMEONE BAIL ME OUT HERE?
BENJAMIN FRANKLIN
I GOT THIS.
ME, TOO!
ALEXANDER HAMILTON
IN MY BOOK, YOU'LL SEE HOW I ARGUED IN LONDON FOR YEARS TO LOWER THESE AWFUL WAR TAXES.
AND TO LET US ELECT REPRESENTATIVES.
HOW'D THAT WORK OUT?
THE COLONISTS HAVE FOUGHT AS FAITHFUL BRITISH CITIZENS.
WE HAVE PAID DEARLY. WE ARE IN DEBT.
WE SHOULD VOTE ON OUR OWN TAXES, AND LET OUR REPRESENTATIVES SPEND THEM.
WHY DOES THE CROWN HAVE THE POWER TO TAX US, BUT NOT LET US BE REPRESENTED?
OH... YOU KNOW... MORE TAXES.
AND THEN, SOLDIERS CAME TO COLLECT THEM.
WELL IN MY BOOK, YOU'LL SEE WHAT HAPPENS WHEN PEOPLE DON'T WANT TO PAY TAXES.
OR DEAL WITH SOLDIERS.
HOW'D THAT WORK OUT, SON?
JUST YOU WAIT.
YOU SHOULD MEET MY DEAR PATSY. SHE'S YOUR AGE.
I HAVE TO GO NOW. IT'S MY BEDTIME.
MINE TOO. DENTIST APPOINTMENT.
MINE, TOO. EARLY TO BED...

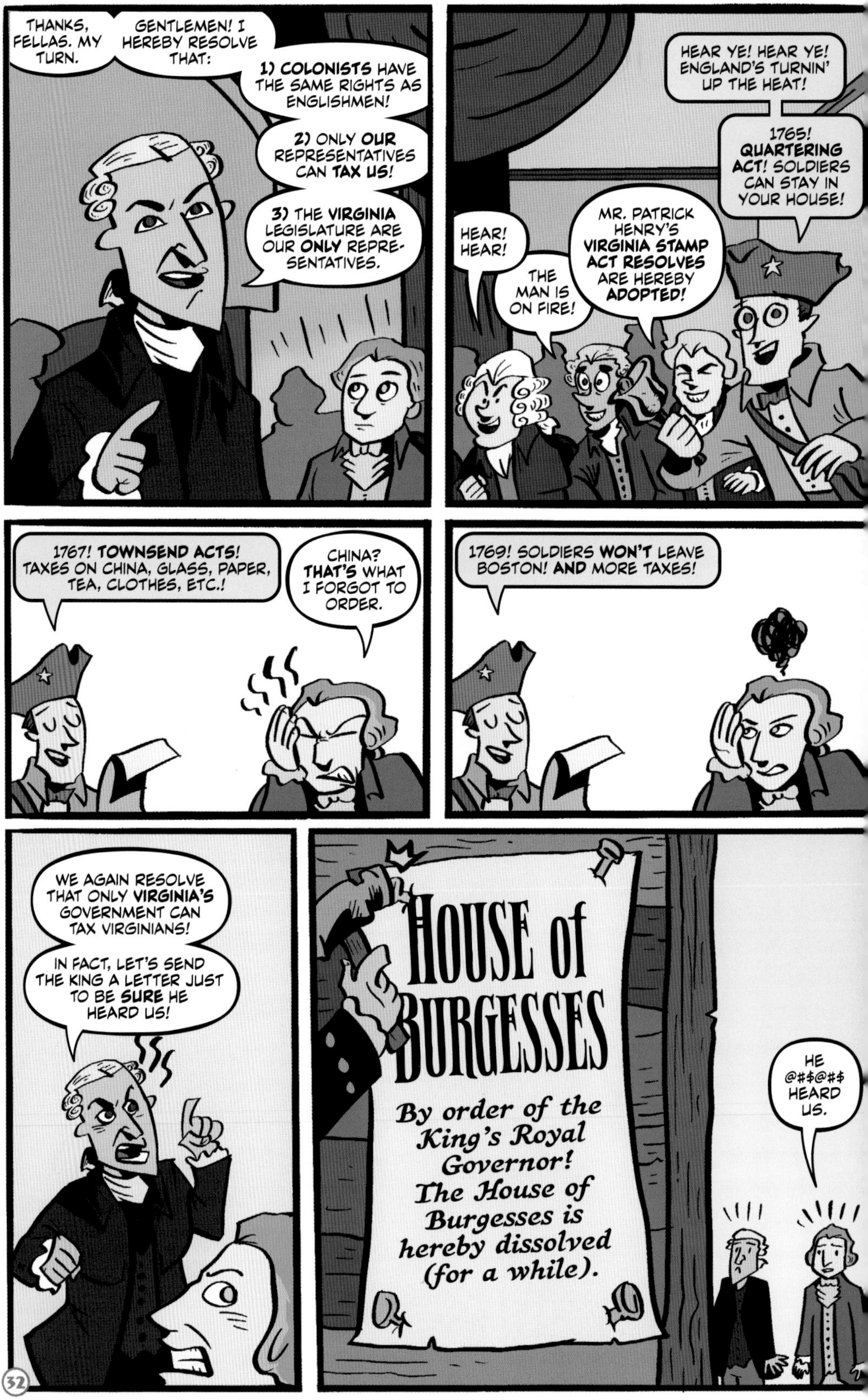
THANKS, FELLAS. MY TURN.
GENTLEMEN! I HEREBY RESOLVE THAT:
1) COLONISTS HAVE THE SAME RIGHTS AS ENGLISHMEN!
2) ONLY OUR REPRESENTATIVES CAN TAX US!
3) THE VIRGINIA LEGISLATURE ARE OUR ONLY REPRE-SENTATIVES.
HEAR! HEAR!
THE MAN IS ON FIRE!
MR. PATRICK HENRY'S VIRGINIA STAMP ACT RESOLVES ARE HEREBY ADOPTED!
HEAR YE! HEAR YE! ENGLAND'S TURNIN' UP THE HEAT!
1765! QUARTERING ACT! SOLDIERS CAN STAY IN YOUR HOUSE!
1767! TOWNSEND ACTS! TAXES ON CHINA, GLASS, PAPER, TEA, CLOTHES, ETC.!
CHINA? THAT'S WHAT I FORGOT TO ORDER.
1769! SOLDIERS WON'T LEAVE BOSTON! AND MORE TAXES!
WE AGAIN RESOLVE THAT ONLY VIRGINIA'S GOVERNMENT CAN TAX VIRGINIANS!
IN FACT, LET'S SEND THE KING A LETTER JUST TO BE SURE HE HEARD US!
HOUSE of BURGESSES
By order of the King's Royal Governor! The House of Burgesses is hereby dissolved (for a while).
HE @#$@#$ HEARD US.

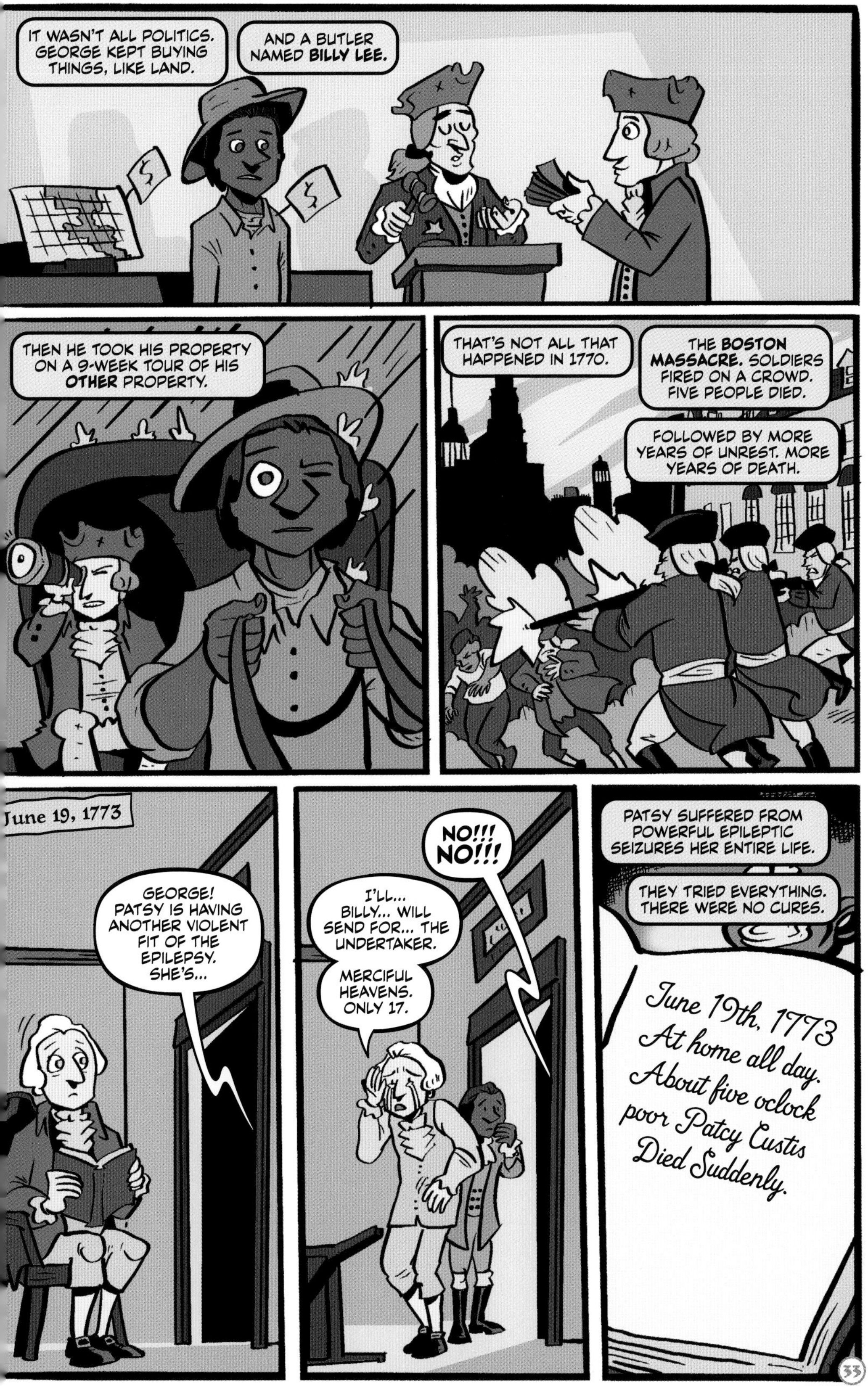
IT WASN'T ALL POLITICS. GEORGE KEPT BUYING THINGS, LIKE LAND.
AND A BUTLER NAMED **BILLY LEE.**
THEN HE TOOK HIS PROPERTY ON A 9-WEEK TOUR OF HIS **OTHER** PROPERTY.
THAT'S NOT ALL THAT HAPPENED IN 1770.
THE **BOSTON MASSACRE.** SOLDIERS FIRED ON A CROWD. FIVE PEOPLE DIED.
FOLLOWED BY MORE YEARS OF UNREST. MORE YEARS OF DEATH.
June 19, 1773
GEORGE! PATSY IS HAVING ANOTHER VIOLENT FIT OF THE EPILEPSY. SHE'S...
NO!!! NO!!!
I'LL... BILLY... WILL SEND FOR... THE UNDERTAKER.
MERCIFUL HEAVENS. ONLY 17.
PATSY SUFFERED FROM POWERFUL EPILEPTIC SEIZURES HER ENTIRE LIFE.
THEY TRIED EVERYTHING. THERE WERE NO CURES.
June 19th, 1773 At home all day. About five oclock poor Patcy Custis Died Suddenly.

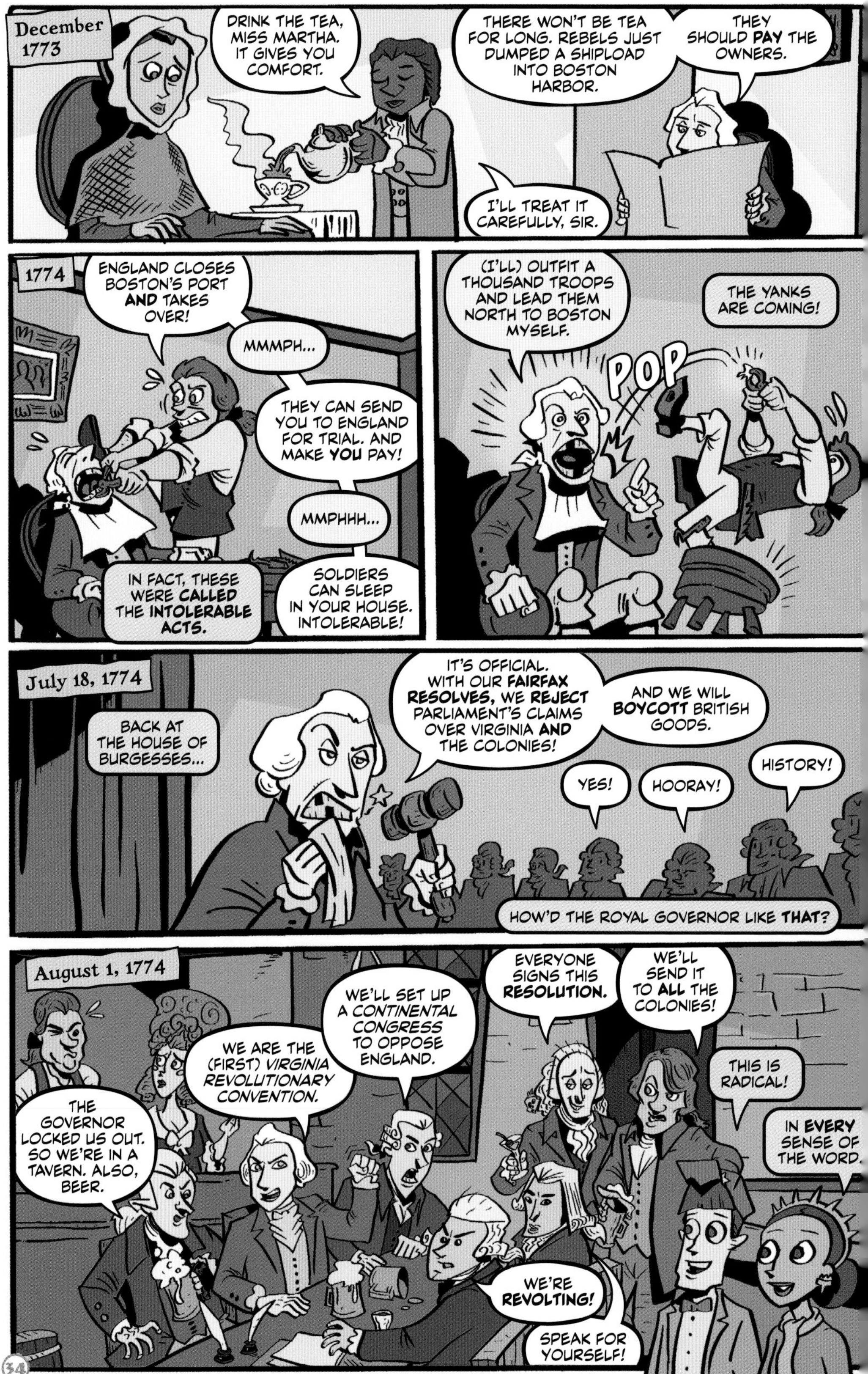
December 1773
DRINK THE TEA, MISS MARTHA. IT GIVES YOU COMFORT.
THERE WON'T BE TEA FOR LONG. REBELS JUST DUMPED A SHIPLOAD INTO BOSTON HARBOR.
THEY SHOULD PAY THE OWNERS.
I'LL TREAT IT CAREFULLY, SIR.
1774
ENGLAND CLOSES BOSTON'S PORT AND TAKES OVER!
MMMPH...
THEY CAN SEND YOU TO ENGLAND FOR TRIAL. AND MAKE YOU PAY!
MMPHHH...
IN FACT, THESE WERE CALLED THE INTOLERABLE ACTS.
SOLDIERS CAN SLEEP IN YOUR HOUSE. INTOLERABLE!
(I'LL) OUTFIT A THOUSAND TROOPS AND LEAD THEM NORTH TO BOSTON MYSELF.
THE YANKS ARE COMING!
POP
July 18, 1774
BACK AT THE HOUSE OF BURGESSES...
IT'S OFFICIAL. WITH OUR FAIRFAX RESOLVES, WE REJECT PARLIAMENT'S CLAIMS OVER VIRGINIA AND THE COLONIES!
AND WE WILL BOYCOTT BRITISH GOODS.
YES!
HOORAY!
HISTORY!
HOW'D THE ROYAL GOVERNOR LIKE THAT?
August 1, 1774
THE GOVERNOR LOCKED US OUT. SO WE'RE IN A TAVERN. ALSO, BEER.
WE ARE THE (FIRST) VIRGINIA REVOLUTIONARY CONVENTION.
WE'LL SET UP A CONTINENTAL CONGRESS TO OPPOSE ENGLAND.
EVERYONE SIGNS THIS RESOLUTION.
WE'LL SEND IT TO ALL THE COLONIES!
THIS IS RADICAL!
IN EVERY SENSE OF THE WORD.
WE'RE REVOLTING!
SPEAK FOR YOURSELF!

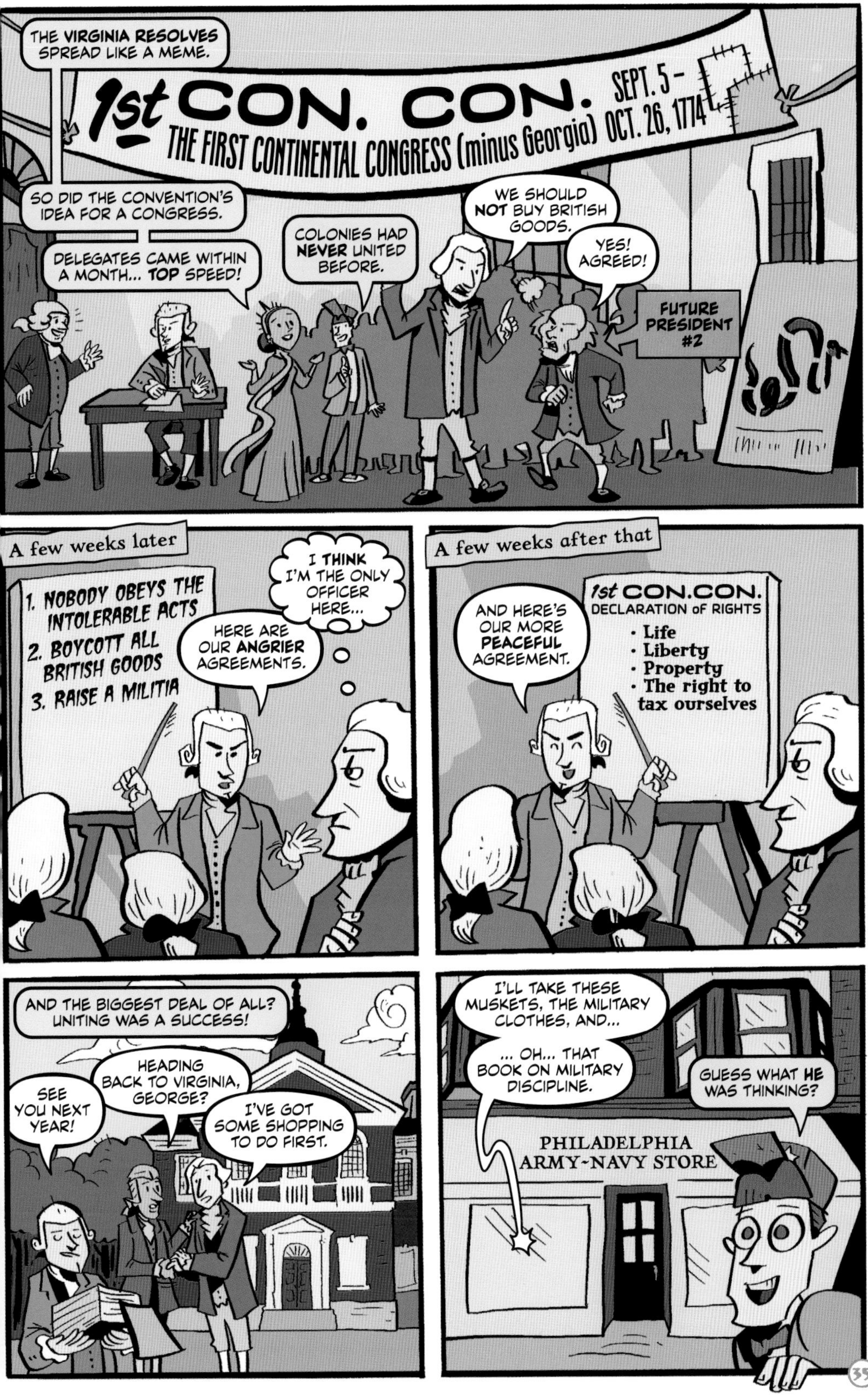

THE VIRGINIA RESOLVES SPREAD LIKE A MEME.
1st CON. CON.
THE FIRST CONTINENTAL CONGRESS (minus Georgia)
SEPT. 5 – OCT. 26, 1774
SO DID THE CONVENTION'S IDEA FOR A CONGRESS.
DELEGATES CAME WITHIN A MONTH... TOP SPEED!
COLONIES HAD NEVER UNITED BEFORE.
WE SHOULD NOT BUY BRITISH GOODS.
YES! AGREED!
FUTURE PRESIDENT #2
A few weeks later
1. NOBODY OBEYS THE INTOLERABLE ACTS
2. BOYCOTT ALL BRITISH GOODS
3. RAISE A MILITIA
HERE ARE OUR ANGRIER AGREEMENTS.
I THINK I'M THE ONLY OFFICER HERE...
A few weeks after that
1st CON.CON.
DECLARATION of RIGHTS
• Life
• Liberty
• Property
• The right to tax ourselves
AND HERE'S OUR MORE PEACEFUL AGREEMENT.
AND THE BIGGEST DEAL OF ALL? UNITING WAS A SUCCESS!
SEE YOU NEXT YEAR!
HEADING BACK TO VIRGINIA, GEORGE?
I'VE GOT SOME SHOPPING TO DO FIRST.
I'LL TAKE THESE MUSKETS, THE MILITARY CLOTHES, AND...
... OH... THAT BOOK ON MILITARY DISCIPLINE.
GUESS WHAT HE WAS THINKING?
PHILADELPHIA ARMY-NAVY STORE

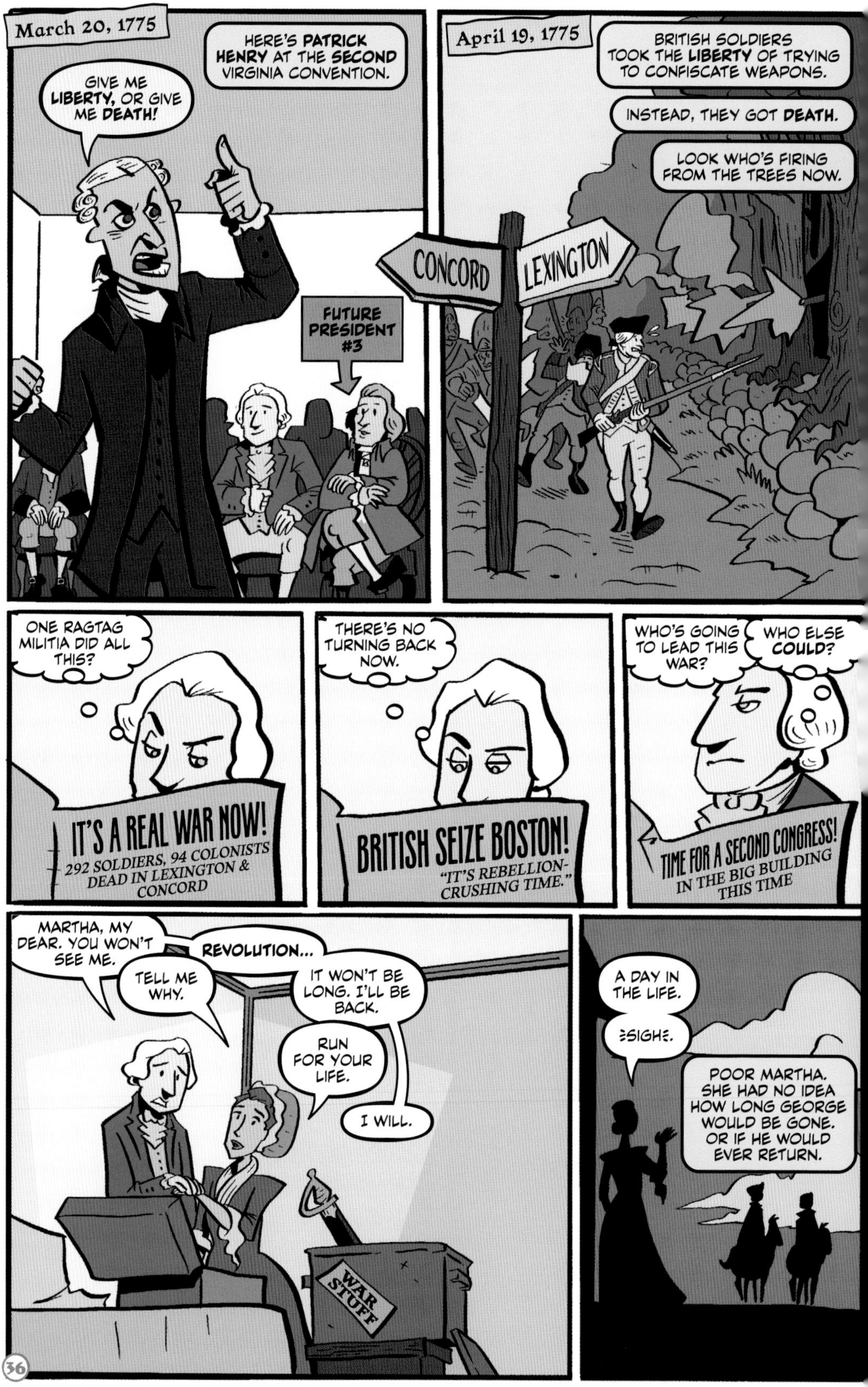

March 20, 1775
HERE'S PATRICK HENRY AT THE SECOND VIRGINIA CONVENTION.
GIVE ME LIBERTY, OR GIVE ME DEATH!
FUTURE PRESIDENT #3
April 19, 1775
BRITISH SOLDIERS TOOK THE LIBERTY OF TRYING TO CONFISCATE WEAPONS.
INSTEAD, THEY GOT DEATH.
LOOK WHO'S FIRING FROM THE TREES NOW.
CONCORD
LEXINGTON
ONE RAGTAG MILITIA DID ALL THIS?
IT'S A REAL WAR NOW!
292 SOLDIERS, 94 COLONISTS DEAD IN LEXINGTON & CONCORD
THERE'S NO TURNING BACK NOW.
BRITISH SEIZE BOSTON!
"IT'S REBELLION-CRUSHING TIME."
WHO'S GOING TO LEAD THIS WAR?
WHO ELSE COULD?
TIME FOR A SECOND CONGRESS!
IN THE BIG BUILDING THIS TIME
MARTHA, MY DEAR. YOU WON'T SEE ME.
REVOLUTION...
TELL ME WHY.
IT WON'T BE LONG. I'LL BE BACK.
RUN FOR YOUR LIFE.
I WILL.
WAR STUFF
A DAY IN THE LIFE.
SIGH.
POOR MARTHA. SHE HAD NO IDEA HOW LONG GEORGE WOULD BE GONE. OR IF HE WOULD EVER RETURN.

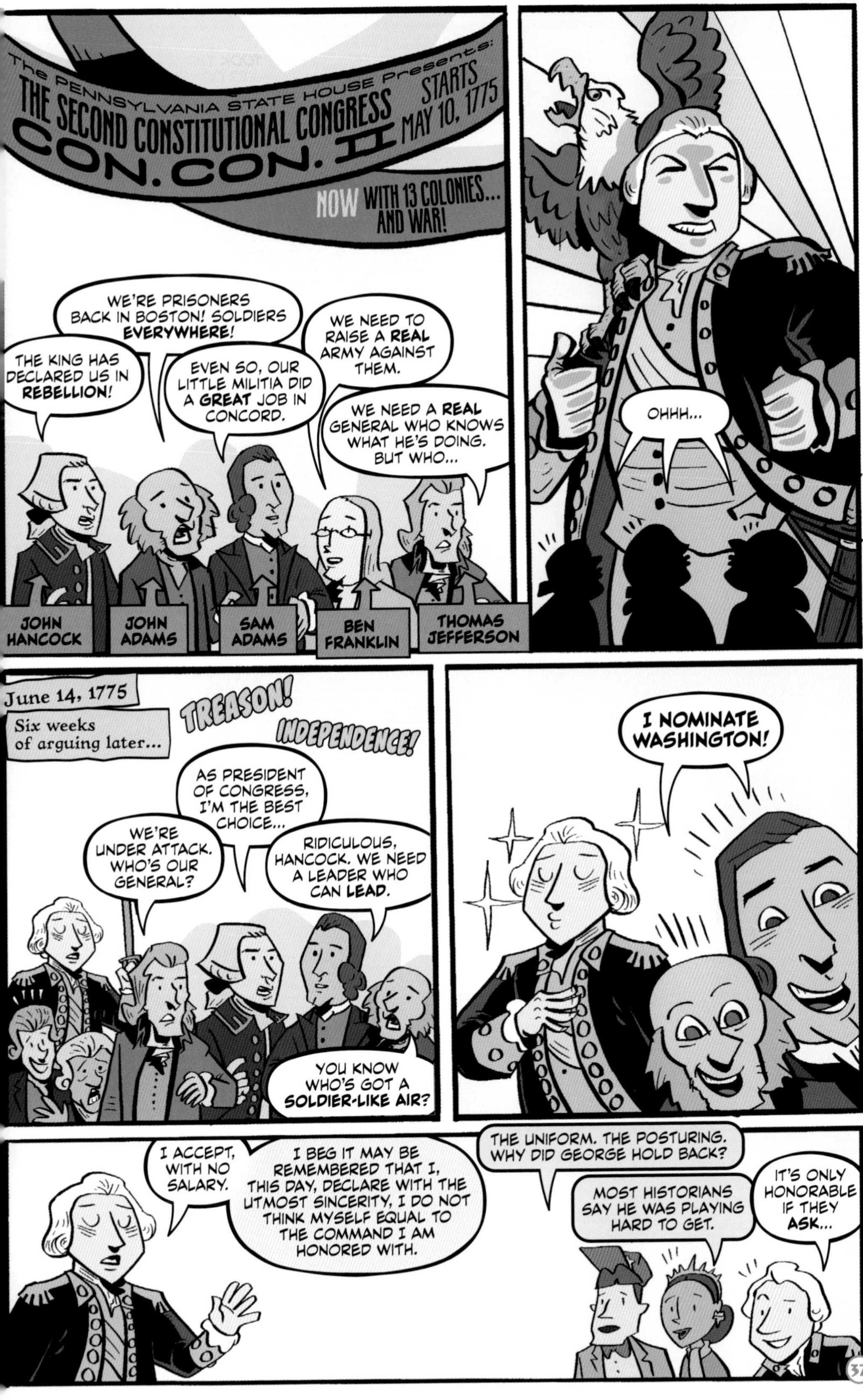
The PENNSYLVANIA STATE HOUSE Presents:
THE SECOND CONSTITUTIONAL CONGRESS
CON. CON. II
STARTS MAY 10, 1775
NOW WITH 13 COLONIES... AND WAR!
THE KING HAS DECLARED US IN REBELLION!
WE'RE PRISONERS BACK IN BOSTON! SOLDIERS EVERYWHERE!
EVEN SO, OUR LITTLE MILITIA DID A GREAT JOB IN CONCORD.
WE NEED TO RAISE A REAL ARMY AGAINST THEM.
WE NEED A REAL GENERAL WHO KNOWS WHAT HE'S DOING. BUT WHO...
JOHN HANCOCK
JOHN ADAMS
SAM ADAMS
BEN FRANKLIN
THOMAS JEFFERSON
OHHH...
June 14, 1775
Six weeks of arguing later...
TREASON!
INDEPENDENCE!
AS PRESIDENT OF CONGRESS, I'M THE BEST CHOICE...
WE'RE UNDER ATTACK. WHO'S OUR GENERAL?
RIDICULOUS, HANCOCK. WE NEED A LEADER WHO CAN LEAD.
YOU KNOW WHO'S GOT A SOLDIER-LIKE AIR?
I NOMINATE WASHINGTON!
I ACCEPT, WITH NO SALARY.
I BEG IT MAY BE REMEMBERED THAT I, THIS DAY, DECLARE WITH THE UTMOST SINCERITY, I DO NOT THINK MYSELF EQUAL TO THE COMMAND I AM HONORED WITH.
THE UNIFORM. THE POSTURING. WHY DID GEORGE HOLD BACK?
MOST HISTORIANS SAY HE WAS PLAYING HARD TO GET.
IT'S ONLY HONORABLE IF THEY ASK...

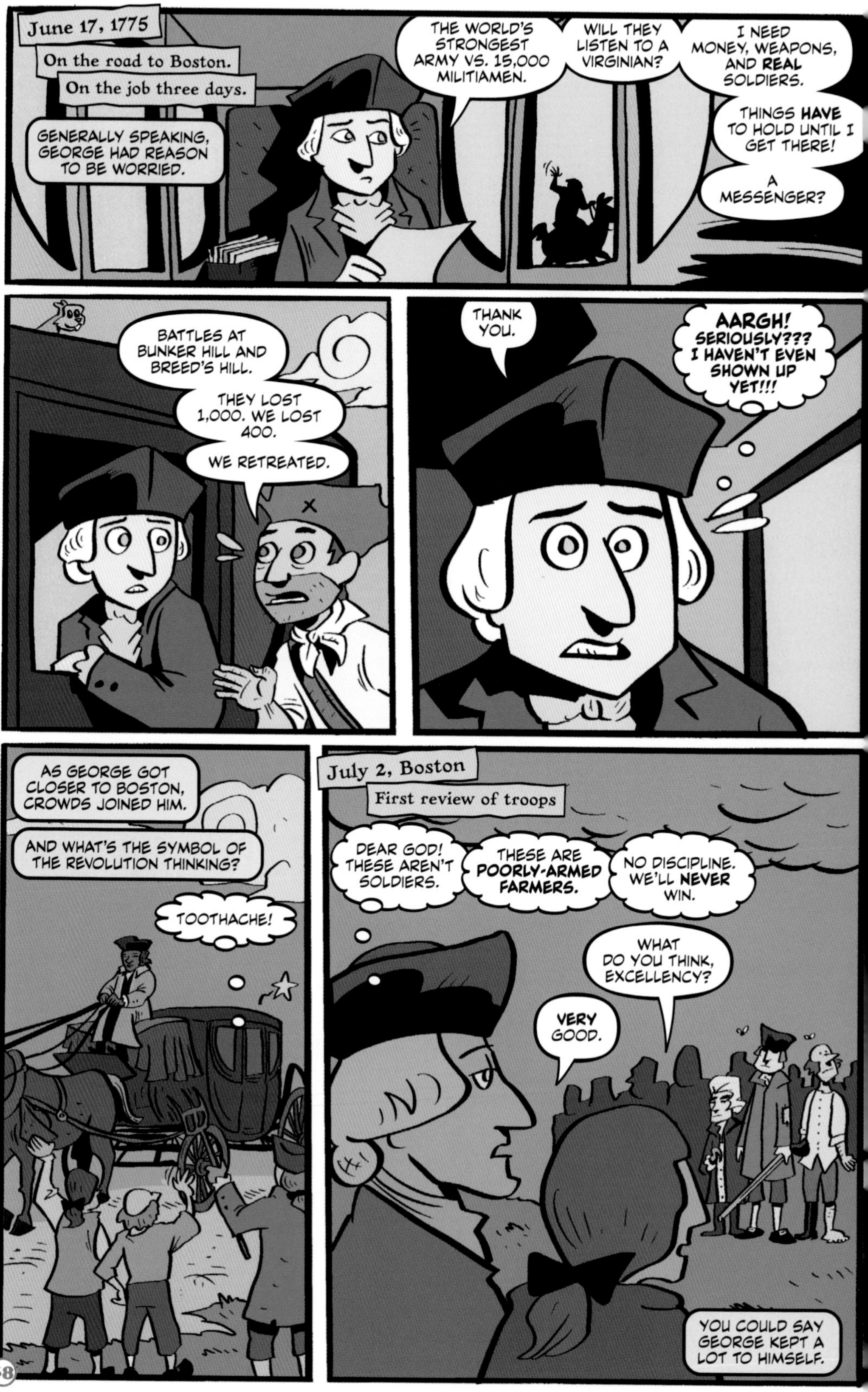
June 17, 1775
On the road to Boston.
On the job three days.
GENERALLY SPEAKING, GEORGE HAD REASON TO BE WORRIED.
THE WORLD'S STRONGEST ARMY VS. 15,000 MILITIAMEN.
WILL THEY LISTEN TO A VIRGINIAN?
I NEED MONEY, WEAPONS, AND **REAL** SOLDIERS.
THINGS **HAVE** TO HOLD UNTIL I GET THERE!
A MESSENGER?
BATTLES AT BUNKER HILL AND BREED'S HILL.
THEY LOST 1,000. WE LOST 400.
WE RETREATED.
THANK YOU.
AARGH! SERIOUSLY??? I HAVEN'T EVEN SHOWN UP YET!!!
AS GEORGE GOT CLOSER TO BOSTON, CROWDS JOINED HIM.
AND WHAT'S THE SYMBOL OF THE REVOLUTION THINKING?
TOOTHACHE!
July 2, Boston
First review of troops
DEAR GOD! THESE AREN'T SOLDIERS.
THESE ARE **POORLY-ARMED FARMERS.**
NO DISCIPLINE. WE'LL **NEVER** WIN.
WHAT DO YOU THINK, EXCELLENCY?
VERY GOOD.
YOU COULD SAY GEORGE KEPT A LOT TO HIMSELF.

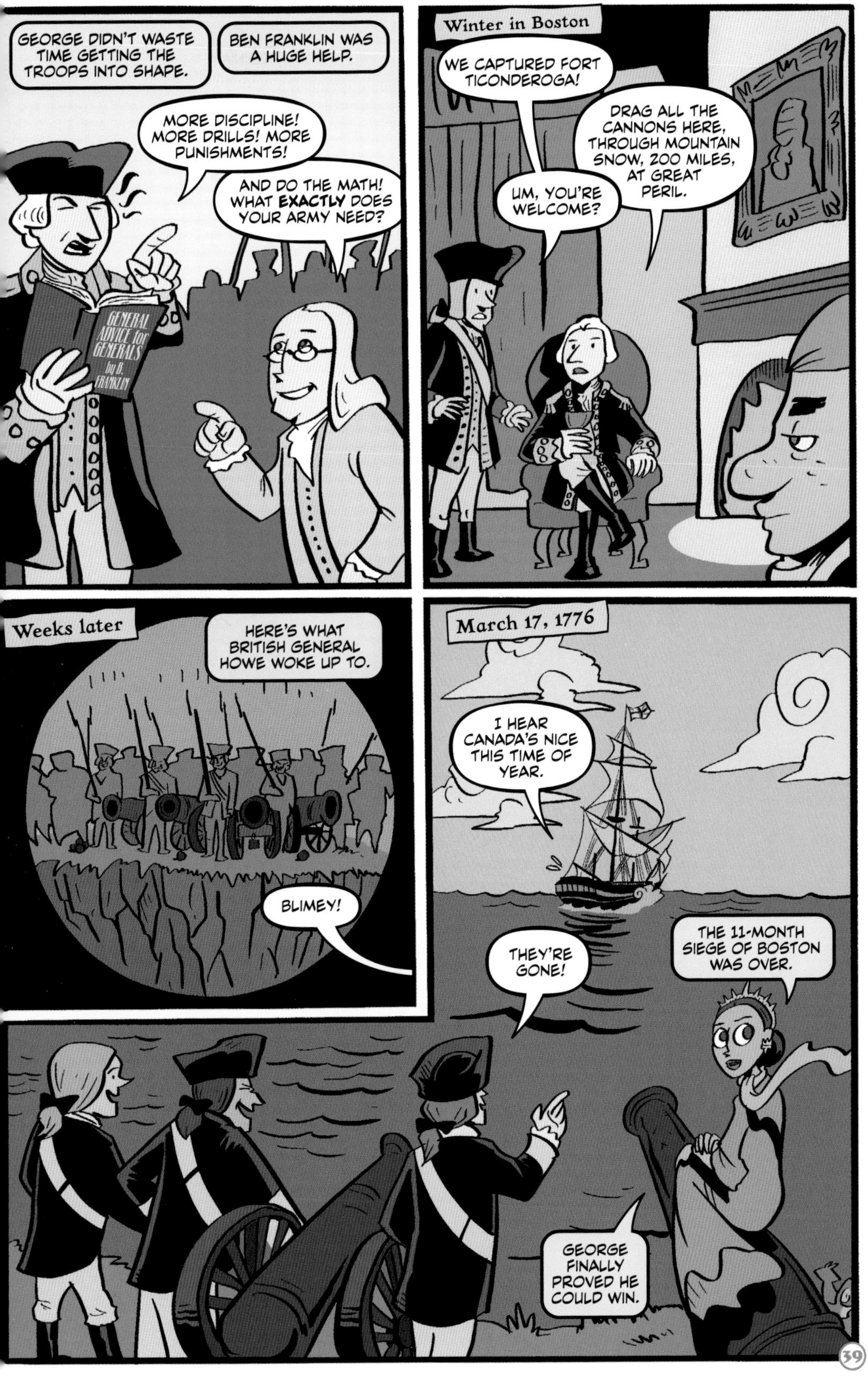
GEORGE DIDN'T WASTE TIME GETTING THE TROOPS INTO SHAPE.
BEN FRANKLIN WAS A HUGE HELP.
MORE DISCIPLINE! MORE DRILLS! MORE PUNISHMENTS!
AND DO THE MATH! WHAT **EXACTLY** DOES YOUR ARMY NEED?
GENERAL ADVICE for GENERALS by B. FRANKLIN
Winter in Boston
WE CAPTURED FORT TICONDEROGA!
DRAG ALL THE CANNONS HERE, THROUGH MOUNTAIN SNOW, 200 MILES, AT GREAT PERIL.
UM, YOU'RE WELCOME?
Weeks later
HERE'S WHAT BRITISH GENERAL HOWE WOKE UP TO.
BLIMEY!
March 17, 1776
I HEAR CANADA'S NICE THIS TIME OF YEAR.
THEY'RE GONE!
THE 11-MONTH SIEGE OF BOSTON WAS OVER.
GEORGE FINALLY PROVED HE COULD WIN.

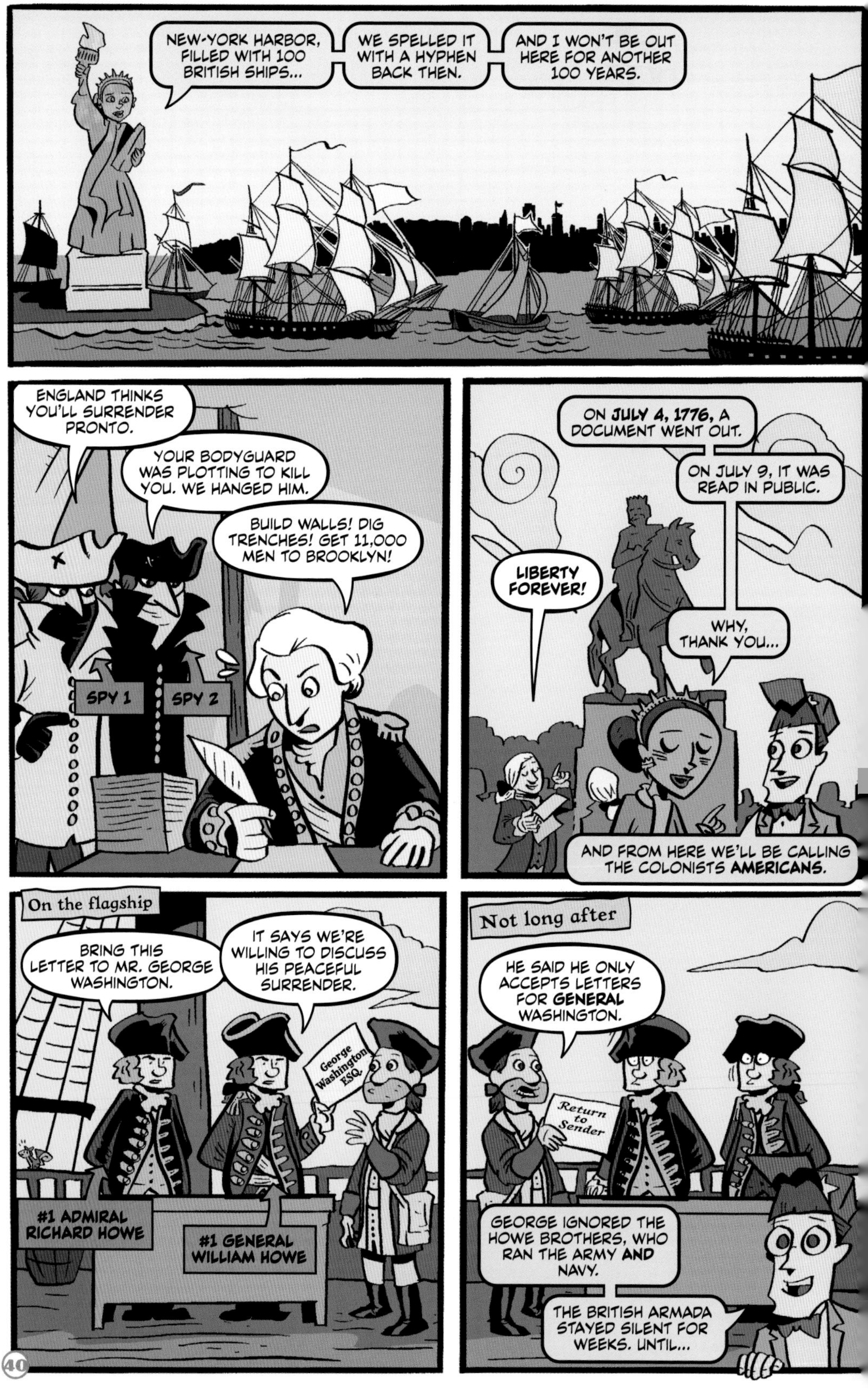
NEW-YORK HARBOR, FILLED WITH 100 BRITISH SHIPS...
WE SPELLED IT WITH A HYPHEN BACK THEN.
AND I WON'T BE OUT HERE FOR ANOTHER 100 YEARS.
ENGLAND THINKS YOU'LL SURRENDER PRONTO.
YOUR BODYGUARD WAS PLOTTING TO KILL YOU. WE HANGED HIM.
BUILD WALLS! DIG TRENCHES! GET 11,000 MEN TO BROOKLYN!
SPY 1
SPY 2
ON JULY 4, 1776, A DOCUMENT WENT OUT.
ON JULY 9, IT WAS READ IN PUBLIC.
LIBERTY FOREVER!
WHY, THANK YOU...
AND FROM HERE WE'LL BE CALLING THE COLONISTS AMERICANS.
On the flagship
BRING THIS LETTER TO MR. GEORGE WASHINGTON.
IT SAYS WE'RE WILLING TO DISCUSS HIS PEACEFUL SURRENDER.
George Washington ESQ.
#1 ADMIRAL RICHARD HOWE
#1 GENERAL WILLIAM HOWE
Not long after
HE SAID HE ONLY ACCEPTS LETTERS FOR GENERAL WASHINGTON.
Return to Sender
GEORGE IGNORED THE HOWE BROTHERS, WHO RAN THE ARMY AND NAVY.
THE BRITISH ARMADA STAYED SILENT FOR WEEKS. UNTIL...

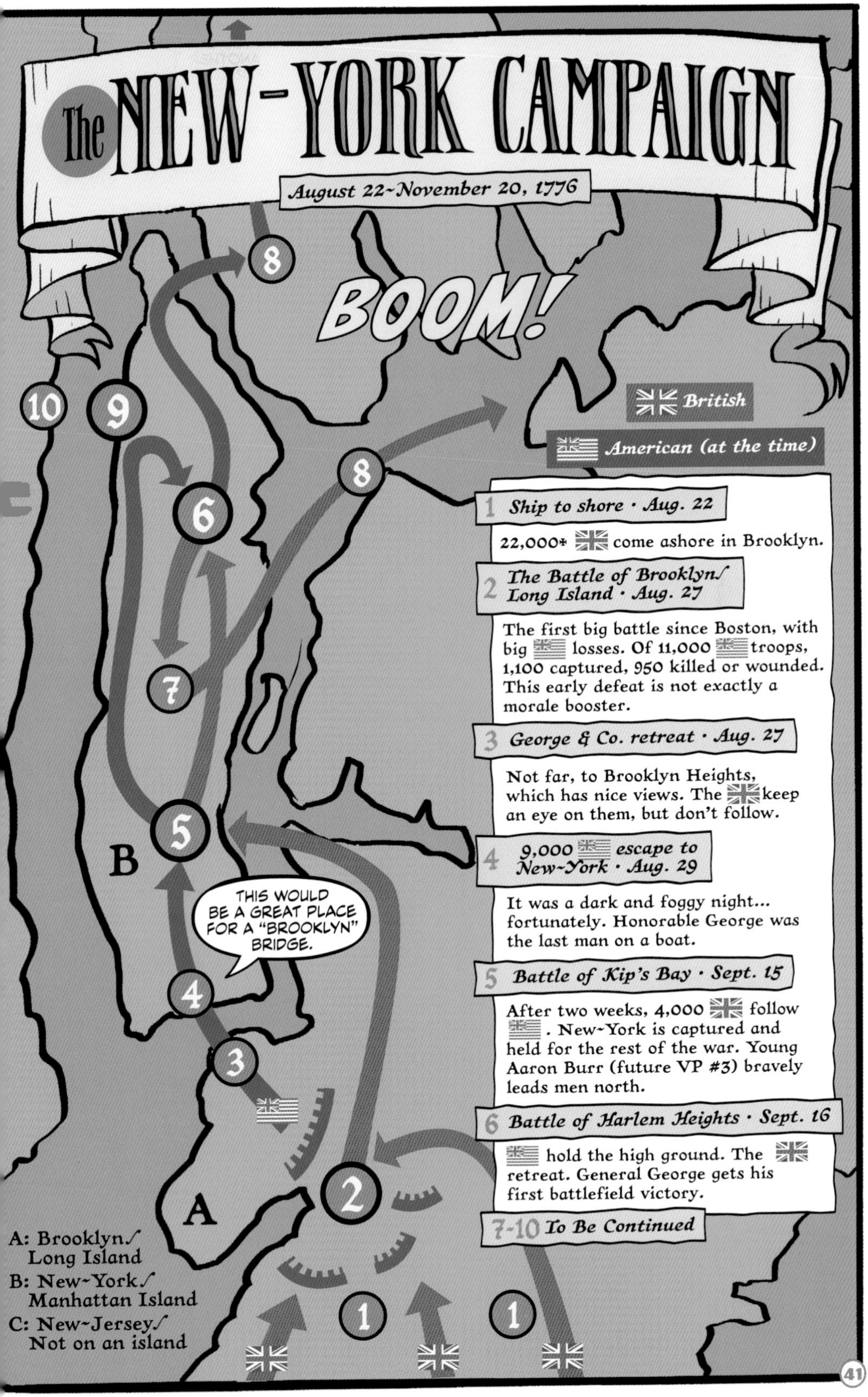
The NEW-YORK CAMPAIGN
August 22~November 20, 1776
BOOM!
British
American (at the time)
1 Ship to shore · Aug. 22
22,000* come ashore in Brooklyn.
2 The Battle of Brooklyn/ Long Island · Aug. 27
The first big battle since Boston, with big losses. Of 11,000 troops, 1,100 captured, 950 killed or wounded. This early defeat is not exactly a morale booster.
3 George & Co. retreat · Aug. 27
Not far, to Brooklyn Heights, which has nice views. The keep an eye on them, but don't follow.
4 9,000 escape to New~York · Aug. 29
It was a dark and foggy night... fortunately. Honorable George was the last man on a boat.
5 Battle of Kip's Bay · Sept. 15
After two weeks, 4,000 follow . New~York is captured and held for the rest of the war. Young Aaron Burr (future VP #3) bravely leads men north.
6 Battle of Harlem Heights · Sept. 16
hold the high ground. The retreat. General George gets his first battlefield victory.
7-10 To Be Continued
THIS WOULD BE A GREAT PLACE FOR A "BROOKLYN" BRIDGE.
A
B
A: Brooklyn/ Long Island
B: New~York/ Manhattan Island
C: New~Jersey/ Not on an island

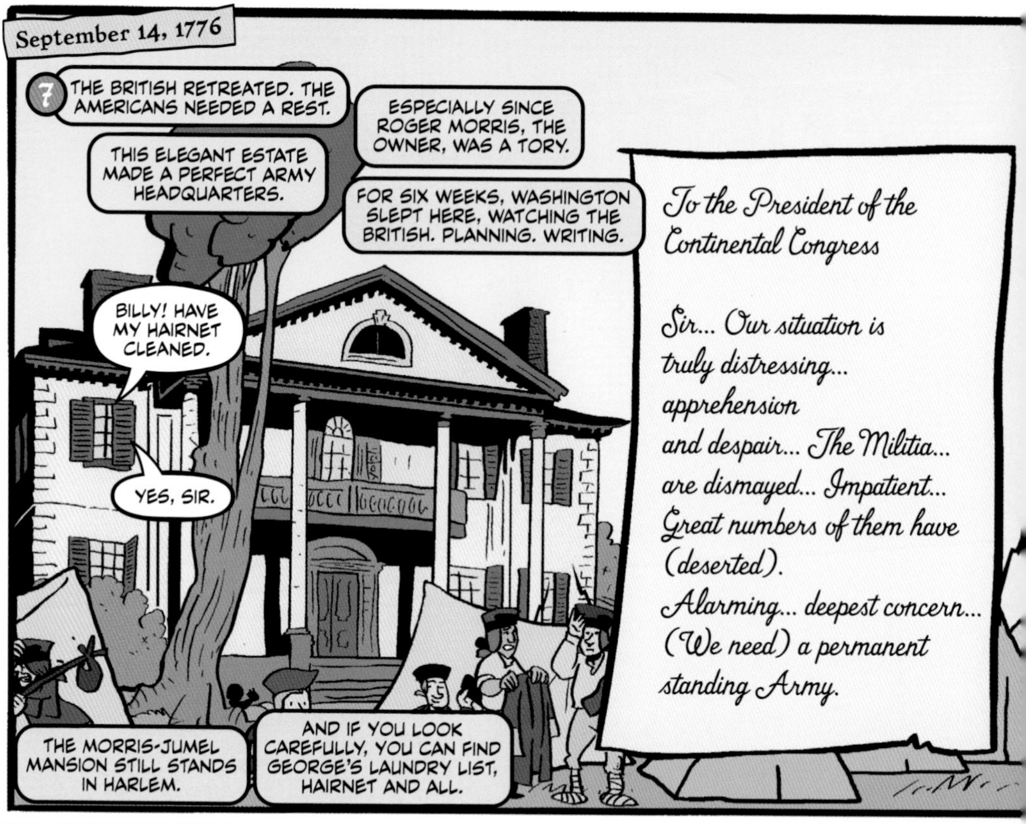
September 14, 1776
7
THE BRITISH RETREATED. THE AMERICANS NEEDED A REST.
THIS ELEGANT ESTATE MADE A PERFECT ARMY HEADQUARTERS.
ESPECIALLY SINCE ROGER MORRIS, THE OWNER, WAS A TORY.
FOR SIX WEEKS, WASHINGTON SLEPT HERE, WATCHING THE BRITISH. PLANNING. WRITING.
To the President of the Continental Congress
Sir... Our situation is truly distressing... apprehension and despair... The Militia... are dismayed... Impatient... Great numbers of them have (deserted).
Alarming... deepest concern... (We need) a permanent standing Army.
BILLY! HAVE MY HAIRNET CLEANED.
YES, SIR.
THE MORRIS-JUMEL MANSION STILL STANDS IN HARLEM.
AND IF YOU LOOK CAREFULLY, YOU CAN FIND GEORGE'S LAUNDRY LIST, HAIRNET AND ALL.

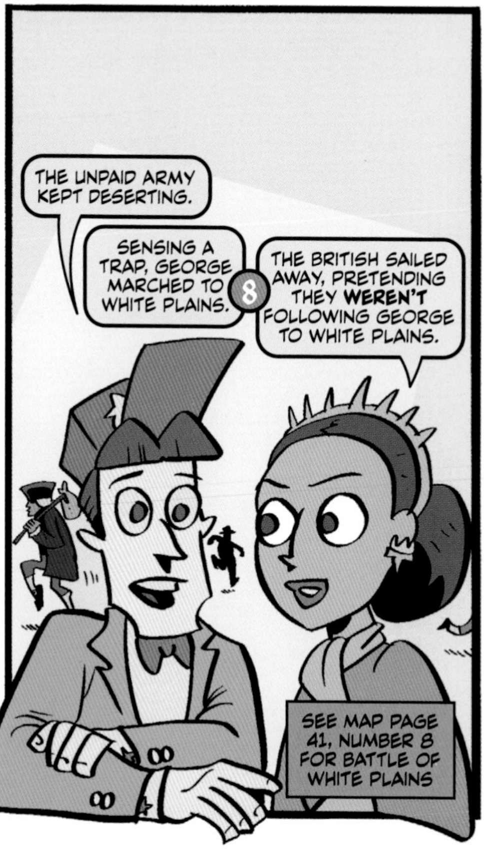
THE UNPAID ARMY KEPT DESERTING.
SENSING A TRAP, GEORGE MARCHED TO WHITE PLAINS.
8
THE BRITISH SAILED AWAY, PRETENDING THEY **WEREN'T** FOLLOWING GEORGE TO WHITE PLAINS.
SEE MAP PAGE 41, NUMBER 8 FOR BATTLE OF WHITE PLAINS

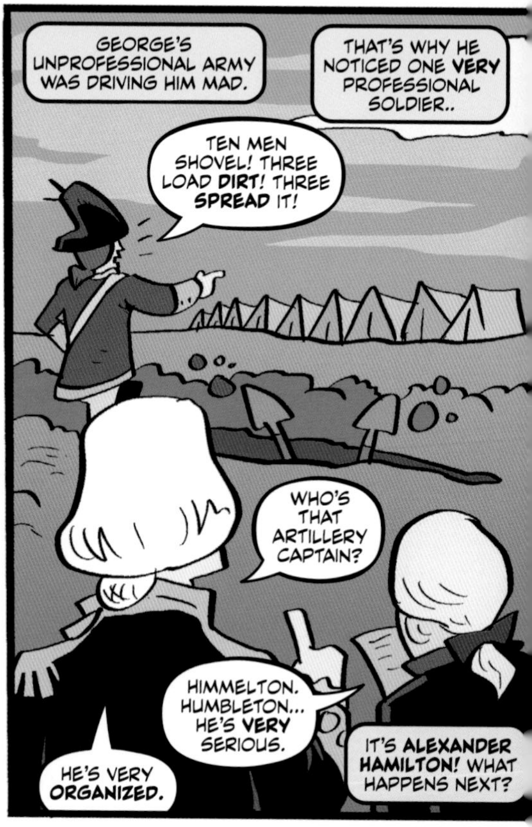
GEORGE'S UNPROFESSIONAL ARMY WAS DRIVING HIM MAD.
THAT'S WHY HE NOTICED ONE **VERY** PROFESSIONAL SOLDIER..
TEN MEN SHOVEL! THREE LOAD **DIRT**! THREE **SPREAD** IT!
WHO'S THAT ARTILLERY CAPTAIN?
HIMMELTON. HUMBLETON... HE'S **VERY** SERIOUS.
HE'S VERY **ORGANIZED.**
IT'S **ALEXANDER HAMILTON!** WHAT HAPPENS NEXT?

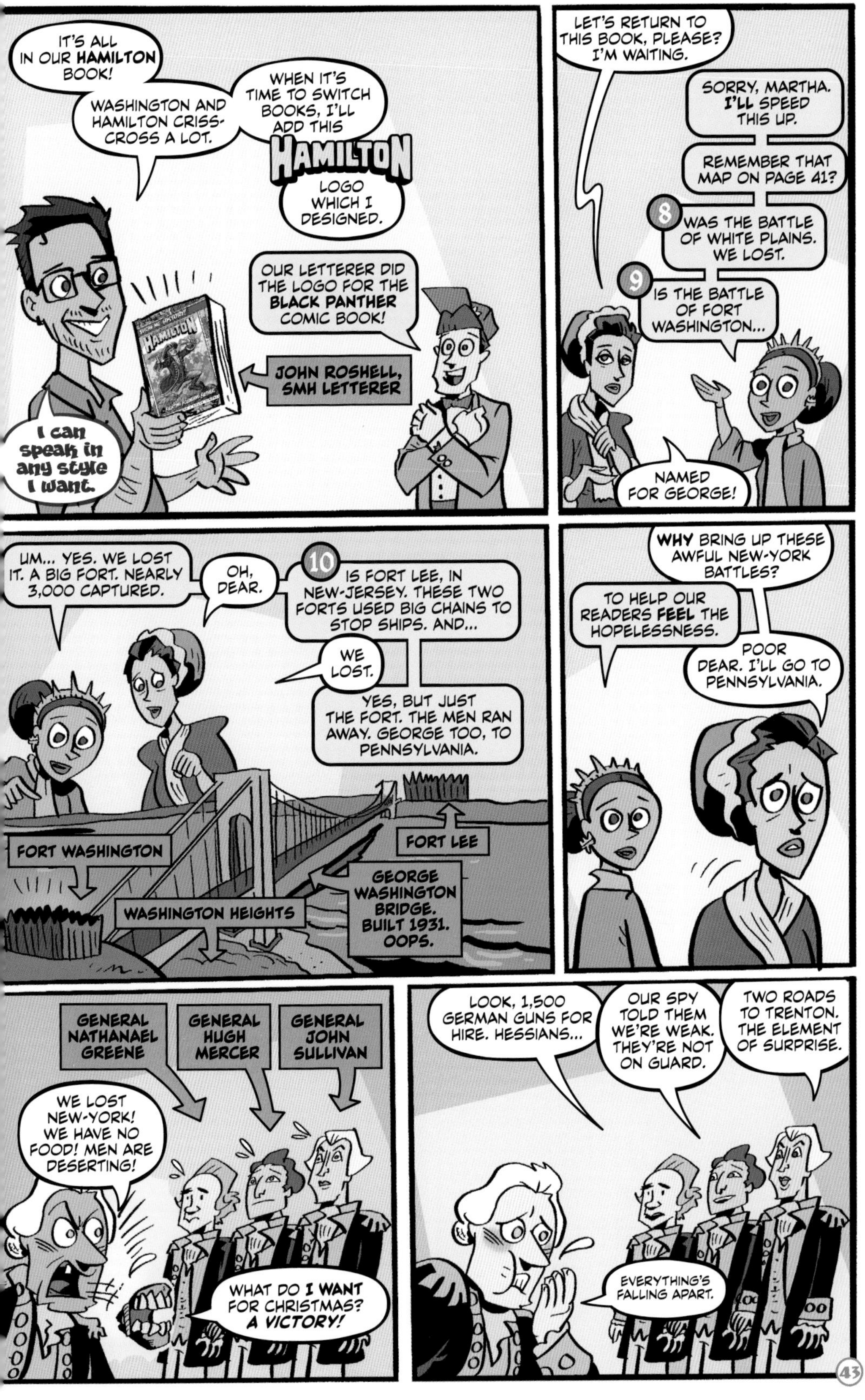
IT'S ALL IN OUR **HAMILTON** BOOK!
WASHINGTON AND HAMILTON CRISS-CROSS A LOT.
WHEN IT'S TIME TO SWITCH BOOKS, I'LL ADD THIS
HAMILTON
LOGO WHICH I DESIGNED.
OUR LETTERER DID THE LOGO FOR THE **BLACK PANTHER** COMIC BOOK!
JOHN ROSHELL, SMH LETTERER
I can speak in any style I want.
LET'S RETURN TO THIS BOOK, PLEASE? I'M WAITING.
SORRY, MARTHA. **I'LL** SPEED THIS UP.
REMEMBER THAT MAP ON PAGE 41?
8 WAS THE BATTLE OF WHITE PLAINS. WE LOST.
9 IS THE BATTLE OF FORT WASHINGTON...
NAMED FOR GEORGE!
UM... YES. WE LOST IT. A BIG FORT. NEARLY 3,000 CAPTURED.
OH, DEAR.
10 IS FORT LEE, IN NEW-JERSEY. THESE TWO FORTS USED BIG CHAINS TO STOP SHIPS. AND...
WE LOST.
YES, BUT JUST THE FORT. THE MEN RAN AWAY. GEORGE TOO, TO PENNSYLVANIA.
FORT WASHINGTON
WASHINGTON HEIGHTS
FORT LEE
GEORGE WASHINGTON BRIDGE. BUILT 1931. OOPS.
WHY BRING UP THESE AWFUL NEW-YORK BATTLES?
TO HELP OUR READERS **FEEL** THE HOPELESSNESS.
POOR DEAR. I'LL GO TO PENNSYLVANIA.
GENERAL NATHANAEL GREENE
GENERAL HUGH MERCER
GENERAL JOHN SULLIVAN
WE LOST NEW-YORK! WE HAVE NO FOOD! MEN ARE DESERTING!
WHAT DO **I WANT** FOR CHRISTMAS? ***A VICTORY!***
LOOK, 1,500 GERMAN GUNS FOR HIRE. HESSIANS...
OUR SPY TOLD THEM WE'RE WEAK. THEY'RE NOT ON GUARD.
TWO ROADS TO TRENTON. THE ELEMENT OF SURPRISE.
EVERYTHING'S FALLING APART.

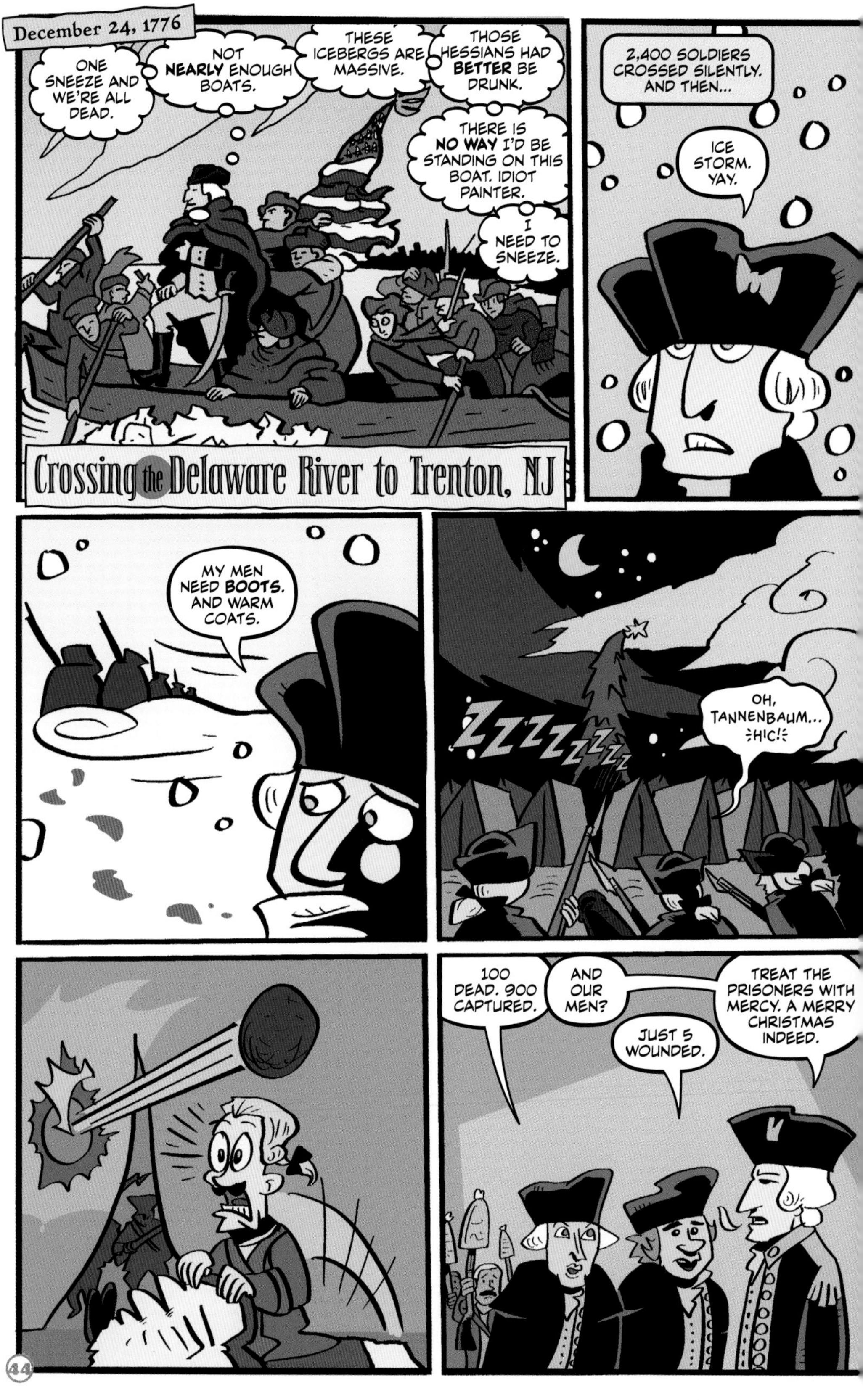

December 24, 1776
ONE SNEEZE AND WE'RE ALL DEAD.
NOT NEARLY ENOUGH BOATS.
THESE ICEBERGS ARE MASSIVE.
THOSE HESSIANS HAD BETTER BE DRUNK.
THERE IS NO WAY I'D BE STANDING ON THIS BOAT. IDIOT PAINTER.
I NEED TO SNEEZE.
Crossing the Delaware River to Trenton, NJ
2,400 SOLDIERS CROSSED SILENTLY. AND THEN...
ICE STORM. YAY.
MY MEN NEED BOOTS. AND WARM COATS.
ZZZZZZZZZ
OH, TANNENBAUM... HIC!
100 DEAD. 900 CAPTURED.
AND OUR MEN?
JUST 5 WOUNDED.
TREAT THE PRISONERS WITH MERCY. A MERRY CHRISTMAS INDEED.

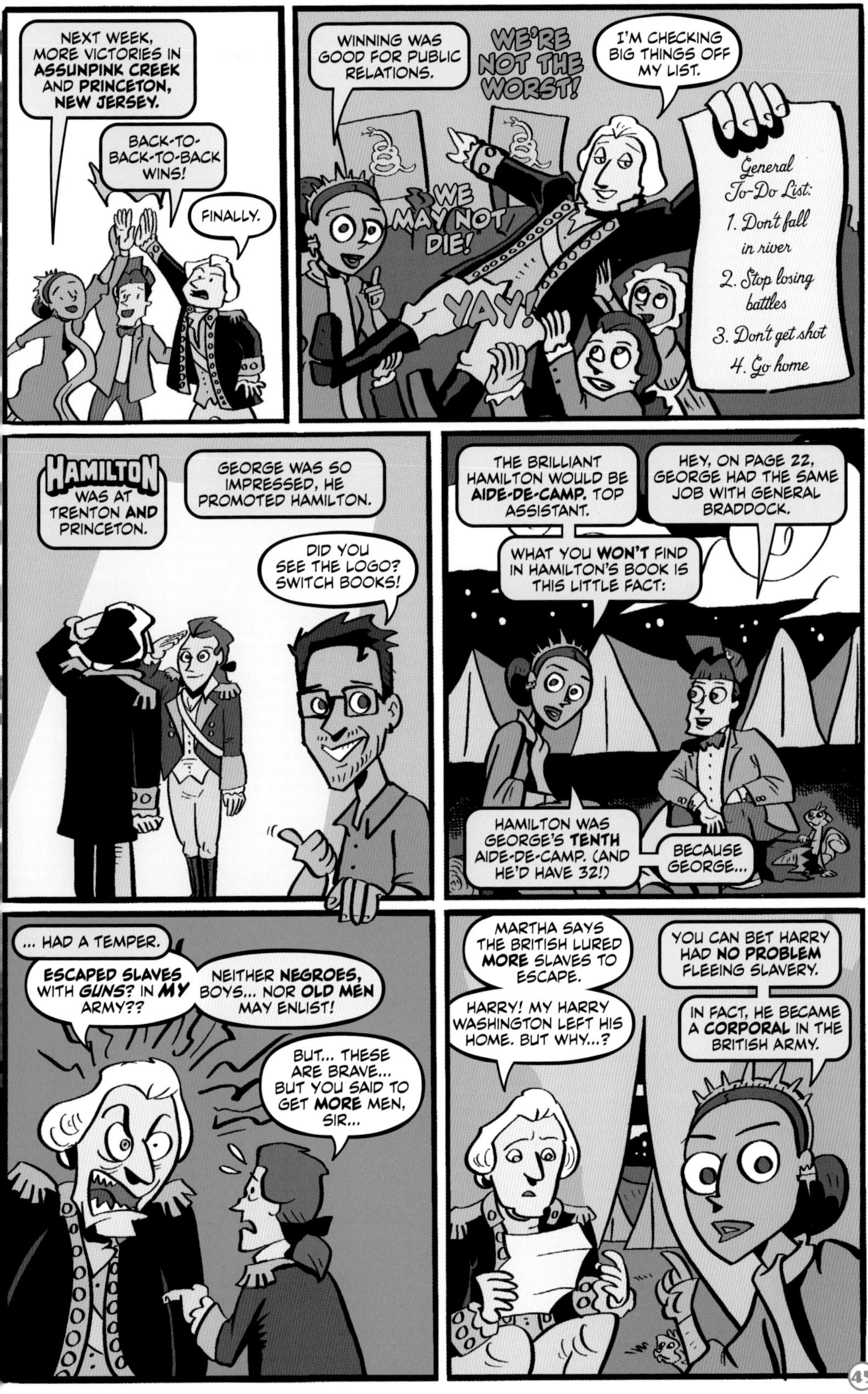
NEXT WEEK, MORE VICTORIES IN ASSUNPINK CREEK AND PRINCETON, NEW JERSEY.
BACK-TO-BACK-TO-BACK WINS!
FINALLY.
WINNING WAS GOOD FOR PUBLIC RELATIONS.
WE'RE NOT THE WORST!
I'M CHECKING BIG THINGS OFF MY LIST.
WE MAY NOT DIE!
YAY!
General To-Do List:
1. Don't fall in river
2. Stop losing battles
3. Don't get shot
4. Go home
HAMILTON WAS AT TRENTON AND PRINCETON.
GEORGE WAS SO IMPRESSED, HE PROMOTED HAMILTON.
DID YOU SEE THE LOGO? SWITCH BOOKS!
THE BRILLIANT HAMILTON WOULD BE AIDE-DE-CAMP. TOP ASSISTANT.
HEY, ON PAGE 22, GEORGE HAD THE SAME JOB WITH GENERAL BRADDOCK.
WHAT YOU WON'T FIND IN HAMILTON'S BOOK IS THIS LITTLE FACT:
HAMILTON WAS GEORGE'S TENTH AIDE-DE-CAMP. (AND HE'D HAVE 32!)
BECAUSE GEORGE...
... HAD A TEMPER.
ESCAPED SLAVES WITH GUNS? IN MY ARMY??
NEITHER NEGROES, BOYS... NOR OLD MEN MAY ENLIST!
BUT... THESE ARE BRAVE... BUT YOU SAID TO GET MORE MEN, SIR...
MARTHA SAYS THE BRITISH LURED MORE SLAVES TO ESCAPE.
HARRY! MY HARRY WASHINGTON LEFT HIS HOME. BUT WHY...?
YOU CAN BET HARRY HAD NO PROBLEM FLEEING SLAVERY.
IN FACT, HE BECAME A CORPORAL IN THE BRITISH ARMY.

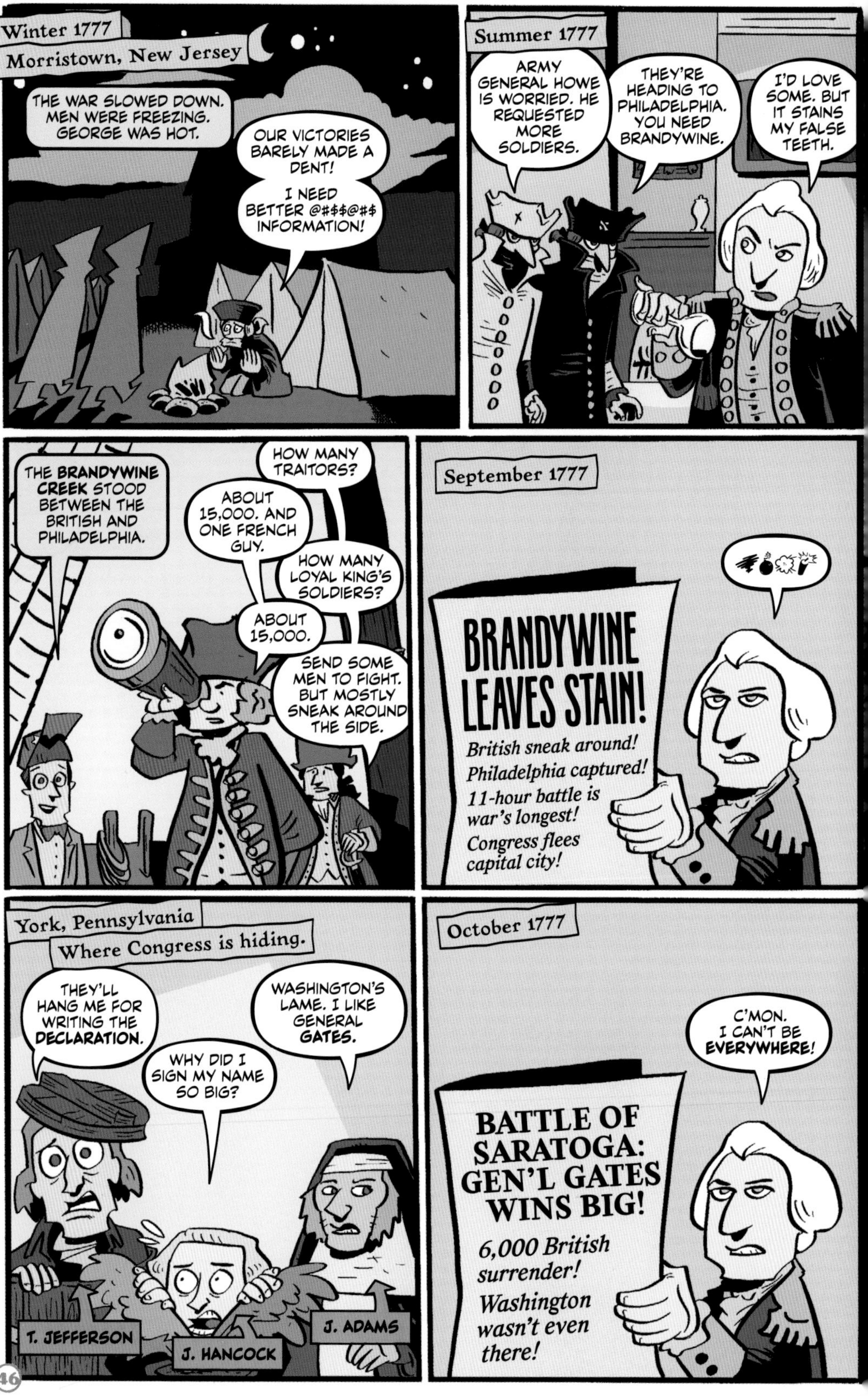

Winter 1777
Morristown, New Jersey
THE WAR SLOWED DOWN. MEN WERE FREEZING. GEORGE WAS HOT.
OUR VICTORIES BARELY MADE A DENT!
I NEED BETTER @#$$@#$ INFORMATION!
Summer 1777
ARMY GENERAL HOWE IS WORRIED. HE REQUESTED MORE SOLDIERS.
THEY'RE HEADING TO PHILADELPHIA. YOU NEED BRANDYWINE.
I'D LOVE SOME. BUT IT STAINS MY FALSE TEETH.
THE BRANDYWINE CREEK STOOD BETWEEN THE BRITISH AND PHILADELPHIA.
HOW MANY TRAITORS?
ABOUT 15,000. AND ONE FRENCH GUY.
HOW MANY LOYAL KING'S SOLDIERS?
ABOUT 15,000.
SEND SOME MEN TO FIGHT. BUT MOSTLY SNEAK AROUND THE SIDE.
September 1777
BRANDYWINE LEAVES STAIN!
British sneak around!
Philadelphia captured!
11-hour battle is war's longest!
Congress flees capital city!
York, Pennsylvania
Where Congress is hiding.
THEY'LL HANG ME FOR WRITING THE DECLARATION.
WHY DID I SIGN MY NAME SO BIG?
WASHINGTON'S LAME. I LIKE GENERAL GATES.
T. JEFFERSON
J. HANCOCK
J. ADAMS
October 1777
C'MON. I CAN'T BE EVERYWHERE!
BATTLE OF SARATOGA: GEN'L GATES WINS BIG!
6,000 British surrender!
Washington wasn't even there!

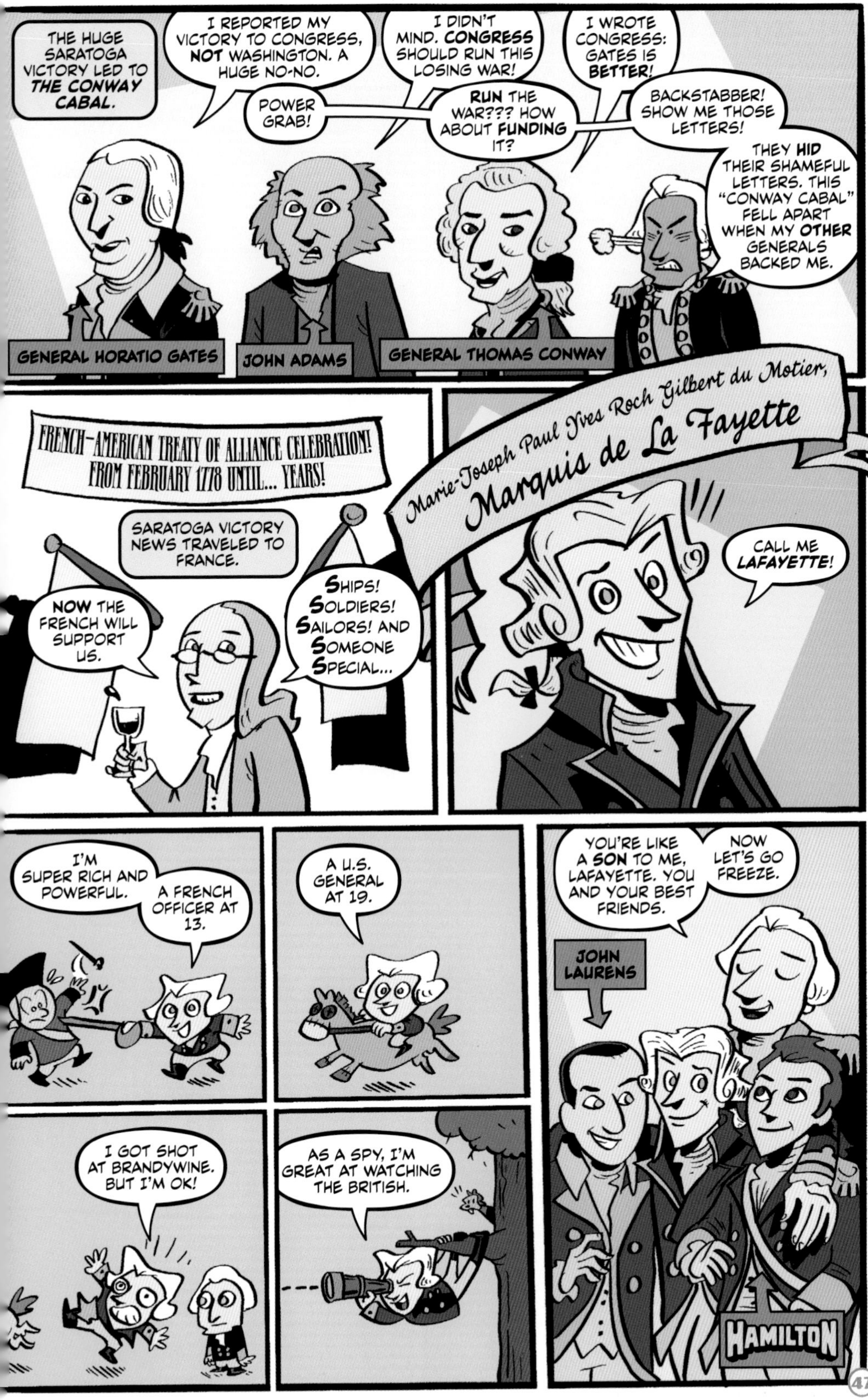
THE HUGE SARATOGA VICTORY LED TO THE CONWAY CABAL.
I REPORTED MY VICTORY TO CONGRESS, NOT WASHINGTON. A HUGE NO-NO.
POWER GRAB!
I DIDN'T MIND. CONGRESS SHOULD RUN THIS LOSING WAR!
RUN THE WAR??? HOW ABOUT FUNDING IT?
I WROTE CONGRESS: GATES IS BETTER!
BACKSTABBER! SHOW ME THOSE LETTERS!
THEY HID THEIR SHAMEFUL LETTERS. THIS "CONWAY CABAL" FELL APART WHEN MY OTHER GENERALS BACKED ME.
GENERAL HORATIO GATES
JOHN ADAMS
GENERAL THOMAS CONWAY
FRENCH-AMERICAN TREATY OF ALLIANCE CELEBRATION! FROM FEBRUARY 1778 UNTIL... YEARS!
SARATOGA VICTORY NEWS TRAVELED TO FRANCE.
NOW THE FRENCH WILL SUPPORT US.
SHIPS! SOLDIERS! SAILORS! AND SOMEONE SPECIAL...
Marie-Joseph Paul Yves Roch Gilbert du Motier, Marquis de La Fayette
CALL ME LAFAYETTE!
I'M SUPER RICH AND POWERFUL.
A FRENCH OFFICER AT 13.
A U.S. GENERAL AT 19.
YOU'RE LIKE A SON TO ME, LAFAYETTE. YOU AND YOUR BEST FRIENDS.
NOW LET'S GO FREEZE.
JOHN LAURENS
I GOT SHOT AT BRANDYWINE. BUT I'M OK!
AS A SPY, I'M GREAT AT WATCHING THE BRITISH.
HAMILTON

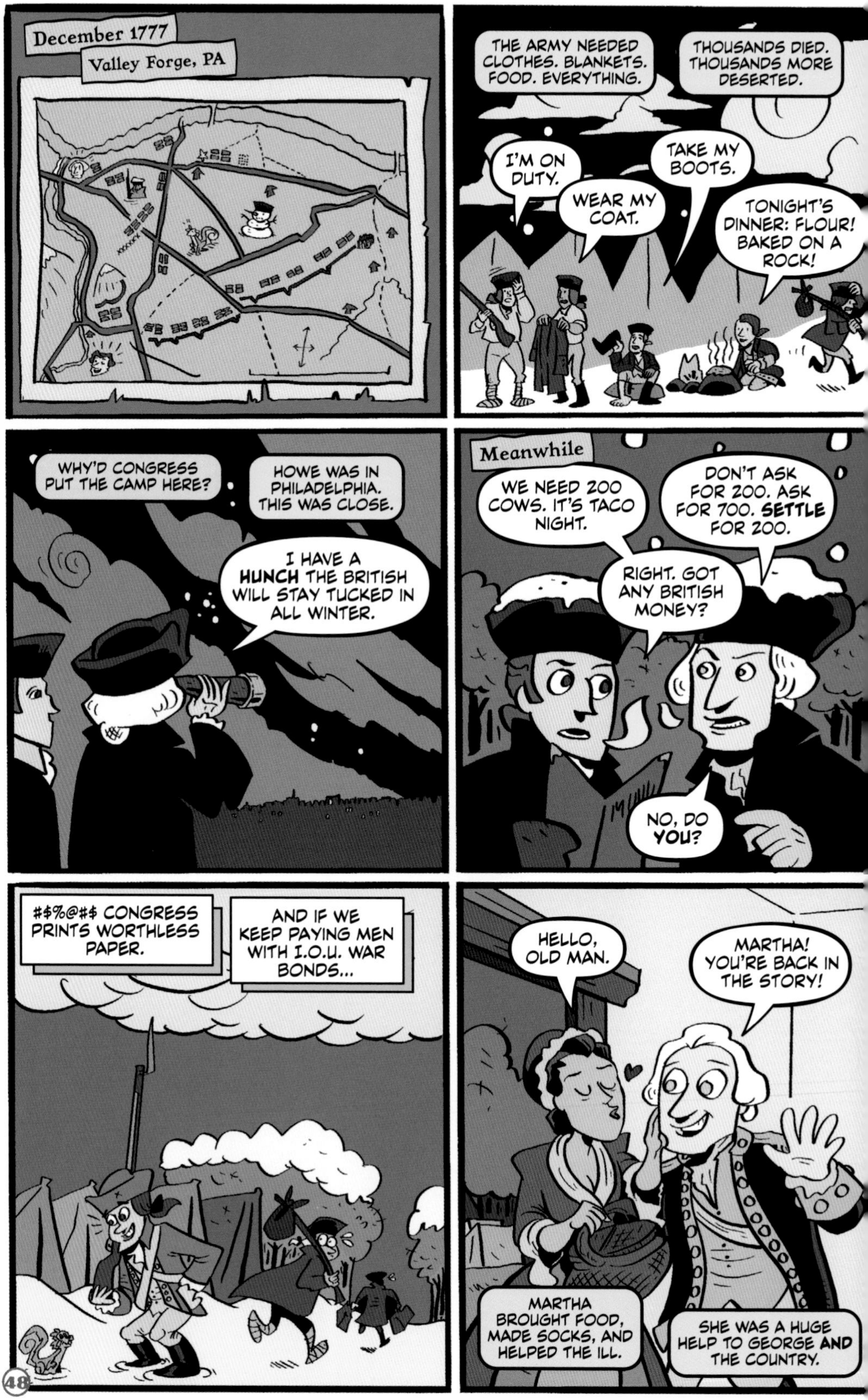
December 1777
Valley Forge, PA
THE ARMY NEEDED CLOTHES. BLANKETS. FOOD. EVERYTHING.
THOUSANDS DIED. THOUSANDS MORE DESERTED.
I'M ON DUTY.
WEAR MY COAT.
TAKE MY BOOTS.
TONIGHT'S DINNER: FLOUR! BAKED ON A ROCK!
WHY'D CONGRESS PUT THE CAMP HERE?
HOWE WAS IN PHILADELPHIA. THIS WAS CLOSE.
I HAVE A **HUNCH** THE BRITISH WILL STAY TUCKED IN ALL WINTER.
Meanwhile
WE NEED 200 COWS. IT'S TACO NIGHT.
DON'T ASK FOR 200. ASK FOR 700. **SETTLE** FOR 200.
RIGHT. GOT ANY BRITISH MONEY?
NO, DO **YOU**?
#$%@#$ CONGRESS PRINTS WORTHLESS PAPER.
AND IF WE KEEP PAYING MEN WITH I.O.U. WAR BONDS...
HELLO, OLD MAN.
MARTHA! YOU'RE BACK IN THE STORY!
MARTHA BROUGHT FOOD, MADE SOCKS, AND HELPED THE ILL.
SHE WAS A HUGE HELP TO GEORGE **AND** THE COUNTRY.

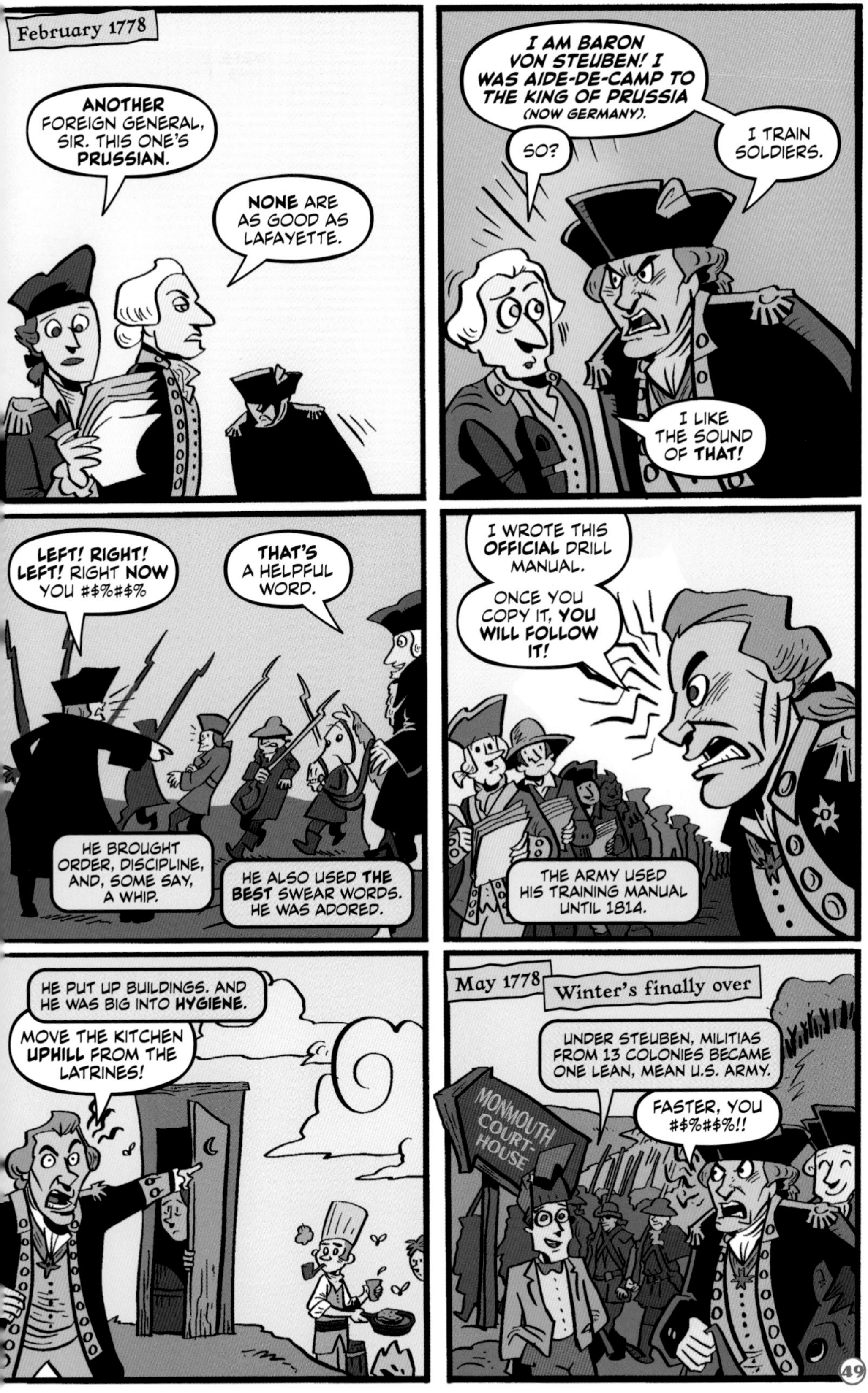
February 1778
ANOTHER FOREIGN GENERAL, SIR. THIS ONE'S PRUSSIAN.
NONE ARE AS GOOD AS LAFAYETTE.
I AM BARON VON STEUBEN! I WAS AIDE-DE-CAMP TO THE KING OF PRUSSIA (NOW GERMANY).
SO?
I TRAIN SOLDIERS.
I LIKE THE SOUND OF THAT!
LEFT! RIGHT! LEFT! RIGHT NOW YOU #$%#$%
THAT'S A HELPFUL WORD.
HE BROUGHT ORDER, DISCIPLINE, AND, SOME SAY, A WHIP.
HE ALSO USED THE BEST SWEAR WORDS. HE WAS ADORED.
I WROTE THIS OFFICIAL DRILL MANUAL.
ONCE YOU COPY IT, YOU WILL FOLLOW IT!
THE ARMY USED HIS TRAINING MANUAL UNTIL 1814.
HE PUT UP BUILDINGS. AND HE WAS BIG INTO HYGIENE.
MOVE THE KITCHEN UPHILL FROM THE LATRINES!
May 1778
Winter's finally over
MONMOUTH COURT-HOUSE
UNDER STEUBEN, MILITIAS FROM 13 COLONIES BECAME ONE LEAN, MEAN U.S. ARMY.
FASTER, YOU #$%#$%!!

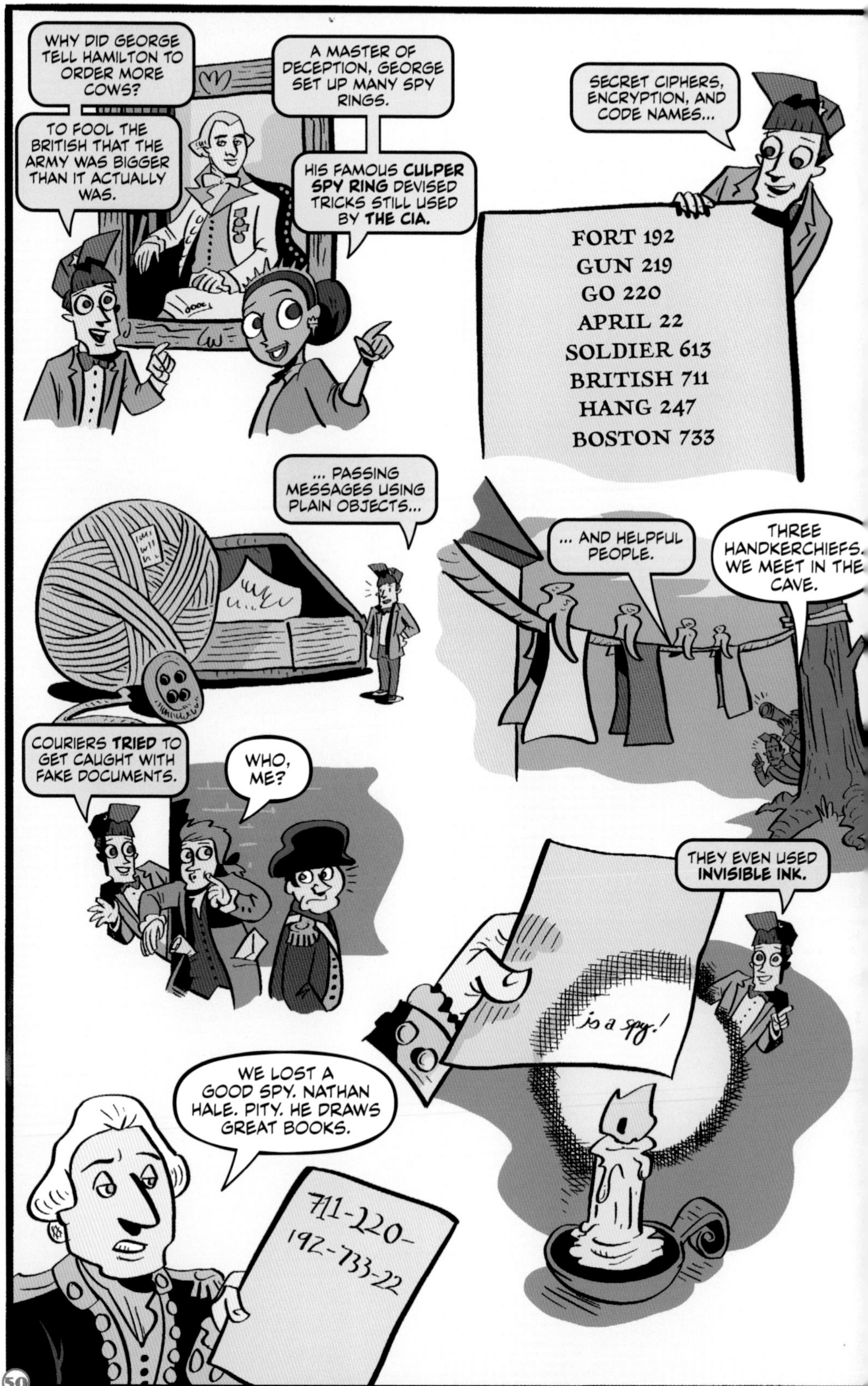
WHY DID GEORGE TELL HAMILTON TO ORDER MORE COWS?
TO FOOL THE BRITISH THAT THE ARMY WAS BIGGER THAN IT ACTUALLY WAS.
A MASTER OF DECEPTION, GEORGE SET UP MANY SPY RINGS.
HIS FAMOUS CULPER SPY RING DEVISED TRICKS STILL USED BY THE CIA.
SECRET CIPHERS, ENCRYPTION, AND CODE NAMES...
FORT 192
GUN 219
GO 220
APRIL 22
SOLDIER 613
BRITISH 711
HANG 247
BOSTON 733
... PASSING MESSAGES USING PLAIN OBJECTS...
... AND HELPFUL PEOPLE.
THREE HANDKERCHIEFS. WE MEET IN THE CAVE.
COURIERS TRIED TO GET CAUGHT WITH FAKE DOCUMENTS.
WHO, ME?
THEY EVEN USED INVISIBLE INK.
is a spy!
WE LOST A GOOD SPY. NATHAN HALE. PITY. HE DRAWS GREAT BOOKS.
711-220-
192-733-22

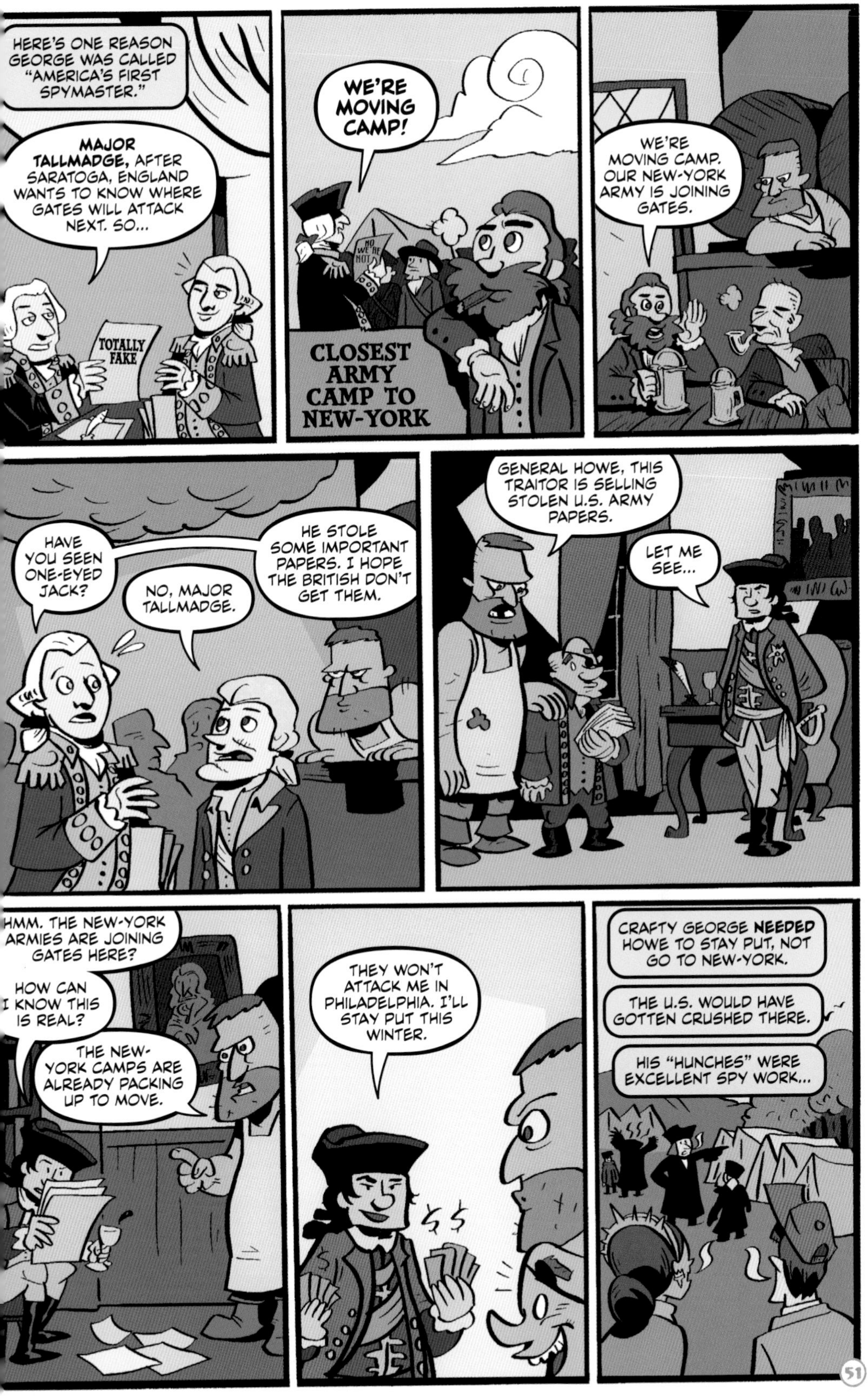
HERE'S ONE REASON GEORGE WAS CALLED "AMERICA'S FIRST SPYMASTER."
MAJOR TALLMADGE, AFTER SARATOGA, ENGLAND WANTS TO KNOW WHERE GATES WILL ATTACK NEXT. SO...
TOTALLY FAKE
WE'RE MOVING CAMP!
NO WE'RE NOT
CLOSEST ARMY CAMP TO NEW-YORK
WE'RE MOVING CAMP. OUR NEW-YORK ARMY IS JOINING GATES.
HAVE YOU SEEN ONE-EYED JACK?
HE STOLE SOME IMPORTANT PAPERS. I HOPE THE BRITISH DON'T GET THEM.
NO, MAJOR TALLMADGE.
GENERAL HOWE, THIS TRAITOR IS SELLING STOLEN U.S. ARMY PAPERS.
LET ME SEE...
HMM. THE NEW-YORK ARMIES ARE JOINING GATES HERE?
HOW CAN I KNOW THIS IS REAL?
THE NEW-YORK CAMPS ARE ALREADY PACKING UP TO MOVE.
THEY WON'T ATTACK ME IN PHILADELPHIA. I'LL STAY PUT THIS WINTER.
CRAFTY GEORGE **NEEDED** HOWE TO STAY PUT, NOT GO TO NEW-YORK.
THE U.S. WOULD HAVE GOTTEN CRUSHED THERE.
HIS "HUNCHES" WERE EXCELLENT SPY WORK...

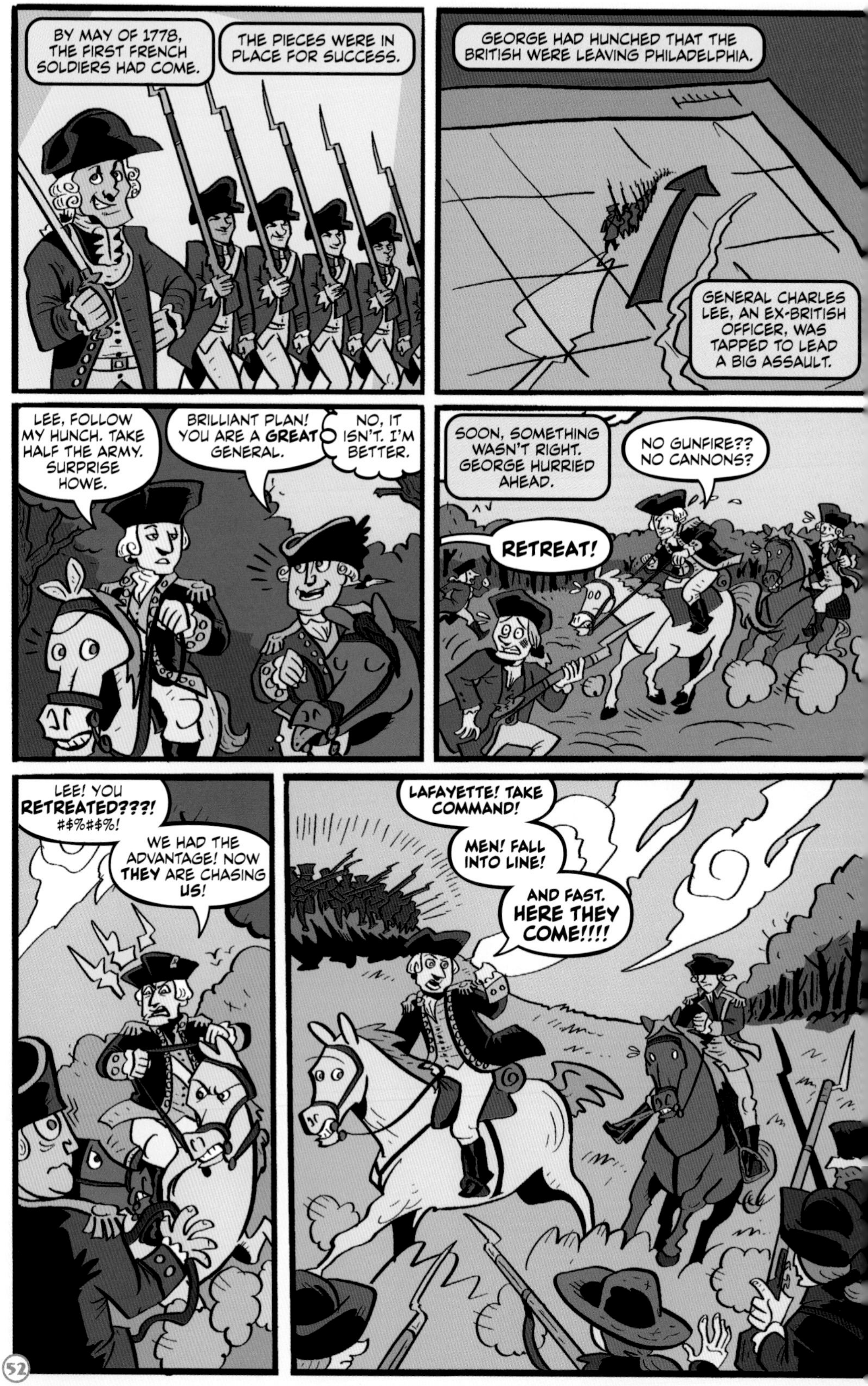
BY MAY OF 1778, THE FIRST FRENCH SOLDIERS HAD COME.
THE PIECES WERE IN PLACE FOR SUCCESS.
GEORGE HAD HUNCHED THAT THE BRITISH WERE LEAVING PHILADELPHIA.
GENERAL CHARLES LEE, AN EX-BRITISH OFFICER, WAS TAPPED TO LEAD A BIG ASSAULT.
LEE, FOLLOW MY HUNCH. TAKE HALF THE ARMY. SURPRISE HOWE.
BRILLIANT PLAN! YOU ARE A GREAT GENERAL.
NO, IT ISN'T. I'M BETTER.
SOON, SOMETHING WASN'T RIGHT. GEORGE HURRIED AHEAD.
NO GUNFIRE?? NO CANNONS?
RETREAT!
LEE! YOU RETREATED???!
#$%#$%!
WE HAD THE ADVANTAGE! NOW THEY ARE CHASING US!
LAFAYETTE! TAKE COMMAND!
MEN! FALL INTO LINE!
AND FAST. HERE THEY COME!!!!

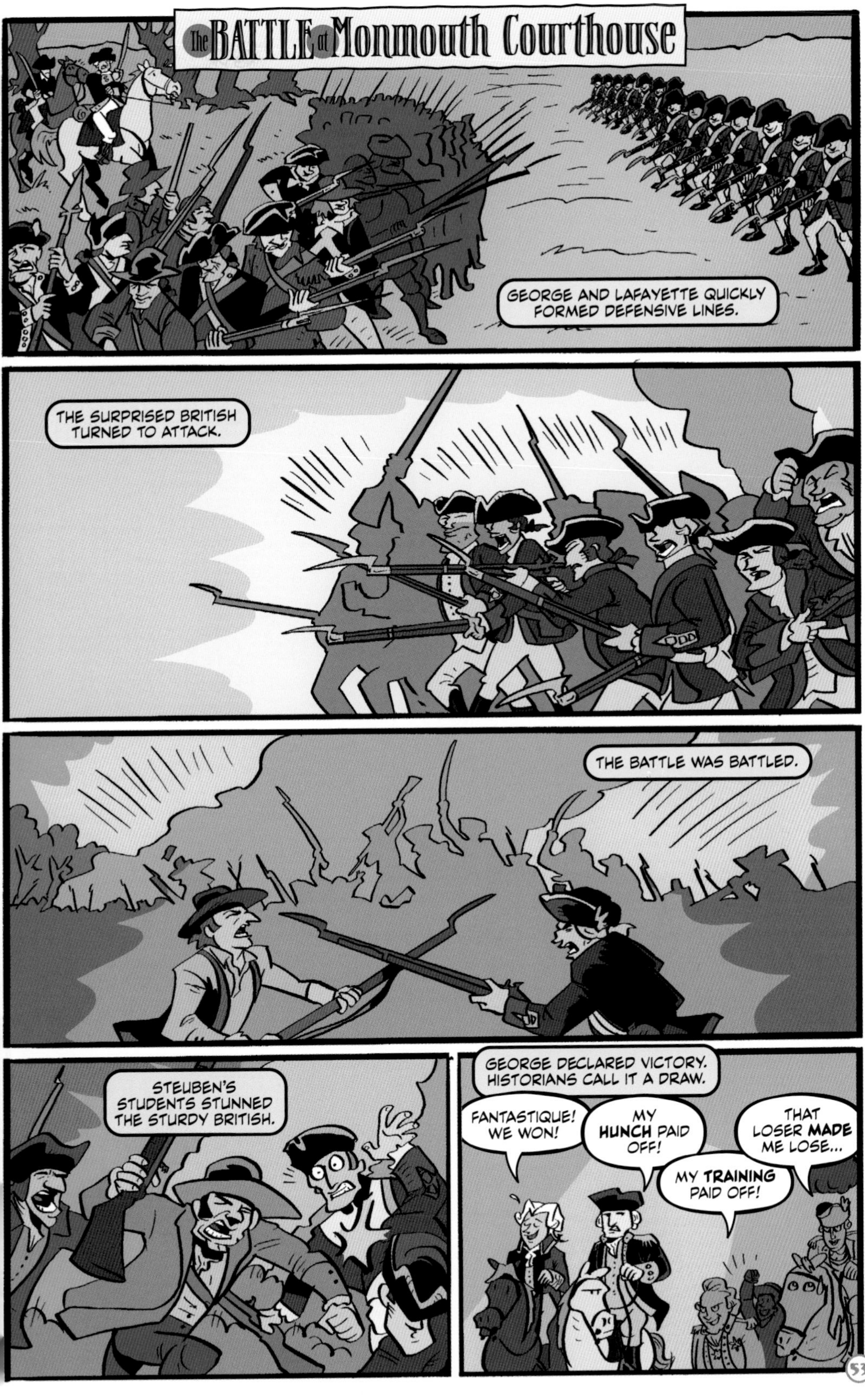
The BATTLE at Monmouth Courthouse
GEORGE AND LAFAYETTE QUICKLY FORMED DEFENSIVE LINES.
THE SURPRISED BRITISH TURNED TO ATTACK.
THE BATTLE WAS BATTLED.
STEUBEN'S STUDENTS STUNNED THE STURDY BRITISH.
GEORGE DECLARED VICTORY. HISTORIANS CALL IT A DRAW.
FANTASTIQUE! WE WON!
MY HUNCH PAID OFF!
MY TRAINING PAID OFF!
THAT LOSER MADE ME LOSE...

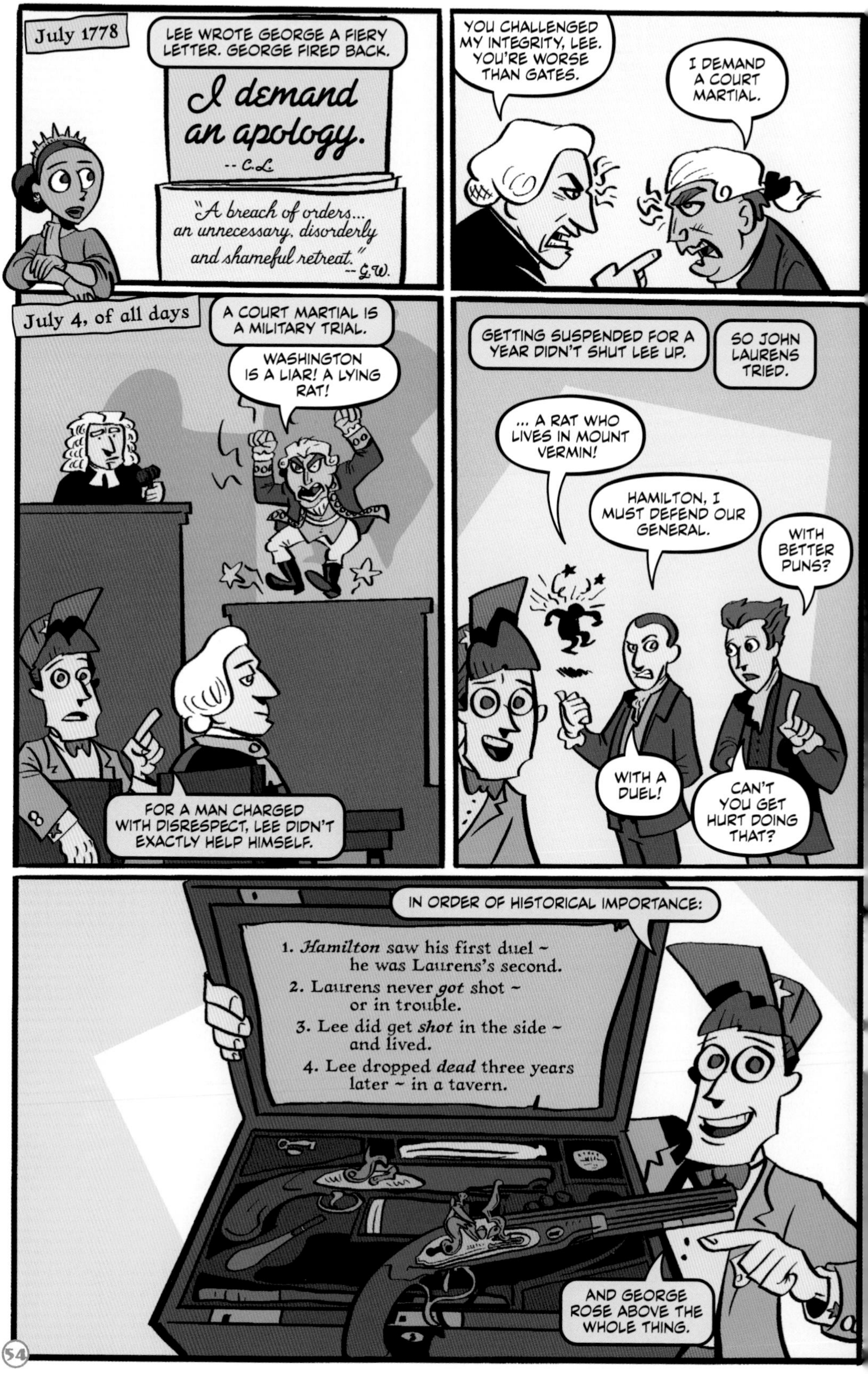

July 1778
LEE WROTE GEORGE A FIERY LETTER. GEORGE FIRED BACK.
I demand an apology. -- C.L.
"A breach of orders... an unnecessary, disorderly and shameful retreat." -- G.W.
YOU CHALLENGED MY INTEGRITY, LEE. YOU'RE WORSE THAN GATES.
I DEMAND A COURT MARTIAL.
July 4, of all days
A COURT MARTIAL IS A MILITARY TRIAL.
WASHINGTON IS A LIAR! A LYING RAT!
FOR A MAN CHARGED WITH DISRESPECT, LEE DIDN'T EXACTLY HELP HIMSELF.
GETTING SUSPENDED FOR A YEAR DIDN'T SHUT LEE UP.
SO JOHN LAURENS TRIED.
... A RAT WHO LIVES IN MOUNT VERMIN!
HAMILTON, I MUST DEFEND OUR GENERAL.
WITH BETTER PUNS?
WITH A DUEL!
CAN'T YOU GET HURT DOING THAT?
IN ORDER OF HISTORICAL IMPORTANCE:
1. Hamilton saw his first duel ~ he was Laurens's second.
2. Laurens never got shot ~ or in trouble.
3. Lee did get shot in the side ~ and lived.
4. Lee dropped dead three years later ~ in a tavern.
AND GEORGE ROSE ABOVE THE WHOLE THING.

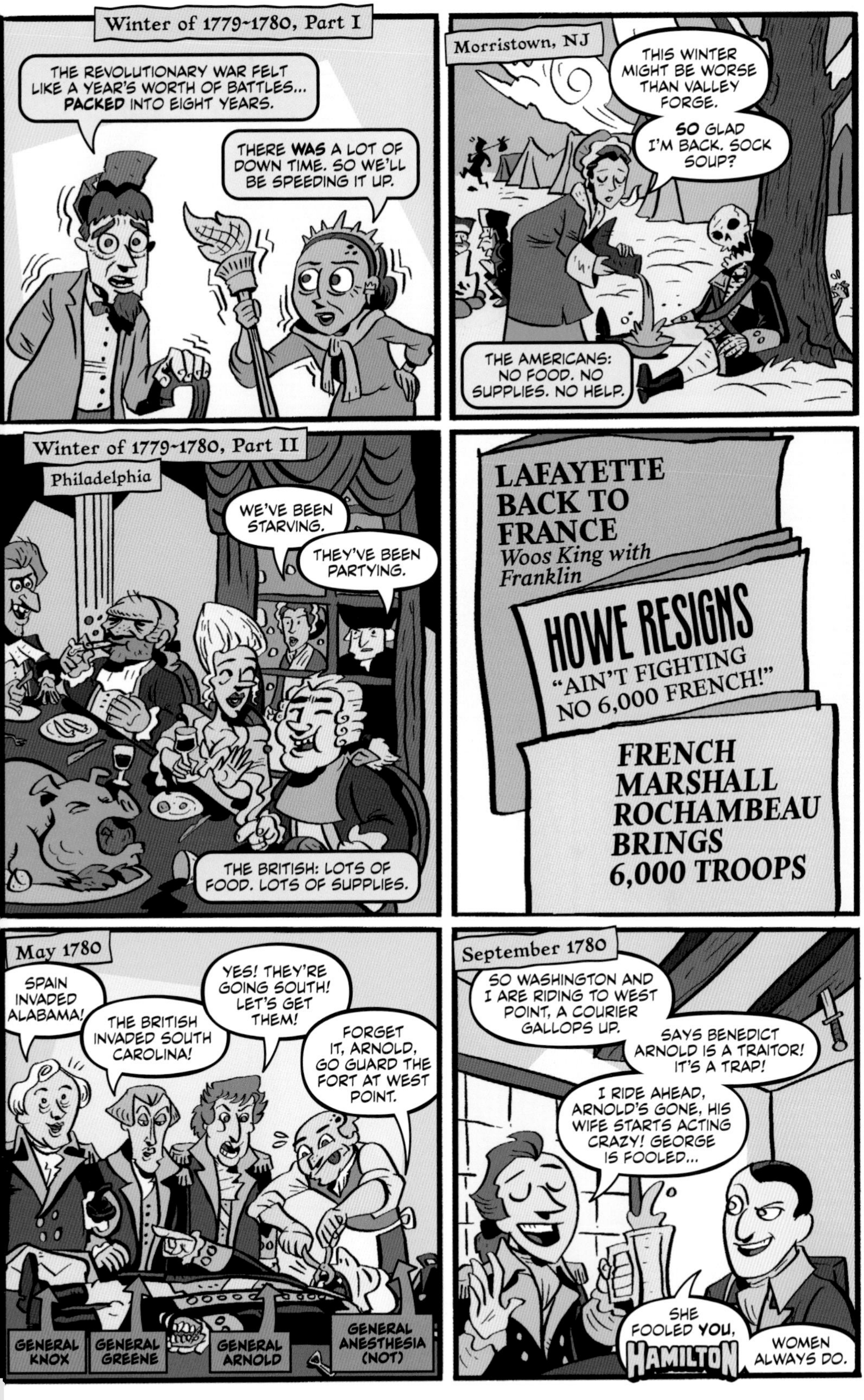
Winter of 1779~1780, Part I
THE REVOLUTIONARY WAR FELT LIKE A YEAR'S WORTH OF BATTLES... PACKED INTO EIGHT YEARS.
THERE WAS A LOT OF DOWN TIME. SO WE'LL BE SPEEDING IT UP.
Morristown, NJ
THIS WINTER MIGHT BE WORSE THAN VALLEY FORGE.
SO GLAD I'M BACK. SOCK SOUP?
THE AMERICANS: NO FOOD. NO SUPPLIES. NO HELP.
Winter of 1779~1780, Part II
Philadelphia
WE'VE BEEN STARVING.
THEY'VE BEEN PARTYING.
THE BRITISH: LOTS OF FOOD. LOTS OF SUPPLIES.
LAFAYETTE BACK TO FRANCE
Woos King with Franklin
HOWE RESIGNS
"AIN'T FIGHTING NO 6,000 FRENCH!"
FRENCH MARSHALL ROCHAMBEAU BRINGS 6,000 TROOPS
May 1780
SPAIN INVADED ALABAMA!
THE BRITISH INVADED SOUTH CAROLINA!
YES! THEY'RE GOING SOUTH! LET'S GET THEM!
FORGET IT, ARNOLD, GO GUARD THE FORT AT WEST POINT.
GENERAL KNOX
GENERAL GREENE
GENERAL ARNOLD
GENERAL ANESTHESIA (NOT)
September 1780
SO WASHINGTON AND I ARE RIDING TO WEST POINT, A COURIER GALLOPS UP.
SAYS BENEDICT ARNOLD IS A TRAITOR! IT'S A TRAP!
I RIDE AHEAD, ARNOLD'S GONE, HIS WIFE STARTS ACTING CRAZY! GEORGE IS FOOLED...
SHE FOOLED YOU, HAMILTON
WOMEN ALWAYS DO.

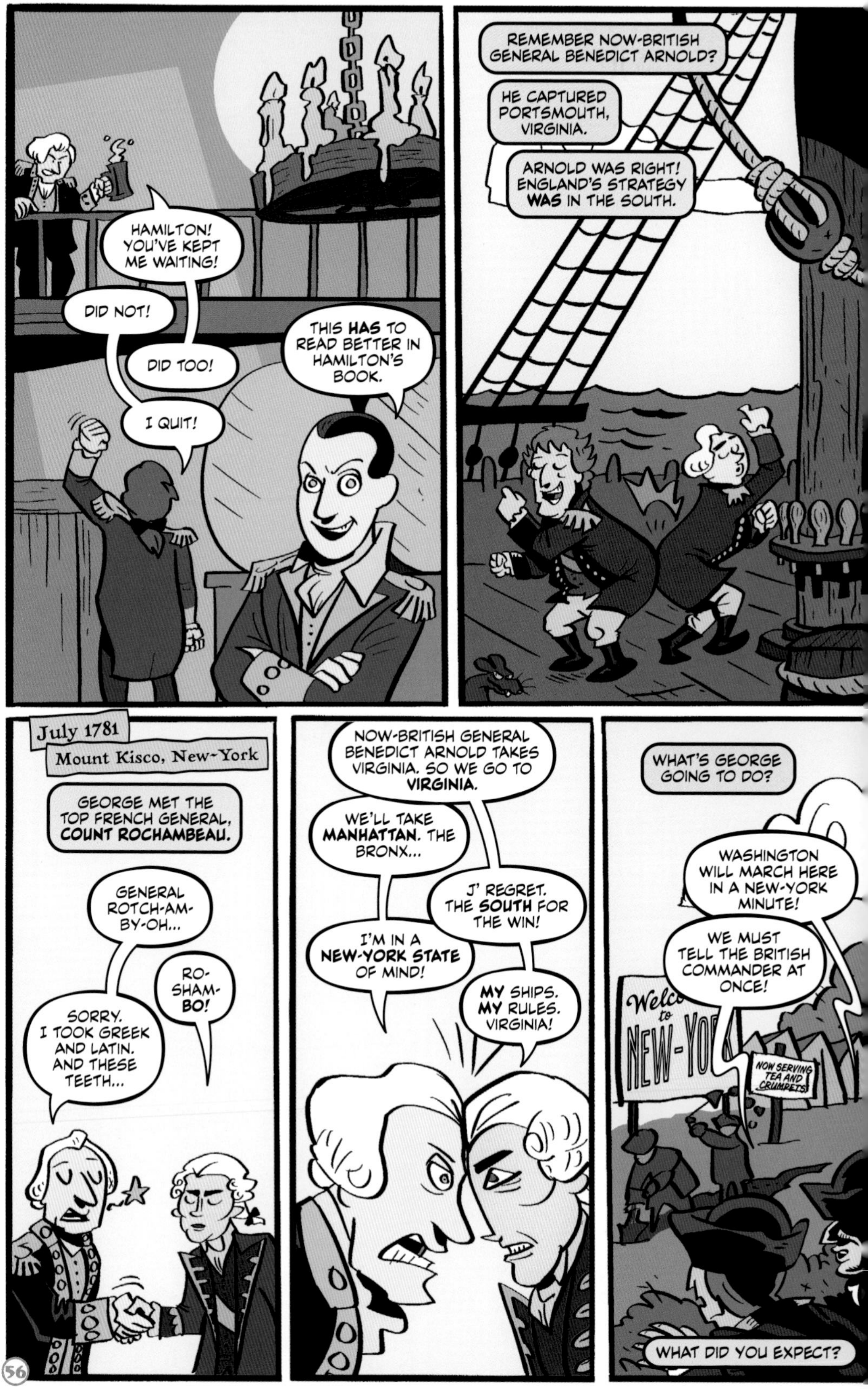
HAMILTON! YOU'VE KEPT ME WAITING!
DID NOT!
DID TOO!
I QUIT!
THIS **HAS** TO READ BETTER IN HAMILTON'S BOOK.
REMEMBER NOW-BRITISH GENERAL BENEDICT ARNOLD?
HE CAPTURED PORTSMOUTH, VIRGINIA.
ARNOLD WAS RIGHT! ENGLAND'S STRATEGY **WAS** IN THE SOUTH.
July 1781
Mount Kisco, New-York
GEORGE MET THE TOP FRENCH GENERAL, **COUNT ROCHAMBEAU.**
GENERAL ROTCH-AM-BY-OH...
RO-SHAM-**BO!**
SORRY. I TOOK GREEK AND LATIN. AND THESE TEETH...
NOW-BRITISH GENERAL BENEDICT ARNOLD TAKES VIRGINIA. SO WE GO TO **VIRGINIA**.
WE'LL TAKE **MANHATTAN**. THE BRONX...
J' REGRET. THE **SOUTH** FOR THE WIN!
I'M IN A **NEW-YORK STATE** OF MIND!
MY SHIPS. **MY** RULES. VIRGINIA!
WHAT'S GEORGE GOING TO DO?
WASHINGTON WILL MARCH HERE IN A NEW-YORK MINUTE!
WE MUST TELL THE BRITISH COMMANDER AT ONCE!
NOW SERVING TEA AND CRUMPETS
WHAT DID YOU EXPECT?

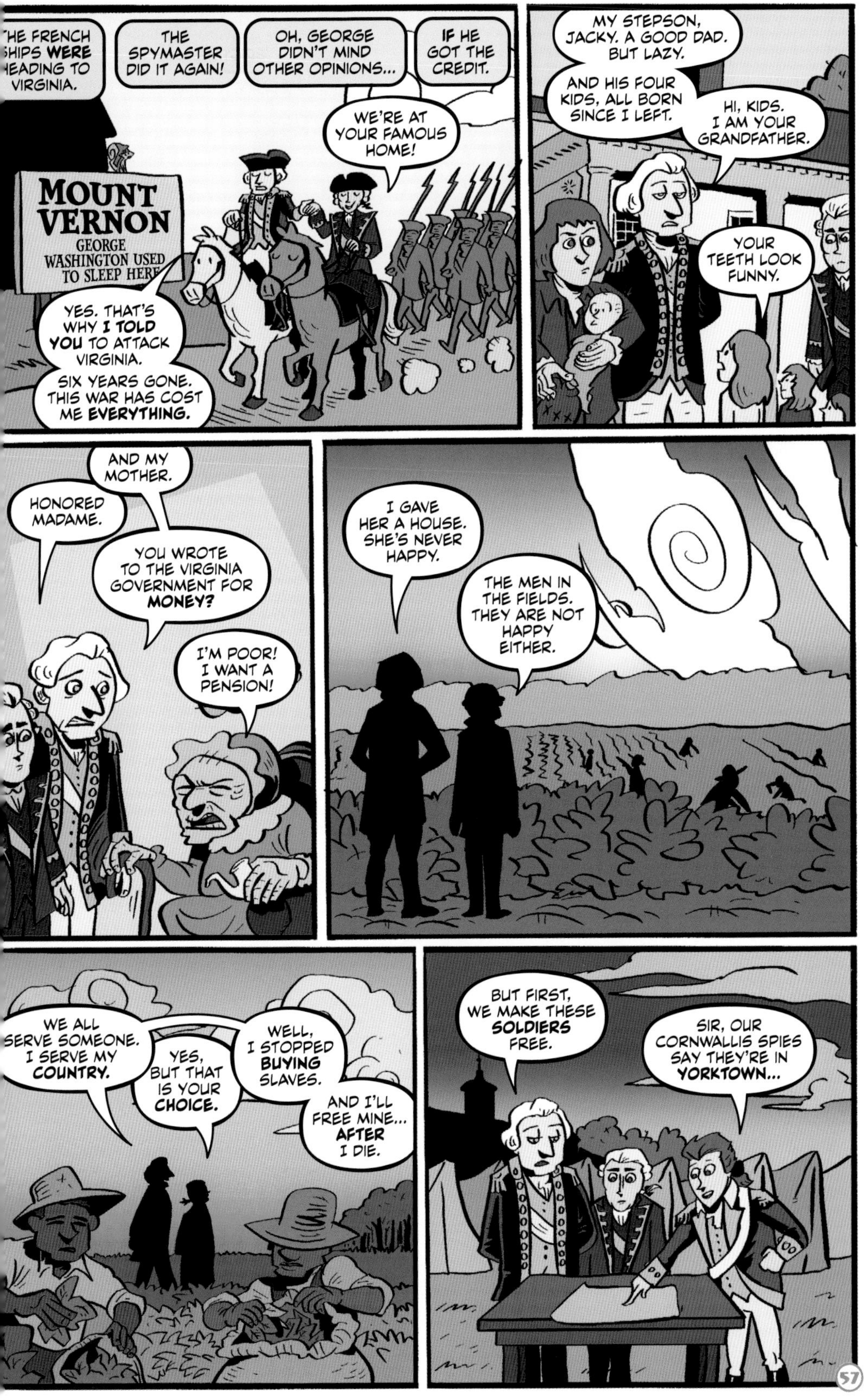

THE FRENCH SHIPS WERE HEADING TO VIRGINIA.
THE SPYMASTER DID IT AGAIN!
OH, GEORGE DIDN'T MIND OTHER OPINIONS...
IF HE GOT THE CREDIT.
WE'RE AT YOUR FAMOUS HOME!
MOUNT VERNON
GEORGE WASHINGTON USED TO SLEEP HERE
YES. THAT'S WHY I TOLD YOU TO ATTACK VIRGINIA.
SIX YEARS GONE. THIS WAR HAS COST ME EVERYTHING.
MY STEPSON, JACKY. A GOOD DAD. BUT LAZY.
AND HIS FOUR KIDS, ALL BORN SINCE I LEFT.
HI, KIDS. I AM YOUR GRANDFATHER.
YOUR TEETH LOOK FUNNY.
HONORED MADAME.
AND MY MOTHER.
YOU WROTE TO THE VIRGINIA GOVERNMENT FOR MONEY?
I'M POOR! I WANT A PENSION!
I GAVE HER A HOUSE. SHE'S NEVER HAPPY.
THE MEN IN THE FIELDS. THEY ARE NOT HAPPY EITHER.
WE ALL SERVE SOMEONE. I SERVE MY COUNTRY.
YES, BUT THAT IS YOUR CHOICE.
WELL, I STOPPED BUYING SLAVES.
AND I'LL FREE MINE... AFTER I DIE.
BUT FIRST, WE MAKE THESE SOLDIERS FREE.
SIR, OUR CORNWALLIS SPIES SAY THEY'RE IN YORKTOWN...

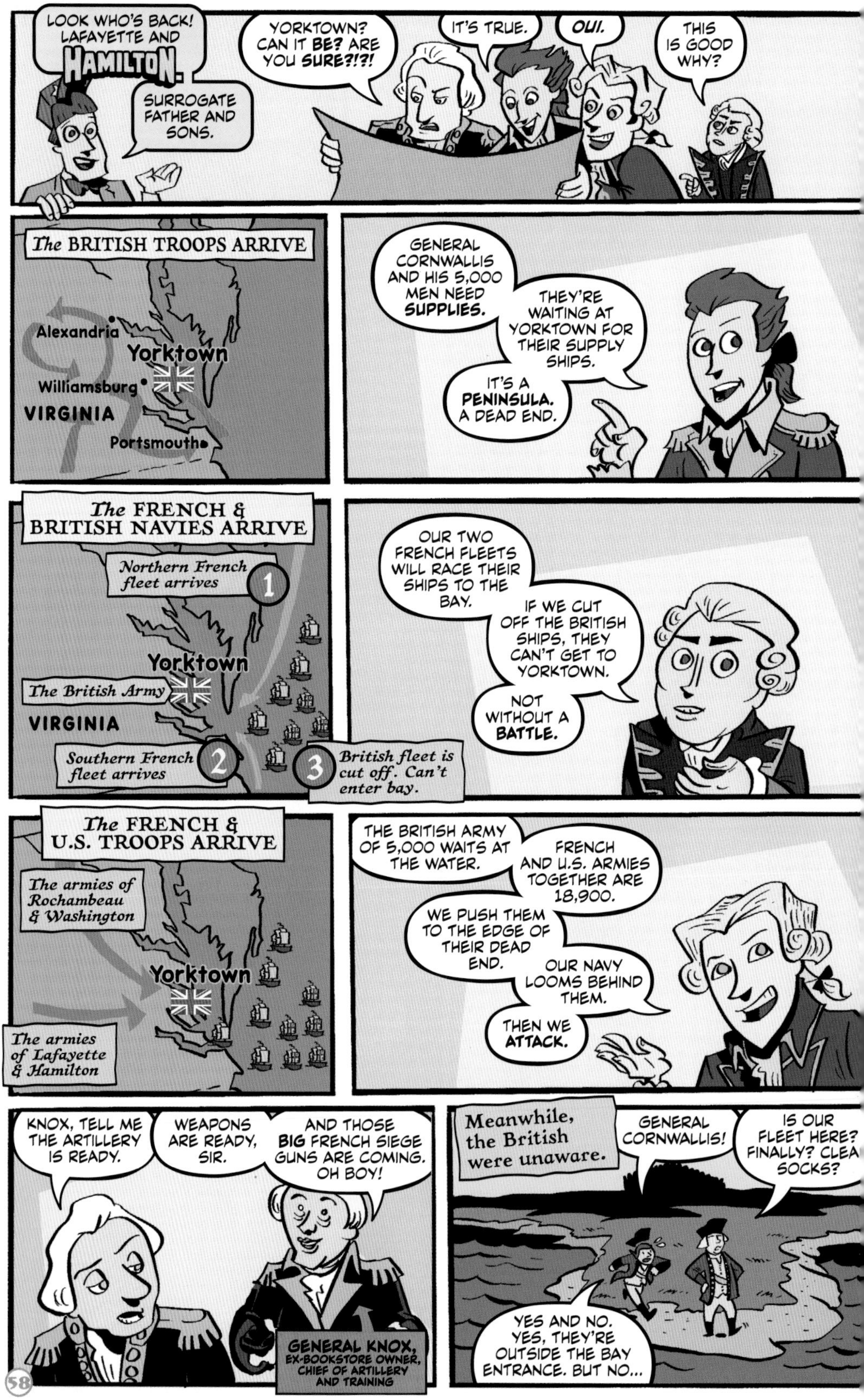
LOOK WHO'S BACK! LAFAYETTE AND HAMILTON.
SURROGATE FATHER AND SONS.
YORKTOWN? CAN IT BE? ARE YOU SURE?!?!
IT'S TRUE.
OUI.
THIS IS GOOD WHY?
The BRITISH TROOPS ARRIVE
Alexandria
Yorktown
Williamsburg
VIRGINIA
Portsmouth
GENERAL CORNWALLIS AND HIS 5,000 MEN NEED SUPPLIES.
THEY'RE WAITING AT YORKTOWN FOR THEIR SUPPLY SHIPS.
IT'S A PENINSULA. A DEAD END.
The FRENCH & BRITISH NAVIES ARRIVE
Northern French fleet arrives
1
Yorktown
The British Army
VIRGINIA
Southern French fleet arrives
2
3
British fleet is cut off. Can't enter bay.
OUR TWO FRENCH FLEETS WILL RACE THEIR SHIPS TO THE BAY.
IF WE CUT OFF THE BRITISH SHIPS, THEY CAN'T GET TO YORKTOWN.
NOT WITHOUT A BATTLE.
The FRENCH & U.S. TROOPS ARRIVE
The armies of Rochambeau & Washington
Yorktown
The armies of Lafayette & Hamilton
THE BRITISH ARMY OF 5,000 WAITS AT THE WATER.
FRENCH AND U.S. ARMIES TOGETHER ARE 18,900.
WE PUSH THEM TO THE EDGE OF THEIR DEAD END.
OUR NAVY LOOMS BEHIND THEM.
THEN WE ATTACK.
KNOX, TELL ME THE ARTILLERY IS READY.
WEAPONS ARE READY, SIR.
AND THOSE BIG FRENCH SIEGE GUNS ARE COMING. OH BOY!
GENERAL KNOX, EX-BOOKSTORE OWNER, CHIEF OF ARTILLERY AND TRAINING
Meanwhile, the British were unaware.
GENERAL CORNWALLIS!
IS OUR FLEET HERE? FINALLY? CLEA SOCKS?
YES AND NO. YES, THEY'RE OUTSIDE THE BAY ENTRANCE. BUT NO...

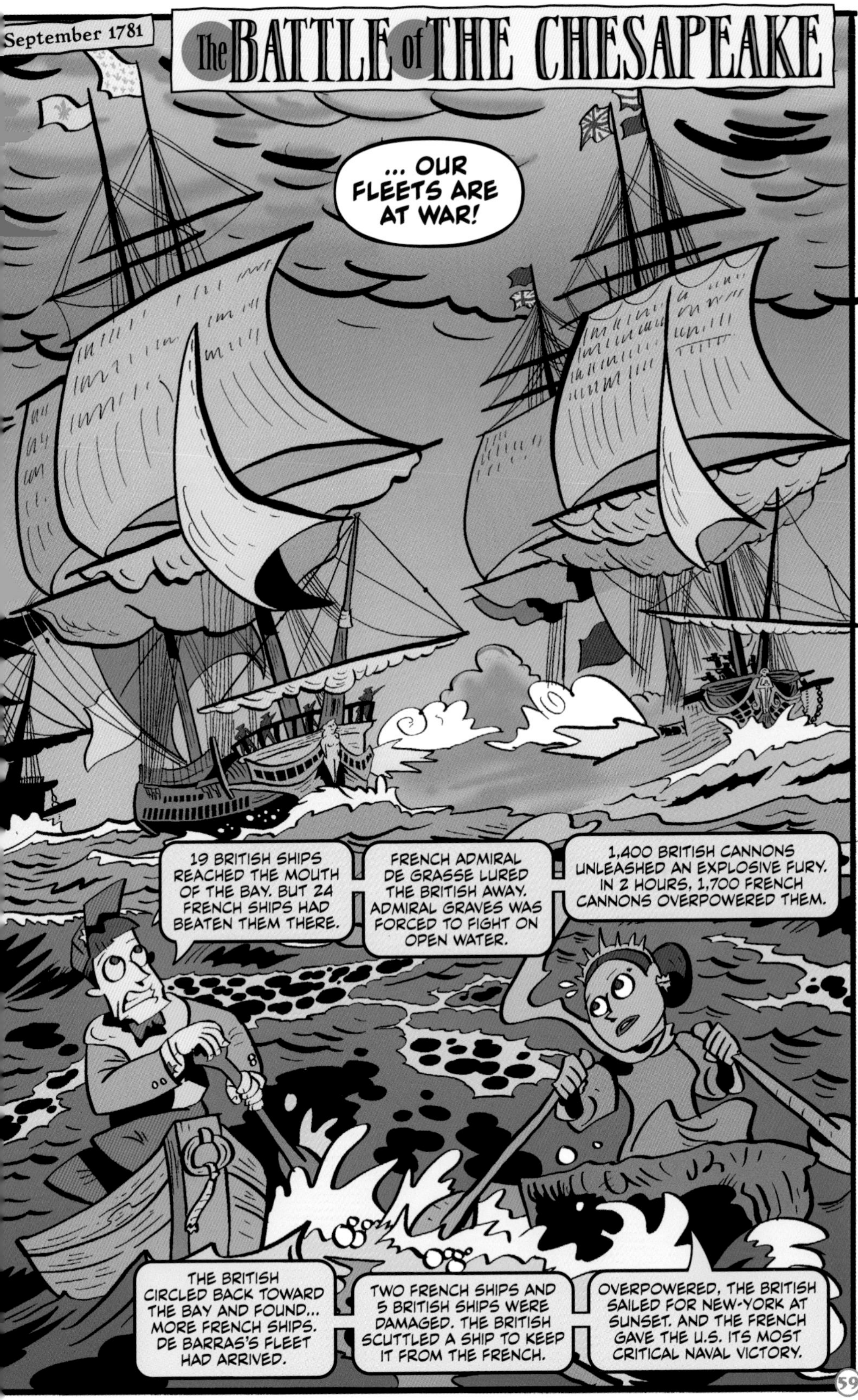
September 1781
The BATTLE of THE CHESAPEAKE
... OUR FLEETS ARE AT WAR!
19 BRITISH SHIPS REACHED THE MOUTH OF THE BAY. BUT 24 FRENCH SHIPS HAD BEATEN THEM THERE.
FRENCH ADMIRAL DE GRASSE LURED THE BRITISH AWAY. ADMIRAL GRAVES WAS FORCED TO FIGHT ON OPEN WATER.
1,400 BRITISH CANNONS UNLEASHED AN EXPLOSIVE FURY. IN 2 HOURS, 1,700 FRENCH CANNONS OVERPOWERED THEM.
THE BRITISH CIRCLED BACK TOWARD THE BAY AND FOUND... MORE FRENCH SHIPS. DE BARRAS'S FLEET HAD ARRIVED.
TWO FRENCH SHIPS AND 5 BRITISH SHIPS WERE DAMAGED. THE BRITISH SCUTTLED A SHIP TO KEEP IT FROM THE FRENCH.
OVERPOWERED, THE BRITISH SAILED FOR NEW-YORK AT SUNSET. AND THE FRENCH GAVE THE U.S. ITS MOST CRITICAL NAVAL VICTORY.

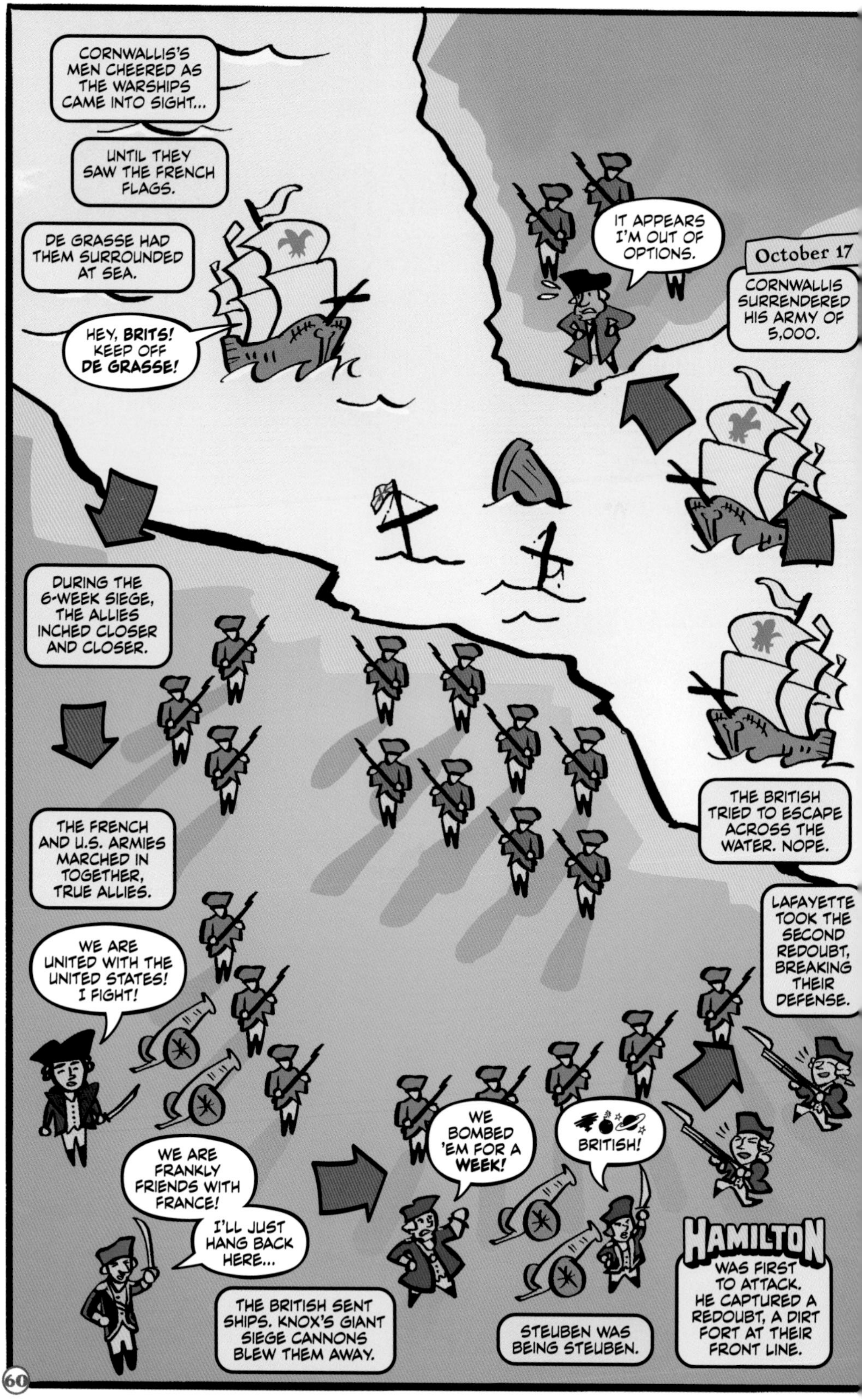

CORNWALLIS'S MEN CHEERED AS THE WARSHIPS CAME INTO SIGHT...
UNTIL THEY SAW THE FRENCH FLAGS.
DE GRASSE HAD THEM SURROUNDED AT SEA.
HEY, BRITS! KEEP OFF DE GRASSE!
IT APPEARS I'M OUT OF OPTIONS.
October 17
CORNWALLIS SURRENDERED HIS ARMY OF 5,000.
DURING THE 6-WEEK SIEGE, THE ALLIES INCHED CLOSER AND CLOSER.
THE BRITISH TRIED TO ESCAPE ACROSS THE WATER. NOPE.
THE FRENCH AND U.S. ARMIES MARCHED IN TOGETHER, TRUE ALLIES.
LAFAYETTE TOOK THE SECOND REDOUBT, BREAKING THEIR DEFENSE.
WE ARE UNITED WITH THE UNITED STATES! I FIGHT!
WE BOMBED 'EM FOR A WEEK!
BRITISH!
WE ARE FRANKLY FRIENDS WITH FRANCE!
I'LL JUST HANG BACK HERE...
HAMILTON WAS FIRST TO ATTACK. HE CAPTURED A REDOUBT, A DIRT FORT AT THEIR FRONT LINE.
THE BRITISH SENT SHIPS. KNOX'S GIANT SIEGE CANNONS BLEW THEM AWAY.
STEUBEN WAS BEING STEUBEN.

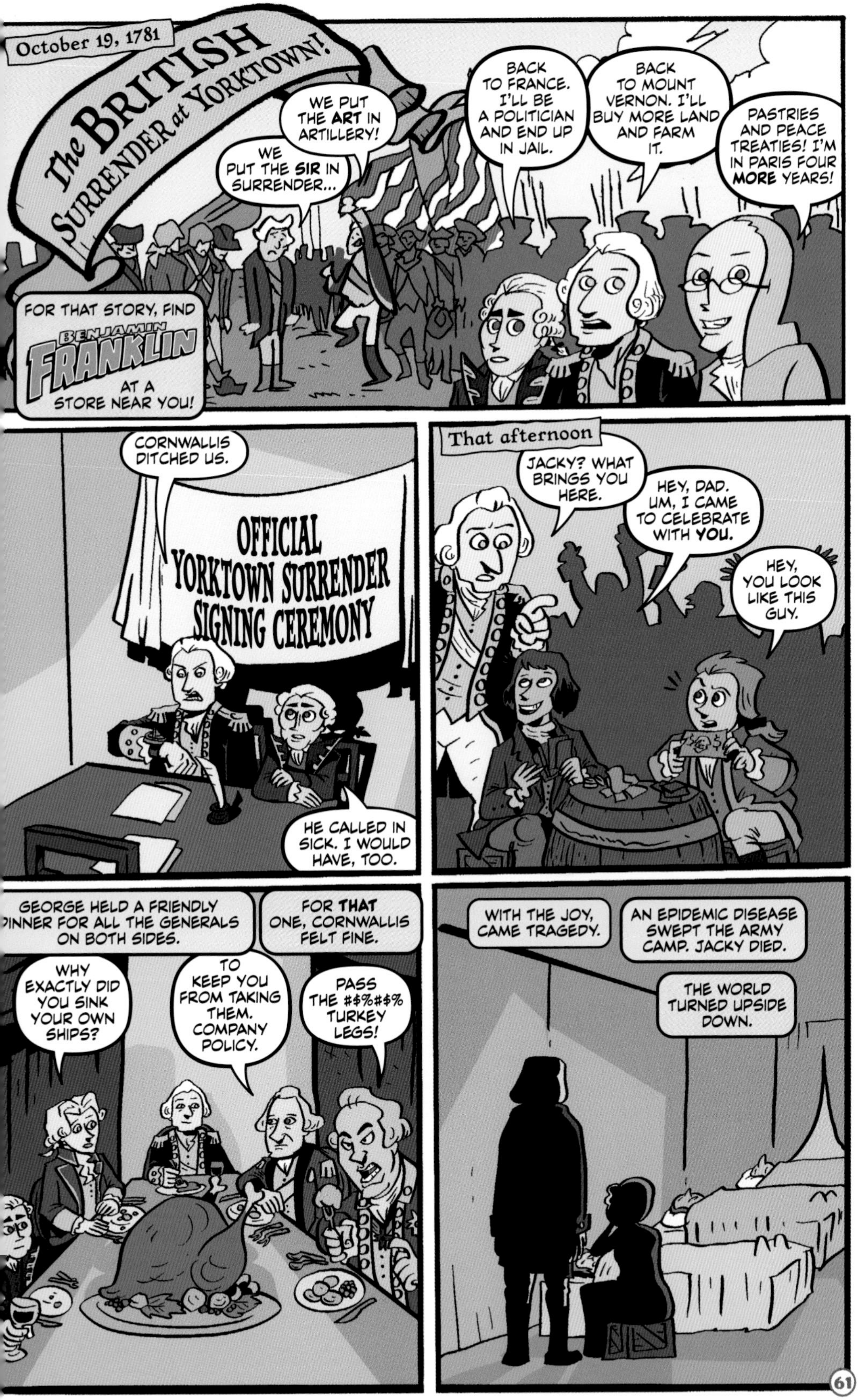
October 19, 1781
The BRITISH SURRENDER at YORKTOWN!
WE PUT THE SIR IN SURRENDER...
WE PUT THE ART IN ARTILLERY!
BACK TO FRANCE. I'LL BE A POLITICIAN AND END UP IN JAIL.
BACK TO MOUNT VERNON. I'LL BUY MORE LAND AND FARM IT.
PASTRIES AND PEACE TREATIES! I'M IN PARIS FOUR MORE YEARS!
FOR THAT STORY, FIND BENJAMIN FRANKLIN AT A STORE NEAR YOU!
CORNWALLIS DITCHED US.
OFFICIAL YORKTOWN SURRENDER SIGNING CEREMONY
HE CALLED IN SICK. I WOULD HAVE, TOO.
That afternoon
JACKY? WHAT BRINGS YOU HERE.
HEY, DAD. UM, I CAME TO CELEBRATE WITH YOU.
HEY, YOU LOOK LIKE THIS GUY.
GEORGE HELD A FRIENDLY DINNER FOR ALL THE GENERALS ON BOTH SIDES.
FOR THAT ONE, CORNWALLIS FELT FINE.
WHY EXACTLY DID YOU SINK YOUR OWN SHIPS?
TO KEEP YOU FROM TAKING THEM. COMPANY POLICY.
PASS THE #$%#$% TURKEY LEGS!
WITH THE JOY, CAME TRAGEDY.
AN EPIDEMIC DISEASE SWEPT THE ARMY CAMP. JACKY DIED.
THE WORLD TURNED UPSIDE DOWN.

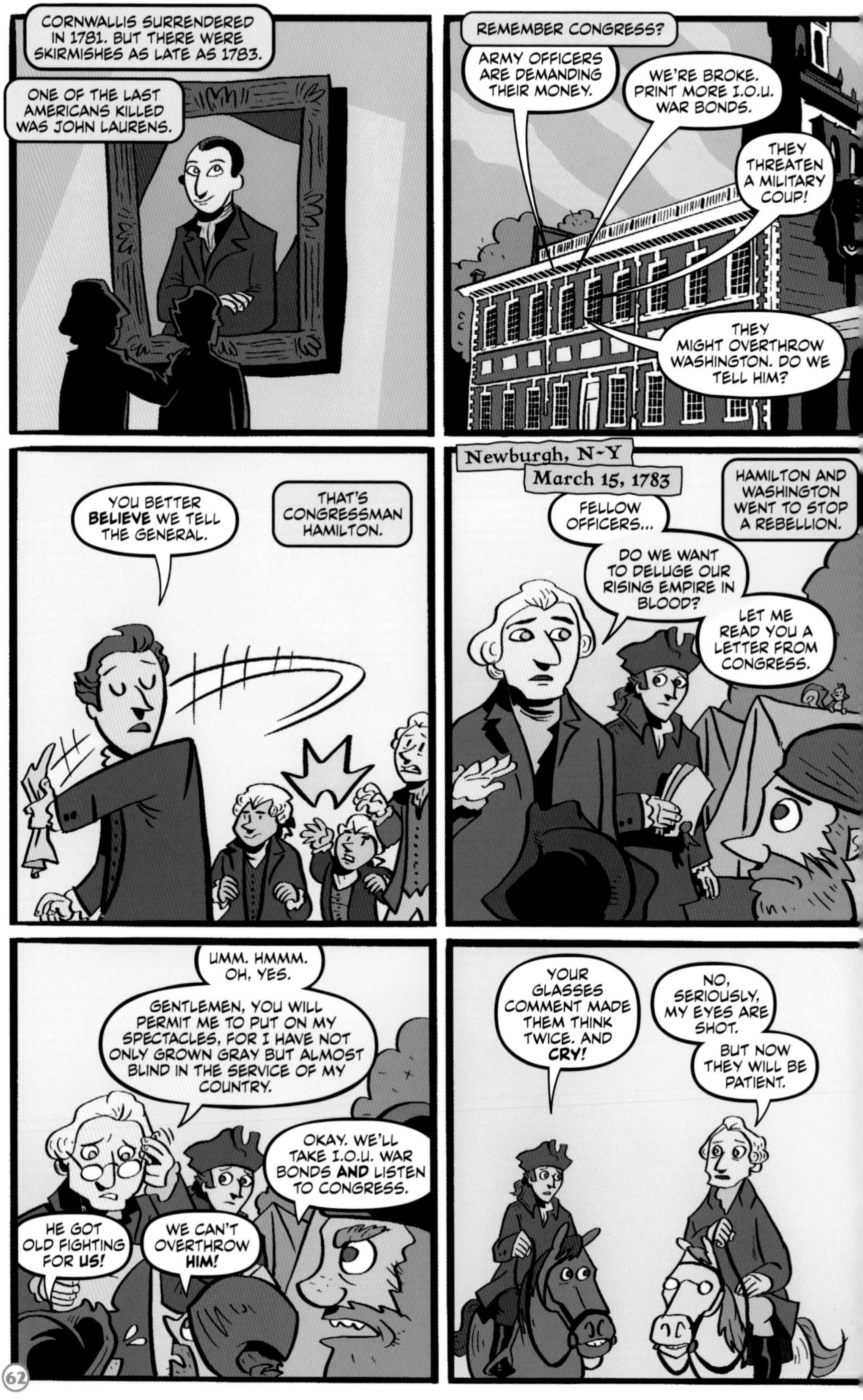
CORNWALLIS SURRENDERED IN 1781. BUT THERE WERE SKIRMISHES AS LATE AS 1783.
ONE OF THE LAST AMERICANS KILLED WAS JOHN LAURENS.
REMEMBER CONGRESS?
ARMY OFFICERS ARE DEMANDING THEIR MONEY.
WE'RE BROKE. PRINT MORE I.O.U. WAR BONDS.
THEY THREATEN A MILITARY COUP!
THEY MIGHT OVERTHROW WASHINGTON. DO WE TELL HIM?
YOU BETTER **BELIEVE** WE TELL THE GENERAL.
THAT'S CONGRESSMAN HAMILTON.
Newburgh, N-Y
March 15, 1783
HAMILTON AND WASHINGTON WENT TO STOP A REBELLION.
FELLOW OFFICERS...
DO WE WANT TO DELUGE OUR RISING EMPIRE IN BLOOD?
LET ME READ YOU A LETTER FROM CONGRESS.
UMM. HMMM. OH, YES.
GENTLEMEN, YOU WILL PERMIT ME TO PUT ON MY SPECTACLES, FOR I HAVE NOT ONLY GROWN GRAY BUT ALMOST BLIND IN THE SERVICE OF MY COUNTRY.
OKAY. WE'LL TAKE I.O.U. WAR BONDS **AND** LISTEN TO CONGRESS.
HE GOT OLD FIGHTING FOR **US!**
WE CAN'T OVERTHROW **HIM!**
YOUR GLASSES COMMENT MADE THEM THINK TWICE. AND **CRY!**
NO, SERIOUSLY, MY EYES ARE SHOT.
BUT NOW THEY WILL BE PATIENT.

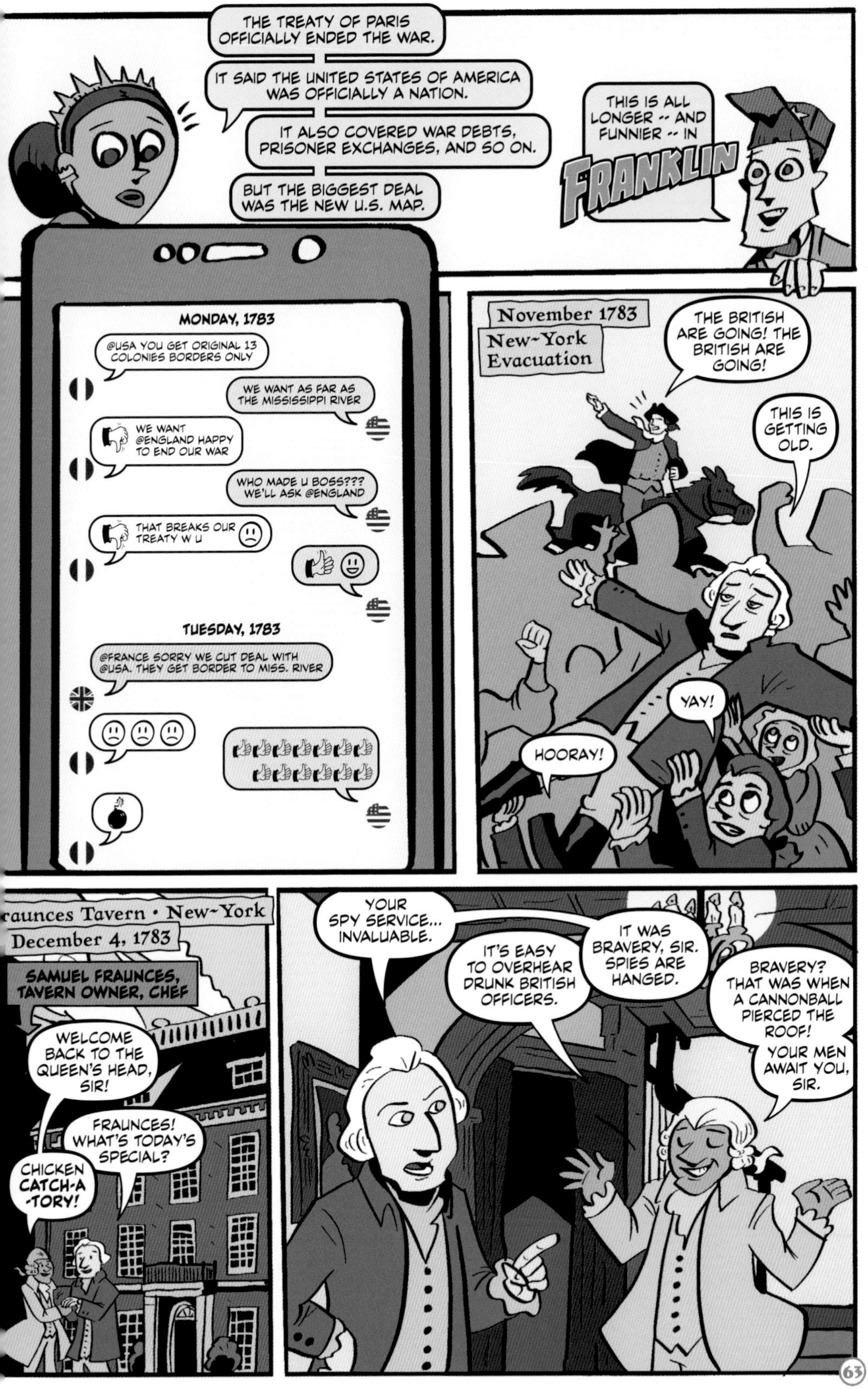
THE TREATY OF PARIS OFFICIALLY ENDED THE WAR.
IT SAID THE UNITED STATES OF AMERICA WAS OFFICIALLY A NATION.
IT ALSO COVERED WAR DEBTS, PRISONER EXCHANGES, AND SO ON.
BUT THE BIGGEST DEAL WAS THE NEW U.S. MAP.
THIS IS ALL LONGER -- AND FUNNIER -- IN FRANKLIN
MONDAY, 1783
@USA YOU GET ORIGINAL 13 COLONIES BORDERS ONLY
WE WANT AS FAR AS THE MISSISSIPPI RIVER
WE WANT @ENGLAND HAPPY TO END OUR WAR
WHO MADE U BOSS??? WE'LL ASK @ENGLAND
THAT BREAKS OUR TREATY W U
TUESDAY, 1783
@FRANCE SORRY WE CUT DEAL WITH @USA. THEY GET BORDER TO MISS. RIVER
November 1783
New-York Evacuation
THE BRITISH ARE GOING! THE BRITISH ARE GOING!
THIS IS GETTING OLD.
YAY!
HOORAY!
Fraunces Tavern • New-York
December 4, 1783
SAMUEL FRAUNCES, TAVERN OWNER, CHEF
WELCOME BACK TO THE QUEEN'S HEAD, SIR!
FRAUNCES! WHAT'S TODAY'S SPECIAL?
CHICKEN CATCH-A-TORY!
YOUR SPY SERVICE... INVALUABLE.
IT'S EASY TO OVERHEAR DRUNK BRITISH OFFICERS.
IT WAS BRAVERY, SIR. SPIES ARE HANGED.
BRAVERY? THAT WAS WHEN A CANNONBALL PIERCED THE ROOF!
YOUR MEN AWAIT YOU, SIR.

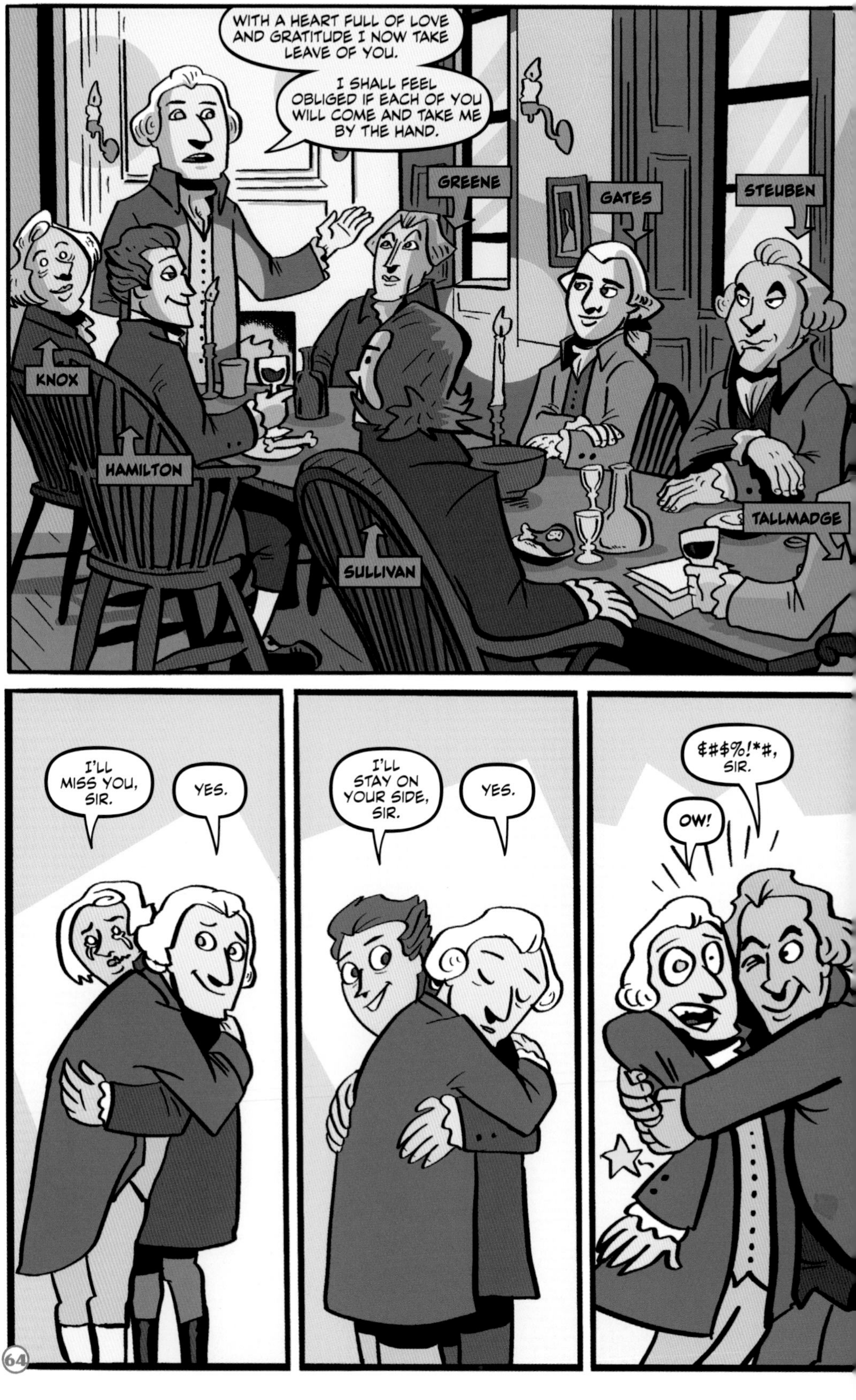
WITH A HEART FULL OF LOVE AND GRATITUDE I NOW TAKE LEAVE OF YOU.
I SHALL FEEL OBLIGED IF EACH OF YOU WILL COME AND TAKE ME BY THE HAND.
GREENE
GATES
STEUBEN
KNOX
HAMILTON
SULLIVAN
TALLMADGE
I'LL MISS YOU, SIR.
YES.
I'LL STAY ON YOUR SIDE, SIR.
YES.
$#$%!*#, SIR.
OW!

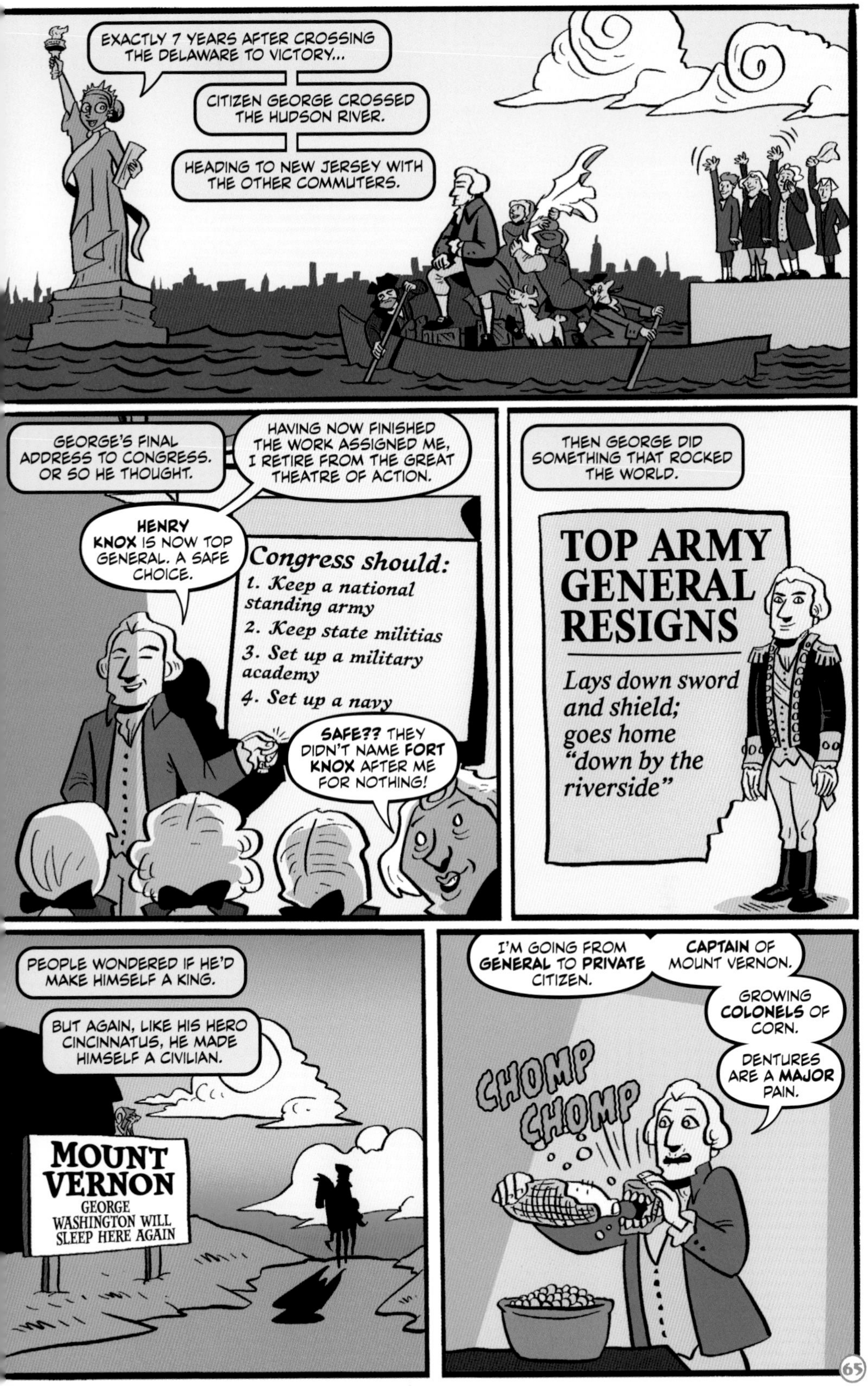
EXACTLY 7 YEARS AFTER CROSSING THE DELAWARE TO VICTORY...
CITIZEN GEORGE CROSSED THE HUDSON RIVER.
HEADING TO NEW JERSEY WITH THE OTHER COMMUTERS.
GEORGE'S FINAL ADDRESS TO CONGRESS. OR SO HE THOUGHT.
HAVING NOW FINISHED THE WORK ASSIGNED ME, I RETIRE FROM THE GREAT THEATRE OF ACTION.
HENRY KNOX IS NOW TOP GENERAL. A SAFE CHOICE.
Congress should:
1. Keep a national standing army
2. Keep state militias
3. Set up a military academy
4. Set up a navy
SAFE?? THEY DIDN'T NAME FORT KNOX AFTER ME FOR NOTHING!
THEN GEORGE DID SOMETHING THAT ROCKED THE WORLD.
TOP ARMY GENERAL RESIGNS
Lays down sword and shield; goes home "down by the riverside"
PEOPLE WONDERED IF HE'D MAKE HIMSELF A KING.
BUT AGAIN, LIKE HIS HERO CINCINNATUS, HE MADE HIMSELF A CIVILIAN.
MOUNT VERNON
GEORGE WASHINGTON WILL SLEEP HERE AGAIN
I'M GOING FROM GENERAL TO PRIVATE CITIZEN.
CAPTAIN OF MOUNT VERNON.
GROWING COLONELS OF CORN.
DENTURES ARE A MAJOR PAIN.
CHOMP CHOMP

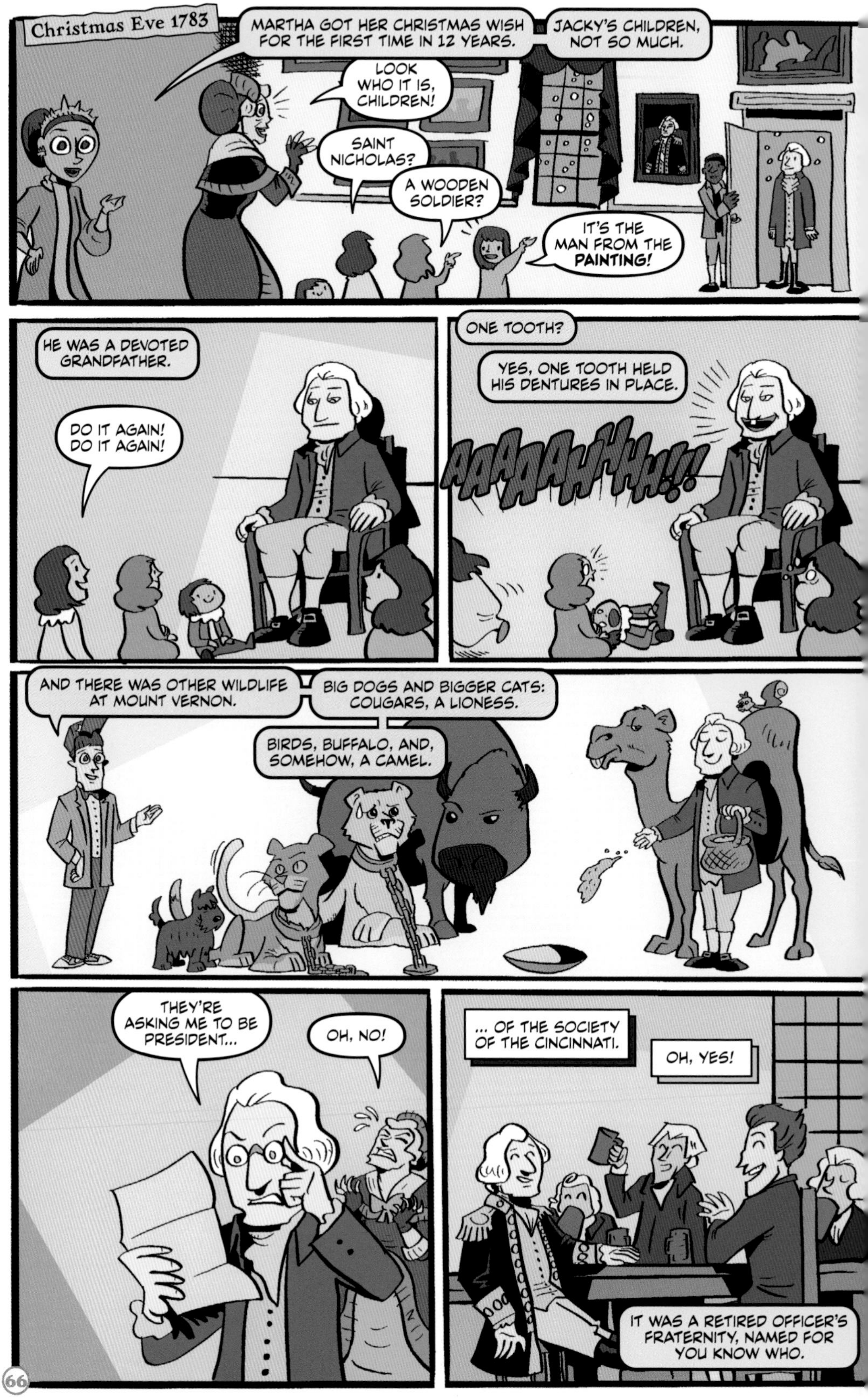
Christmas Eve 1783
MARTHA GOT HER CHRISTMAS WISH FOR THE FIRST TIME IN 12 YEARS.
JACKY'S CHILDREN, NOT SO MUCH.
LOOK WHO IT IS, CHILDREN!
SAINT NICHOLAS?
A WOODEN SOLDIER?
IT'S THE MAN FROM THE **PAINTING!**
HE WAS A DEVOTED GRANDFATHER.
DO IT AGAIN! DO IT AGAIN!
ONE TOOTH?
YES, ONE TOOTH HELD HIS DENTURES IN PLACE.
AAAAAHHHH!!!
AND THERE WAS OTHER WILDLIFE AT MOUNT VERNON.
BIG DOGS AND BIGGER CATS: COUGARS, A LIONESS.
BIRDS, BUFFALO, AND, SOMEHOW, A CAMEL.
THEY'RE ASKING ME TO BE PRESIDENT...
OH, NO!
... OF THE SOCIETY OF THE CINCINNATI.
OH, YES!
IT WAS A RETIRED OFFICER'S FRATERNITY, NAMED FOR YOU KNOW WHO.

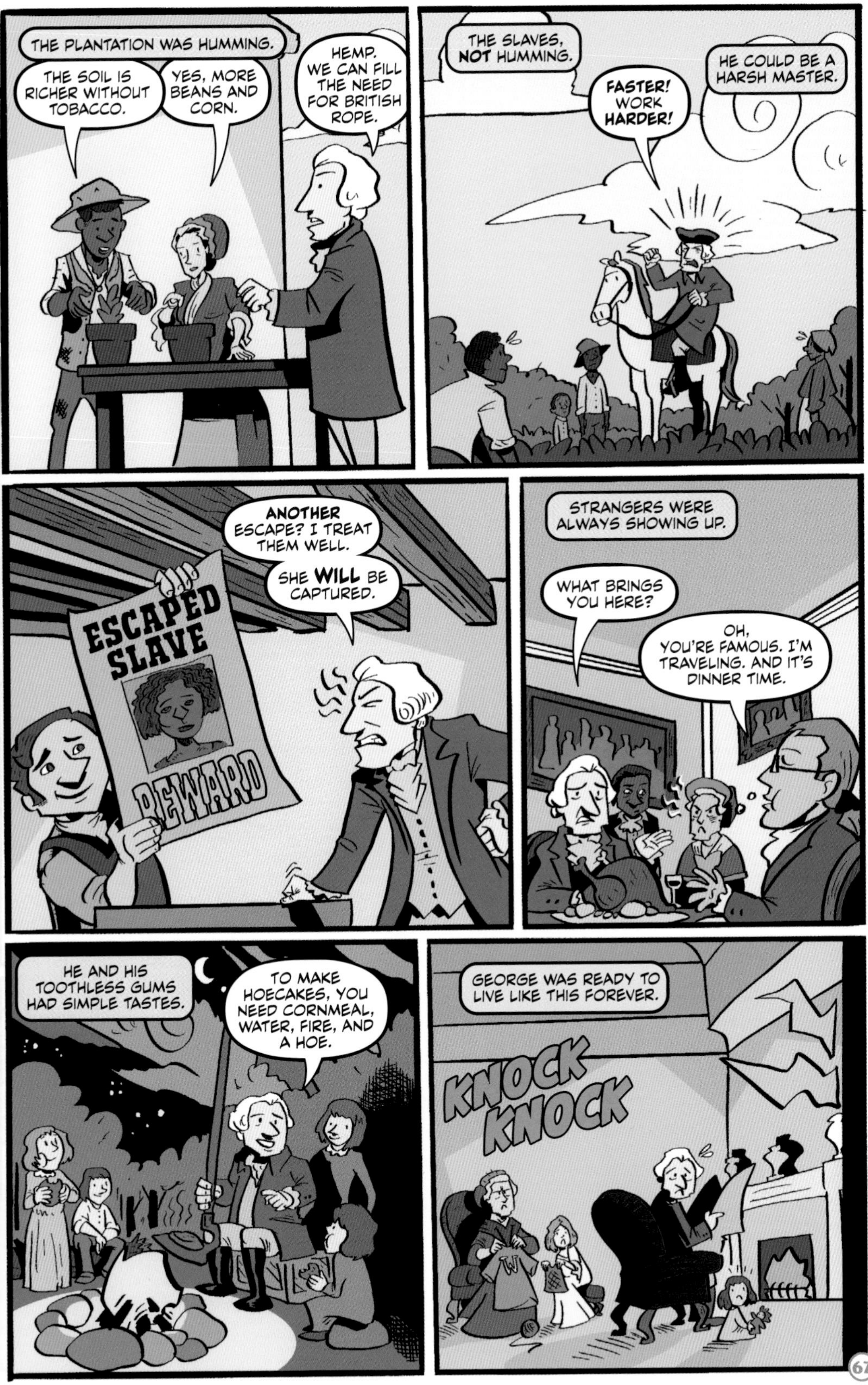
THE PLANTATION WAS HUMMING.
THE SOIL IS RICHER WITHOUT TOBACCO.
YES, MORE BEANS AND CORN.
HEMP. WE CAN FILL THE NEED FOR BRITISH ROPE.
THE SLAVES, NOT HUMMING.
FASTER! WORK HARDER!
HE COULD BE A HARSH MASTER.
ANOTHER ESCAPE? I TREAT THEM WELL.
SHE WILL BE CAPTURED.
ESCAPED SLAVE
REWARD
STRANGERS WERE ALWAYS SHOWING UP.
WHAT BRINGS YOU HERE?
OH, YOU'RE FAMOUS. I'M TRAVELING. AND IT'S DINNER TIME.
HE AND HIS TOOTHLESS GUMS HAD SIMPLE TASTES.
TO MAKE HOECAKES, YOU NEED CORNMEAL, WATER, FIRE, AND A HOE.
GEORGE WAS READY TO LIVE LIKE THIS FOREVER.
KNOCK KNOCK

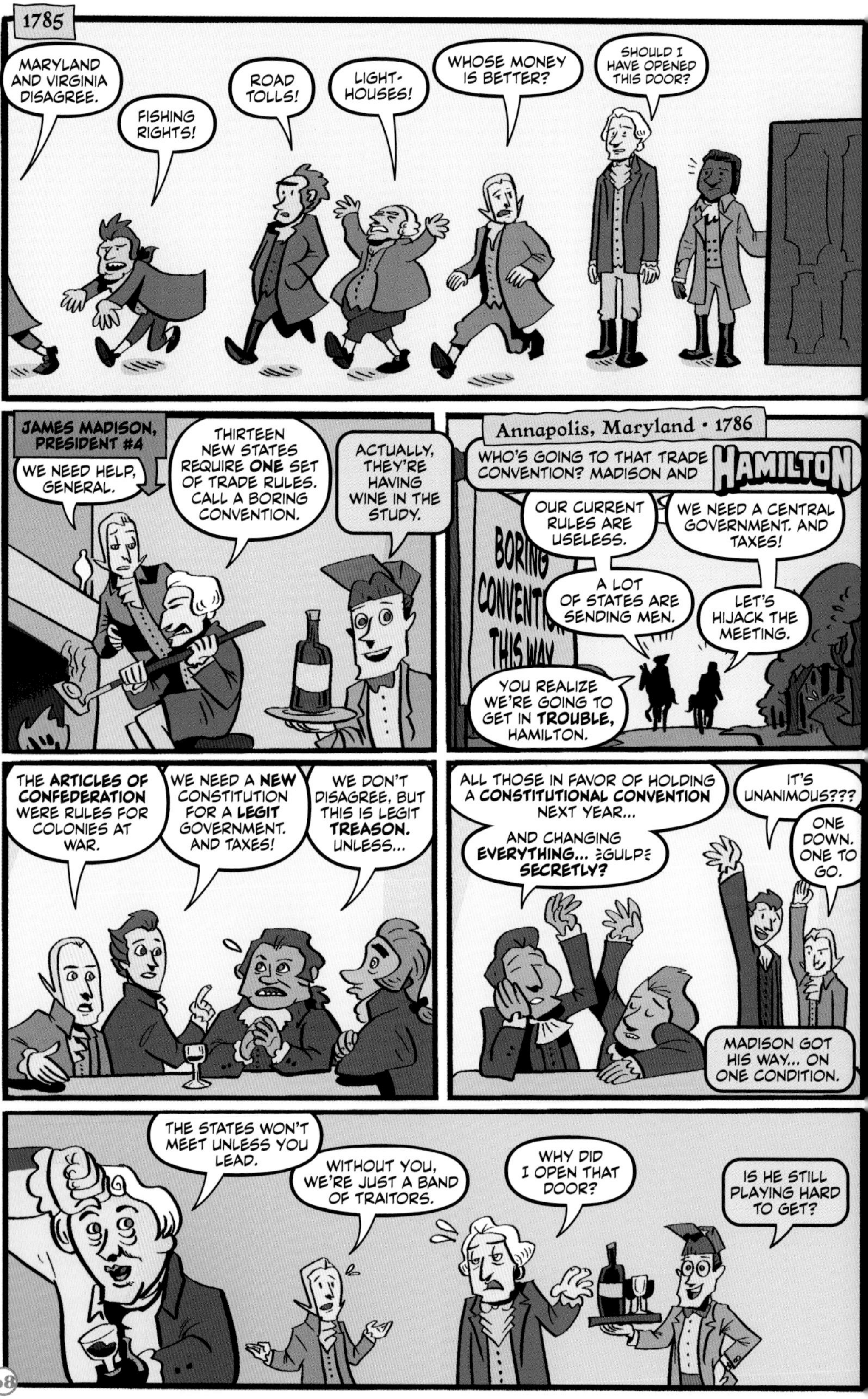
1785
MARYLAND AND VIRGINIA DISAGREE.
FISHING RIGHTS!
ROAD TOLLS!
LIGHT-HOUSES!
WHOSE MONEY IS BETTER?
SHOULD I HAVE OPENED THIS DOOR?
JAMES MADISON, PRESIDENT #4
WE NEED HELP, GENERAL.
THIRTEEN NEW STATES REQUIRE **ONE** SET OF TRADE RULES. CALL A BORING CONVENTION.
ACTUALLY, THEY'RE HAVING WINE IN THE STUDY.
Annapolis, Maryland • 1786
WHO'S GOING TO THAT TRADE CONVENTION? MADISON AND HAMILTON
OUR CURRENT RULES ARE USELESS.
WE NEED A CENTRAL GOVERNMENT. AND TAXES!
BORING CONVENTION THIS WAY
A LOT OF STATES ARE SENDING MEN.
LET'S HIJACK THE MEETING.
YOU REALIZE WE'RE GOING TO GET IN **TROUBLE,** HAMILTON.
THE **ARTICLES OF CONFEDERATION** WERE RULES FOR COLONIES AT WAR.
WE NEED A **NEW** CONSTITUTION FOR A **LEGIT** GOVERNMENT. AND TAXES!
WE DON'T DISAGREE, BUT THIS IS LEGIT **TREASON.** UNLESS...
ALL THOSE IN FAVOR OF HOLDING A **CONSTITUTIONAL CONVENTION** NEXT YEAR...
AND CHANGING **EVERYTHING...** GULP **SECRETLY?**
IT'S UNANIMOUS???
ONE DOWN. ONE TO GO.
MADISON GOT HIS WAY... ON ONE CONDITION.
THE STATES WON'T MEET UNLESS YOU LEAD.
WITHOUT YOU, WE'RE JUST A BAND OF TRAITORS.
WHY DID I OPEN THAT DOOR?
IS HE STILL PLAYING HARD TO GET?

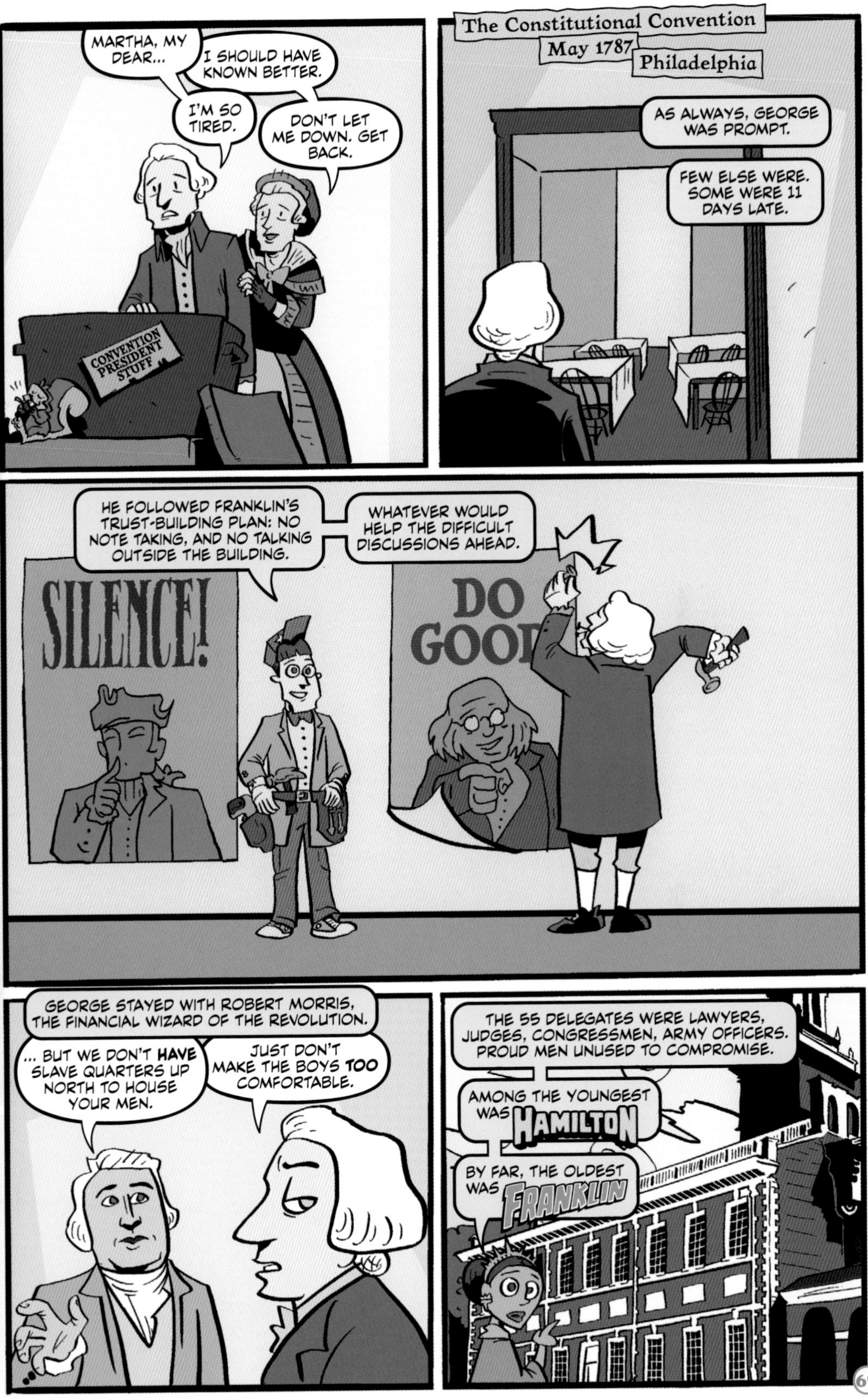

MARTHA, MY DEAR...
I SHOULD HAVE KNOWN BETTER.
I'M SO TIRED.
DON'T LET ME DOWN. GET BACK.
CONVENTION PRESIDENT STUFF
The Constitutional Convention
May 1787
Philadelphia
AS ALWAYS, GEORGE WAS PROMPT.
FEW ELSE WERE. SOME WERE 11 DAYS LATE.
HE FOLLOWED FRANKLIN'S TRUST-BUILDING PLAN: NO NOTE TAKING, AND NO TALKING OUTSIDE THE BUILDING.
WHATEVER WOULD HELP THE DIFFICULT DISCUSSIONS AHEAD.
SILENCE!
DO GOO
GEORGE STAYED WITH ROBERT MORRIS, THE FINANCIAL WIZARD OF THE REVOLUTION.
... BUT WE DON'T **HAVE** SLAVE QUARTERS UP NORTH TO HOUSE YOUR MEN.
JUST DON'T MAKE THE BOYS **TOO** COMFORTABLE.
THE 55 DELEGATES WERE LAWYERS, JUDGES, CONGRESSMEN, ARMY OFFICERS. PROUD MEN UNUSED TO COMPROMISE.
AMONG THE YOUNGEST WAS HAMILTON
BY FAR, THE OLDEST WAS FRANKLIN

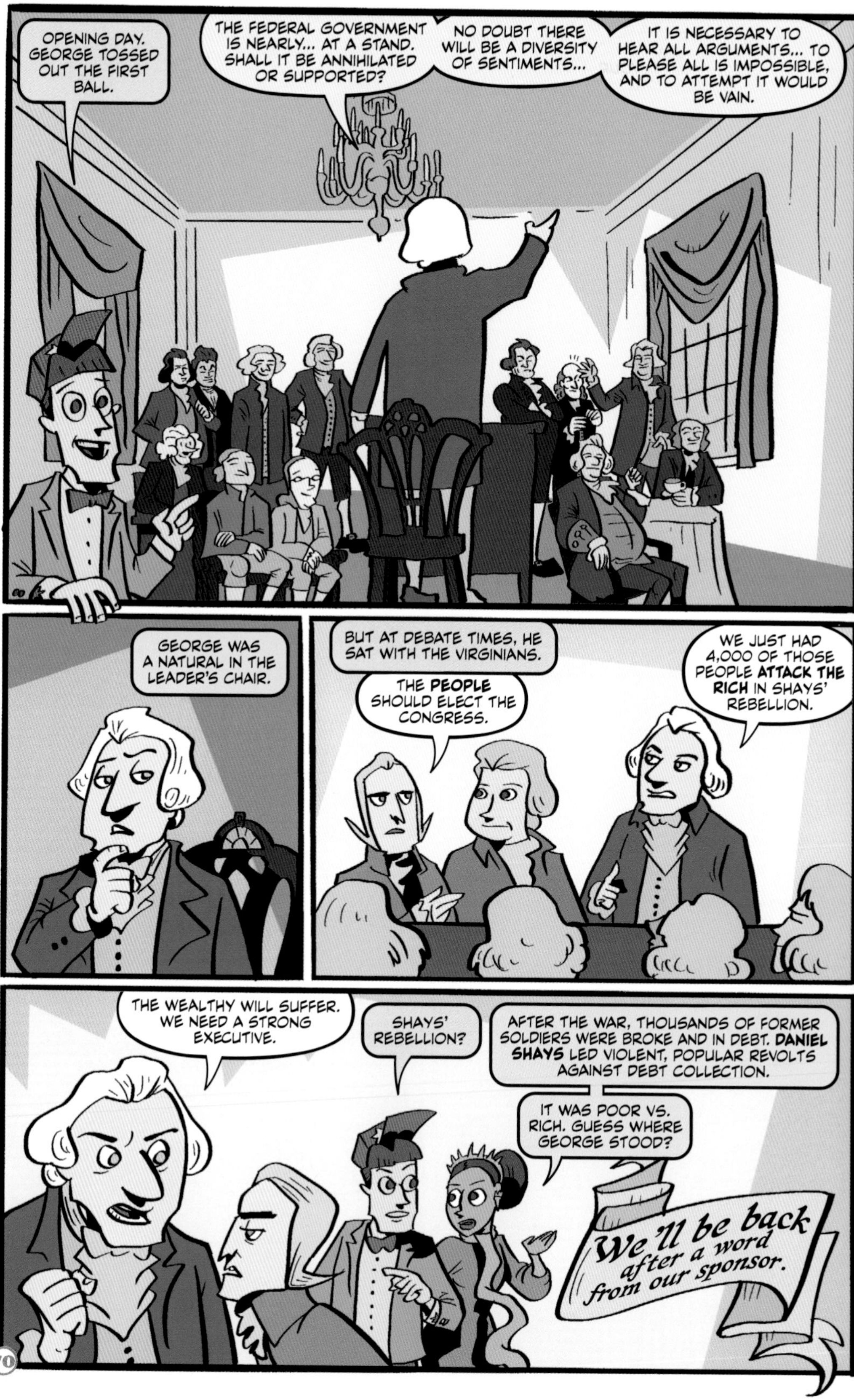
OPENING DAY. GEORGE TOSSED OUT THE FIRST BALL.
THE FEDERAL GOVERNMENT IS NEARLY... AT A STAND. SHALL IT BE ANNIHILATED OR SUPPORTED?
NO DOUBT THERE WILL BE A DIVERSITY OF SENTIMENTS...
IT IS NECESSARY TO HEAR ALL ARGUMENTS... TO PLEASE ALL IS IMPOSSIBLE, AND TO ATTEMPT IT WOULD BE VAIN.
GEORGE WAS A NATURAL IN THE LEADER'S CHAIR.
BUT AT DEBATE TIMES, HE SAT WITH THE VIRGINIANS.
THE **PEOPLE** SHOULD ELECT THE CONGRESS.
WE JUST HAD 4,000 OF THOSE PEOPLE **ATTACK THE RICH** IN SHAYS' REBELLION.
THE WEALTHY WILL SUFFER. WE NEED A STRONG EXECUTIVE.
SHAYS' REBELLION?
AFTER THE WAR, THOUSANDS OF FORMER SOLDIERS WERE BROKE AND IN DEBT. **DANIEL SHAYS** LED VIOLENT, POPULAR REVOLTS AGAINST DEBT COLLECTION.
IT WAS POOR VS. RICH. GUESS WHERE GEORGE STOOD?
We'll be back after a word from our sponsor.

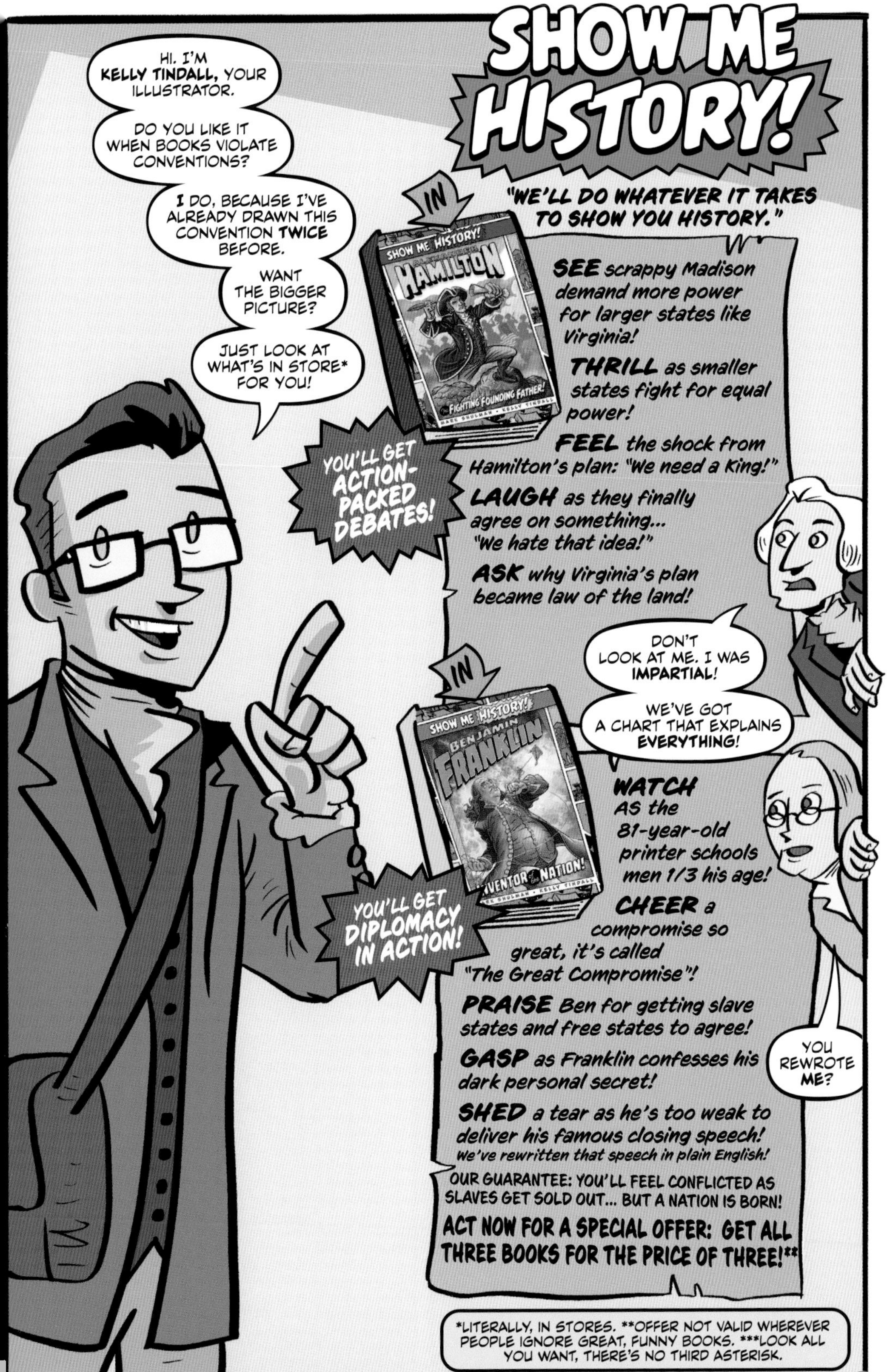

SHOW ME HISTORY!
HI. I'M KELLY TINDALL, YOUR ILLUSTRATOR.
DO YOU LIKE IT WHEN BOOKS VIOLATE CONVENTIONS?
I DO, BECAUSE I'VE ALREADY DRAWN THIS CONVENTION TWICE BEFORE.
WANT THE BIGGER PICTURE?
JUST LOOK AT WHAT'S IN STORE* FOR YOU!
"WE'LL DO WHATEVER IT TAKES TO SHOW YOU HISTORY."
IN
SHOW ME HISTORY! HAMILTON THE FIGHTING FOUNDING FATHER!
SEE scrappy Madison demand more power for larger states like Virginia!
THRILL as smaller states fight for equal power!
FEEL the shock from Hamilton's plan: "We need a King!"
LAUGH as they finally agree on something... "We hate that idea!"
ASK why Virginia's plan became law of the land!
YOU'LL GET ACTION-PACKED DEBATES!
DON'T LOOK AT ME. I WAS IMPARTIAL!
WE'VE GOT A CHART THAT EXPLAINS EVERYTHING!
IN
SHOW ME HISTORY! BENJAMIN FRANKLIN INVENTOR OF THE NATION!
WATCH AS the 81-year-old printer schools men 1/3 his age!
CHEER a compromise so great, it's called "The Great Compromise"!
YOU'LL GET DIPLOMACY IN ACTION!
PRAISE Ben for getting slave states and free states to agree!
GASP as Franklin confesses his dark personal secret!
YOU REWROTE ME?
SHED a tear as he's too weak to deliver his famous closing speech!
We've rewritten that speech in plain English!
OUR GUARANTEE: YOU'LL FEEL CONFLICTED AS SLAVES GET SOLD OUT... BUT A NATION IS BORN!
ACT NOW FOR A SPECIAL OFFER: GET ALL THREE BOOKS FOR THE PRICE OF THREE!**
*LITERALLY, IN STORES. **OFFER NOT VALID WHEREVER PEOPLE IGNORE GREAT, FUNNY BOOKS. ***LOOK ALL YOU WANT, THERE'S NO THIRD ASTERISK.

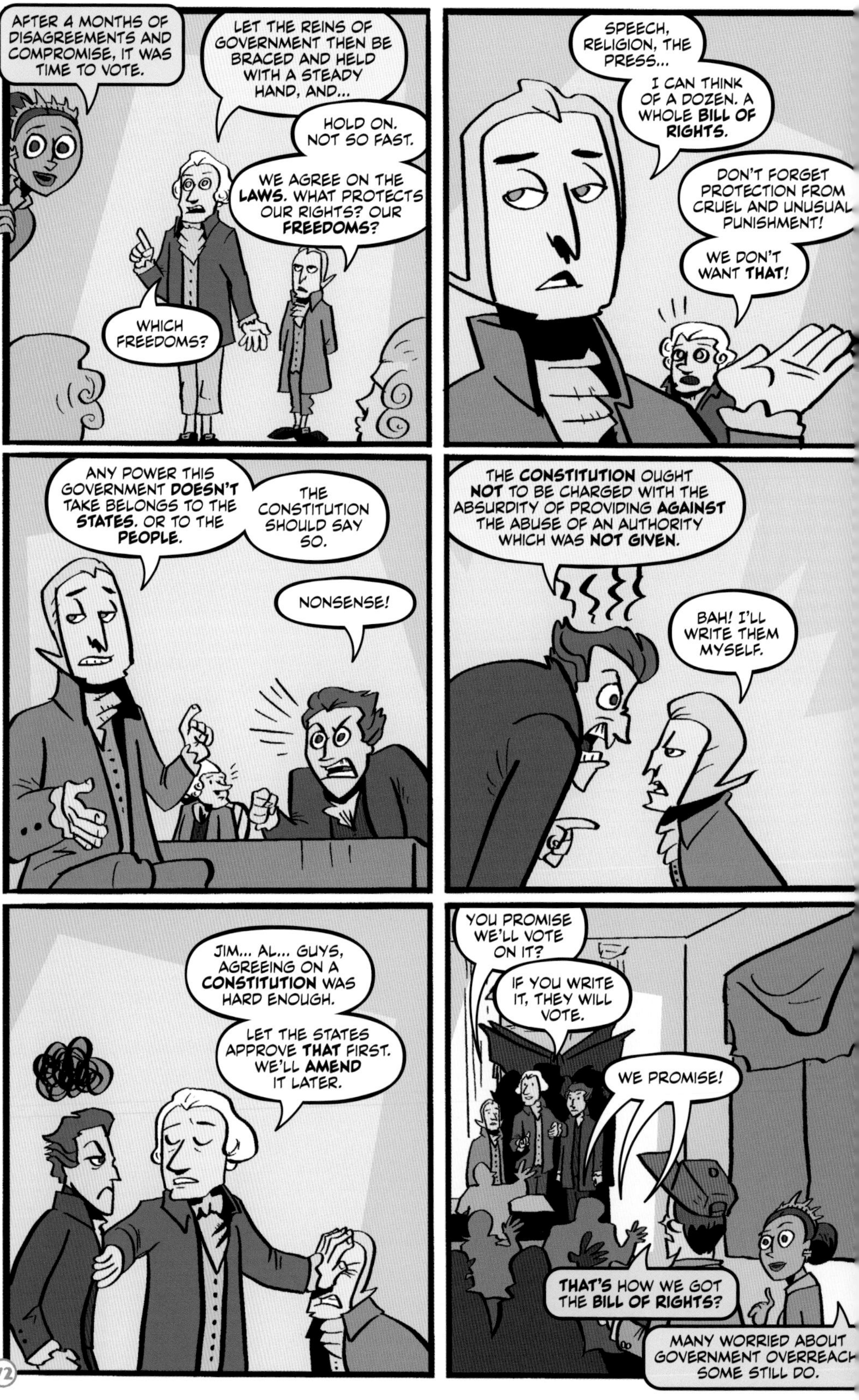

AFTER 4 MONTHS OF DISAGREEMENTS AND COMPROMISE, IT WAS TIME TO VOTE.
LET THE REINS OF GOVERNMENT THEN BE BRACED AND HELD WITH A STEADY HAND, AND...
HOLD ON. NOT SO FAST.
WE AGREE ON THE **LAWS**. WHAT PROTECTS OUR RIGHTS? OUR **FREEDOMS**?
WHICH FREEDOMS?
SPEECH, RELIGION, THE PRESS...
I CAN THINK OF A DOZEN. A WHOLE **BILL OF RIGHTS**.
DON'T FORGET PROTECTION FROM CRUEL AND UNUSUAL PUNISHMENT!
WE DON'T WANT **THAT**!
ANY POWER THIS GOVERNMENT **DOESN'T** TAKE BELONGS TO THE **STATES**. OR TO THE **PEOPLE**.
THE CONSTITUTION SHOULD SAY SO.
NONSENSE!
THE **CONSTITUTION** OUGHT **NOT** TO BE CHARGED WITH THE ABSURDITY OF PROVIDING **AGAINST** THE ABUSE OF AN AUTHORITY WHICH WAS **NOT GIVEN**.
BAH! I'LL WRITE THEM MYSELF.
JIM... AL... GUYS, AGREEING ON A **CONSTITUTION** WAS HARD ENOUGH.
LET THE STATES APPROVE **THAT** FIRST. WE'LL **AMEND** IT LATER.
YOU PROMISE WE'LL VOTE ON IT?
IF YOU WRITE IT, THEY WILL VOTE.
WE PROMISE!
THAT'S HOW WE GOT THE **BILL OF RIGHTS**?
MANY WORRIED ABOUT GOVERNMENT OVERREACH. SOME STILL DO.

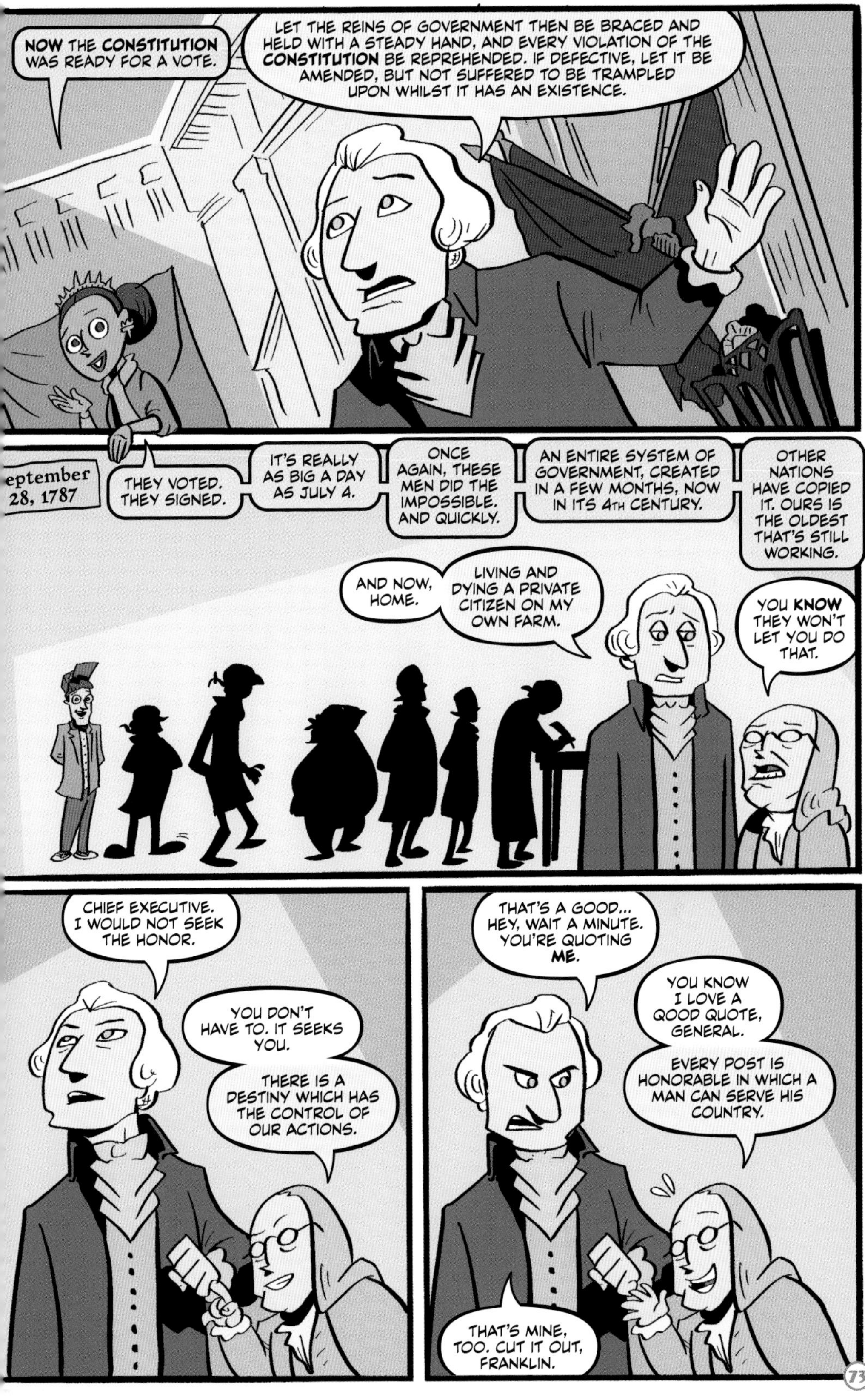
NOW THE CONSTITUTION WAS READY FOR A VOTE.
LET THE REINS OF GOVERNMENT THEN BE BRACED AND HELD WITH A STEADY HAND, AND EVERY VIOLATION OF THE CONSTITUTION BE REPREHENDED. IF DEFECTIVE, LET IT BE AMENDED, BUT NOT SUFFERED TO BE TRAMPLED UPON WHILST IT HAS AN EXISTENCE.
eptember 28, 1787
THEY VOTED. THEY SIGNED.
IT'S REALLY AS BIG A DAY AS JULY 4.
ONCE AGAIN, THESE MEN DID THE IMPOSSIBLE. AND QUICKLY.
AN ENTIRE SYSTEM OF GOVERNMENT, CREATED IN A FEW MONTHS, NOW IN ITS 4TH CENTURY.
OTHER NATIONS HAVE COPIED IT. OURS IS THE OLDEST THAT'S STILL WORKING.
AND NOW, HOME.
LIVING AND DYING A PRIVATE CITIZEN ON MY OWN FARM.
YOU KNOW THEY WON'T LET YOU DO THAT.
CHIEF EXECUTIVE. I WOULD NOT SEEK THE HONOR.
YOU DON'T HAVE TO. IT SEEKS YOU.
THERE IS A DESTINY WHICH HAS THE CONTROL OF OUR ACTIONS.
THAT'S A GOOD... HEY, WAIT A MINUTE. YOU'RE QUOTING ME.
YOU KNOW I LOVE A GOOD QUOTE, GENERAL.
EVERY POST IS HONORABLE IN WHICH A MAN CAN SERVE HIS COUNTRY.
THAT'S MINE, TOO. CUT IT OUT, FRANKLIN.

IN UNDER A YEAR, 11 STATES **RATIFIED THE CONSTITUTION.**

THINGS WERE HAPPENING **VERY** FAST.

THEIR LEGISLATURES ALSO ELECTED THE FIRST U.S. CONGRESS.

EXCEPT GEORGE **STILL** WASN'T SAYING YES TO BEING PRESIDENT.

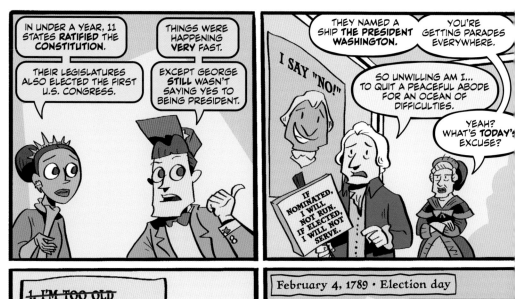

THEY NAMED A SHIP **THE PRESIDENT WASHINGTON.**

YOU'RE GETTING PARADES EVERYWHERE.

I SAY "NO!"

SO UNWILLING AM I... TO QUIT A PEACEFUL ABODE FOR AN OCEAN OF DIFFICULTIES.

YEAH? WHAT'S **TODAY'S** EXCUSE?

IF NOMINATED, I WILL NOT RUN. IF ELECTED, I WILL NOT SERVE.

1. I'M TOO OLD
2. I'M AMUSED BY AGRICULTURE
3. I LOVE RETIREMENT
4. I DON'T WANT ANY OPPOSITION
5. I RETIRED ONCE PEOPLE WILL GOSSIP
6. SOMEONE ELSE COULD DO IT AS WELL

YOU DIDN'T SAY THEY COULD DO IT **BETTER.**

February 4, 1789 • Election day

THE FIRST ELECTION WASN'T OF, BY, OR FOR THE PEOPLE.

IT WAS DONE BY STATE ELECTORS. THEY SENT THE RESULTS TO CONGRESS.

March 4, 1789

New~York Federal Hall

THE FIRST-EVER TASK OF THE U.S. SENATE.

I HAVE THE BALLOTS FOR THE EXECUTIVE.

OF 69 POSSIBLE VOTES, MR. WASHINGTON RECEIVES...

69. IT'S **UNANIMOUS.**

THE ONLY PRESIDENT EVER ELECTED UNANIMOUSLY.

WASHINGTON MIGHT NOT HAVE AGREED OTHERWISE.

I HAVE THE ELECTION RESULTS.

KNOCK KNOCK

NOOOOO!

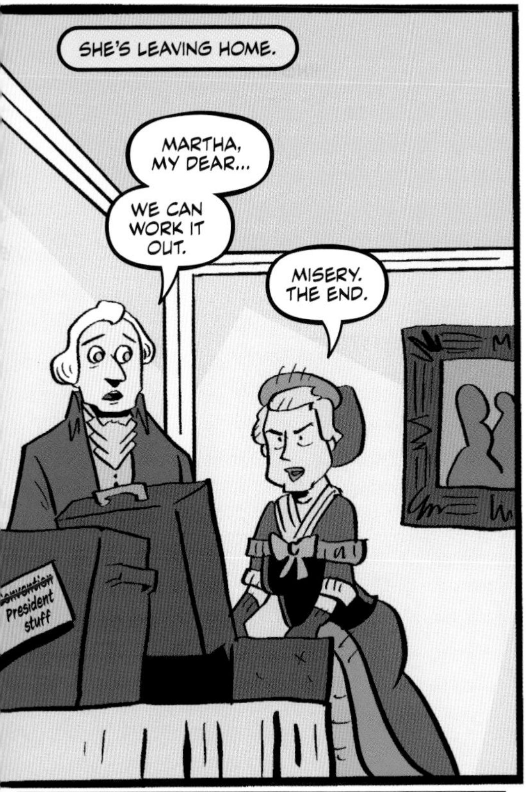
SHE'S LEAVING HOME.
MARTHA, MY DEAR...
WE CAN WORK IT OUT.
MISERY. THE END.
~~Convention~~ President stuff

What George said privately.

About ten o'clock I bade adieu to Mount Vernon, to private life, and to domestic felicity; and with a mind oppressed with more anxious and painful sensations than I have words to express, set out for New York... to render service to my country in obedience to its call, but with less hope of answering its expectations.

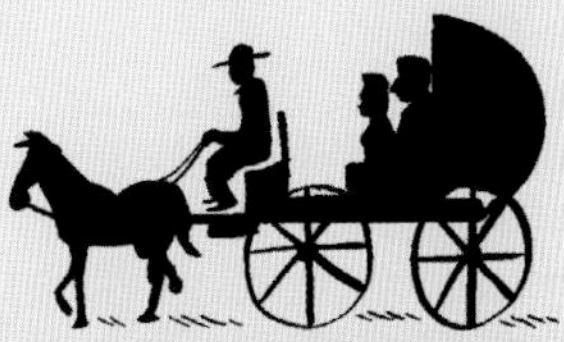

What George said publicly.

I do solemnly swear that I will faithfully execute the Office of President of the United States, and will to the best of my Ability, preserve, protect and defend the Constitution of the United States.

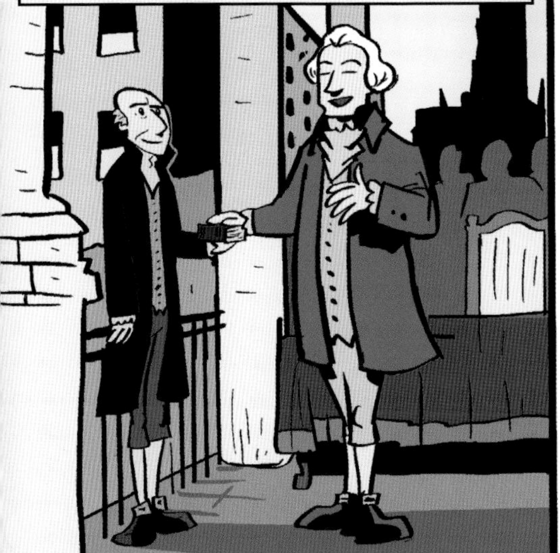

FUN FACTS:

- George most likely didn't say his name, kiss the Bible, or add "So help me, God."
- His original inaugural address ran 70 pages. Madison cut it drastically.
- Attendance in 1789 was 10,000. Record attendance, in 2009, was 1,800,000.
- The streets were so crowded, George had to walk home.
- Martha called in sick; George danced for a while at his ball, then ate alone.
- The Washingtons had to borrow big money just to get to New-York.

HOW TO START? THE **CONSTITUTION** DEVOTES JUST 1,025 WORDS TO THE EXECUTIVE BRANCH.

IN OTHER WORDS, NOT ENOUGH WORDS.

I WALK ON UNTRODDEN GROUND.

NEED HELP?

YES. GO AWAY, ADAMS.

VICE PRESIDENT #1

WHAT ARE THE BASICS OF RUNNING A NATION?

WAR. DIPLOMACY. LAW. MONEY.

HELP!!

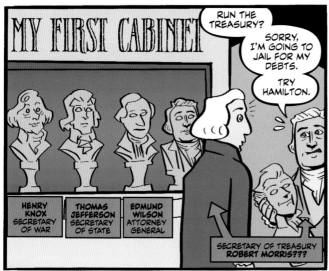

MY FIRST CABINET

RUN THE TREASURY?

SORRY, I'M GOING TO JAIL FOR MY DEBTS.

TRY HAMILTON.

HENRY KNOX SECRETARY OF WAR

THOMAS JEFFERSON SECRETARY OF STATE

EDMUND WILSON ATTORNEY GENERAL

SECRETARY OF TREASURY ROBERT MORRIS???

AM I DONE YET?

NO! PICK JUDGES!

AMBASSADORS! THE POSTMASTER! ETC!

AND THE SENATE WILL "ADVISE AND CONSENT."

THAT MEANS FOLLOW OUR **ADVICE** OR WE WON'T **CONSENT!**

NO, IT MEANS YOU GIVE **ADVICE**, THEN SAY **YES**.

List of Guys I Want

CONGRESS WANTS ME TO SHARE **EVERYTHING!**

NO. THAT WILL... UM... DAMAGE THE... UM... NATIONAL INTEREST.

CALL IT **EXECUTIVE PRIVILEGE.**

THAT'S HOW **THAT** GOT STARTED.

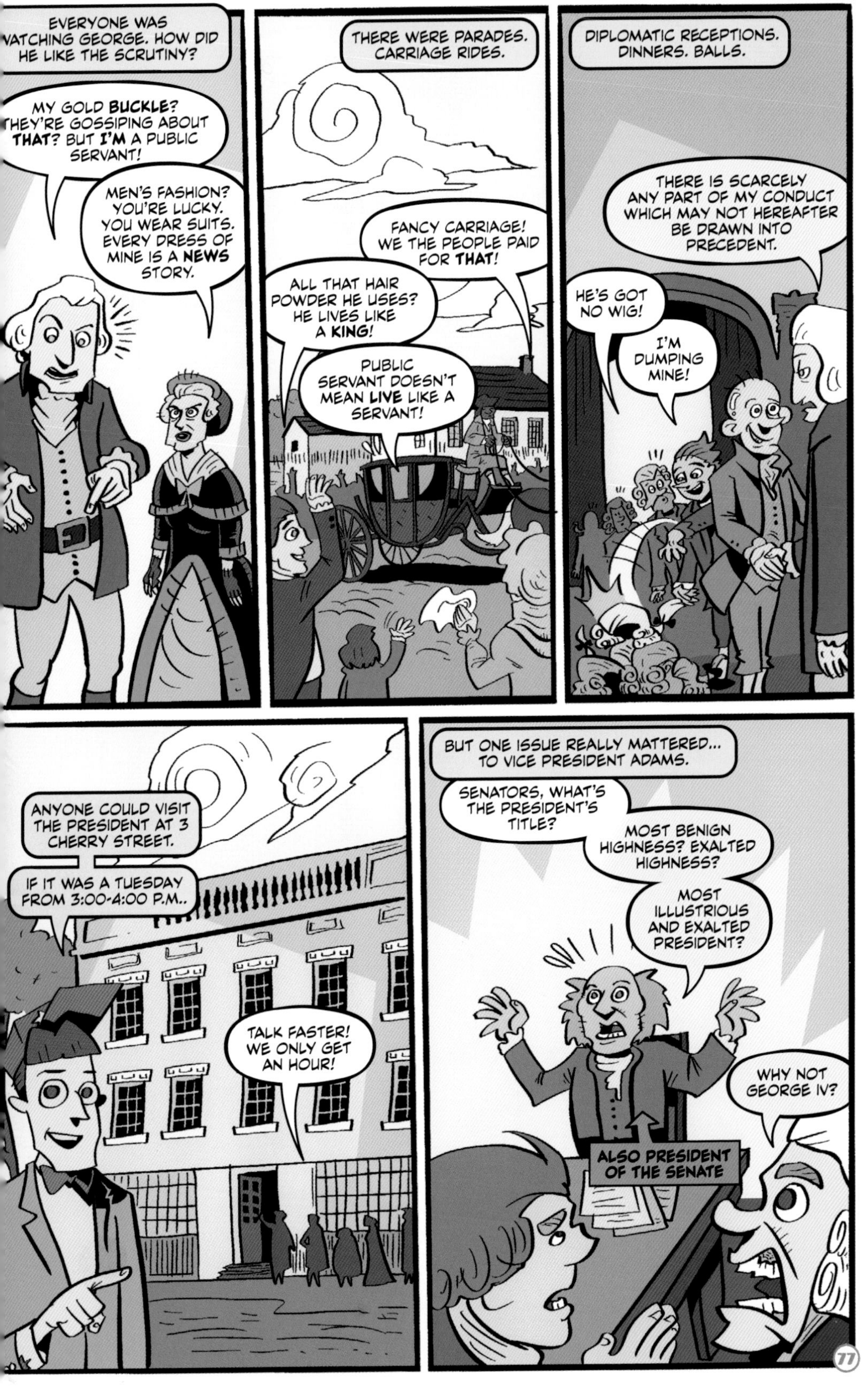
EVERYONE WAS WATCHING GEORGE. HOW DID HE LIKE THE SCRUTINY?
MY GOLD BUCKLE? THEY'RE GOSSIPING ABOUT THAT? BUT I'M A PUBLIC SERVANT!
MEN'S FASHION? YOU'RE LUCKY. YOU WEAR SUITS. EVERY DRESS OF MINE IS A NEWS STORY.
THERE WERE PARADES. CARRIAGE RIDES.
FANCY CARRIAGE! WE THE PEOPLE PAID FOR THAT!
ALL THAT HAIR POWDER HE USES? HE LIVES LIKE A KING!
PUBLIC SERVANT DOESN'T MEAN LIVE LIKE A SERVANT!
DIPLOMATIC RECEPTIONS. DINNERS. BALLS.
THERE IS SCARCELY ANY PART OF MY CONDUCT WHICH MAY NOT HEREAFTER BE DRAWN INTO PRECEDENT.
HE'S GOT NO WIG!
I'M DUMPING MINE!
ANYONE COULD VISIT THE PRESIDENT AT 3 CHERRY STREET.
IF IT WAS A TUESDAY FROM 3:00-4:00 P.M..
TALK FASTER! WE ONLY GET AN HOUR!
BUT ONE ISSUE REALLY MATTERED... TO VICE PRESIDENT ADAMS.
SENATORS, WHAT'S THE PRESIDENT'S TITLE?
MOST BENIGN HIGHNESS? EXALTED HIGHNESS?
MOST ILLUSTRIOUS AND EXALTED PRESIDENT?
WHY NOT GEORGE IV?
ALSO PRESIDENT OF THE SENATE

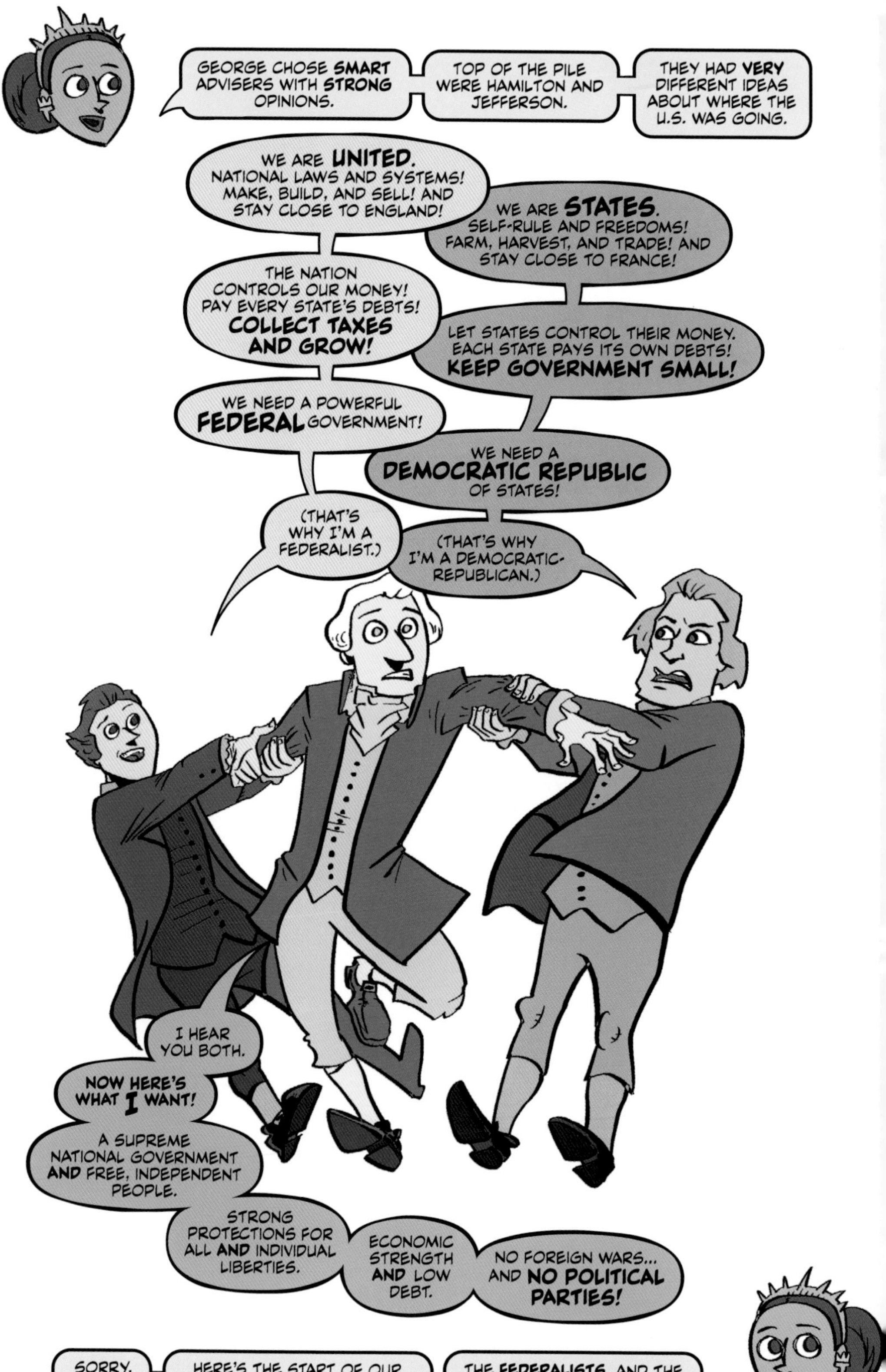
GEORGE CHOSE SMART ADVISERS WITH STRONG OPINIONS.
TOP OF THE PILE WERE HAMILTON AND JEFFERSON.
THEY HAD VERY DIFFERENT IDEAS ABOUT WHERE THE U.S. WAS GOING.
WE ARE UNITED. NATIONAL LAWS AND SYSTEMS! MAKE, BUILD, AND SELL! AND STAY CLOSE TO ENGLAND!
WE ARE STATES. SELF-RULE AND FREEDOMS! FARM, HARVEST, AND TRADE! AND STAY CLOSE TO FRANCE!
THE NATION CONTROLS OUR MONEY! PAY EVERY STATE'S DEBTS! COLLECT TAXES AND GROW!
LET STATES CONTROL THEIR MONEY. EACH STATE PAYS ITS OWN DEBTS! KEEP GOVERNMENT SMALL!
WE NEED A POWERFUL FEDERAL GOVERNMENT!
WE NEED A DEMOCRATIC REPUBLIC OF STATES!
(THAT'S WHY I'M A FEDERALIST.)
(THAT'S WHY I'M A DEMOCRATIC-REPUBLICAN.)
I HEAR YOU BOTH.
NOW HERE'S WHAT I WANT!
A SUPREME NATIONAL GOVERNMENT AND FREE, INDEPENDENT PEOPLE.
STRONG PROTECTIONS FOR ALL AND INDIVIDUAL LIBERTIES.
ECONOMIC STRENGTH AND LOW DEBT.
NO FOREIGN WARS... AND NO POLITICAL PARTIES!
SORRY, GEORGE.
HERE'S THE START OF OUR FIRST TWO POLITICAL PARTIES.
THE FEDERALISTS, AND THE DEMOCRATIC-REPUBLICANS.

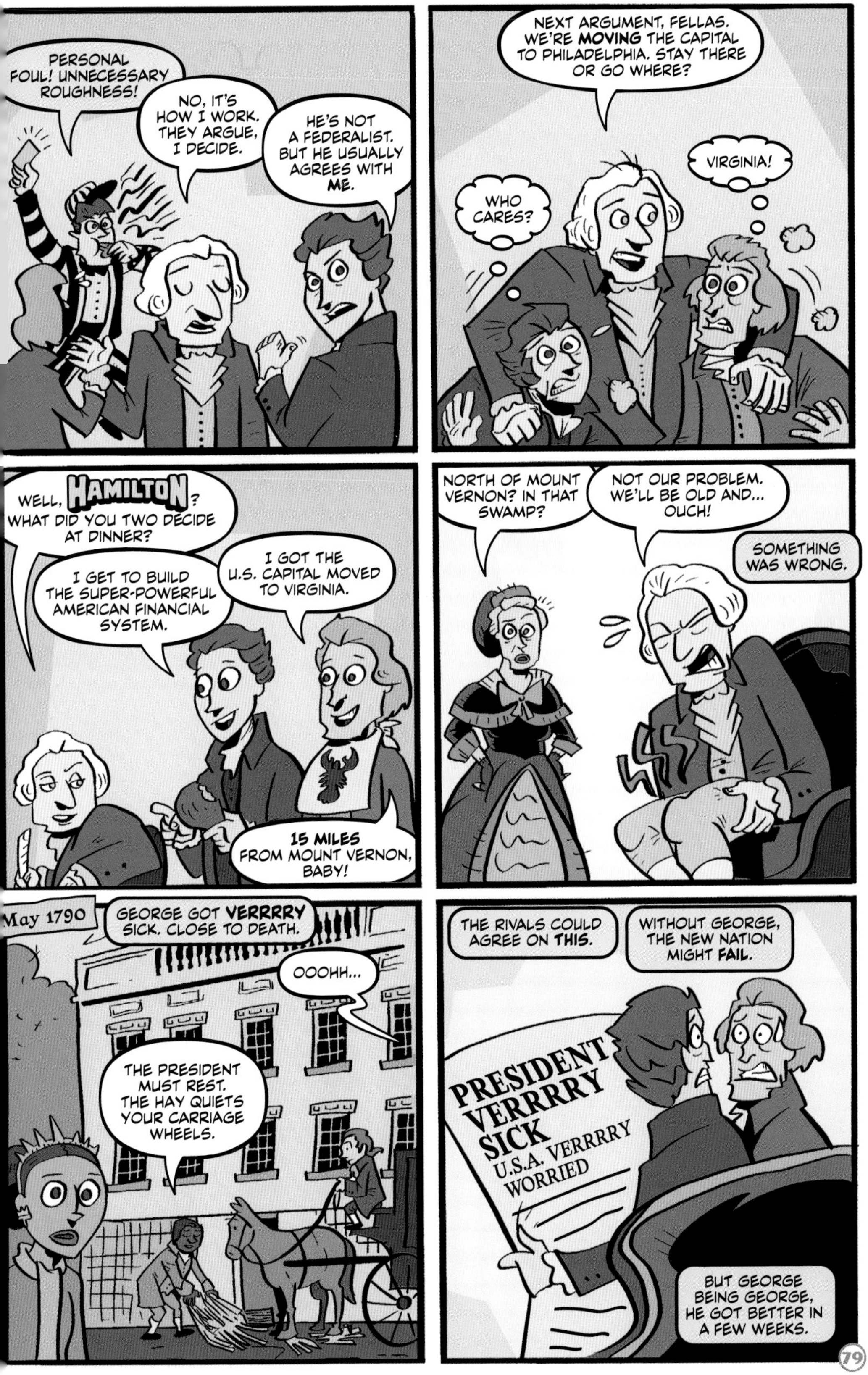
PERSONAL FOUL! UNNECESSARY ROUGHNESS!
NO, IT'S HOW I WORK. THEY ARGUE, I DECIDE.
HE'S NOT A FEDERALIST. BUT HE USUALLY AGREES WITH **ME.**
NEXT ARGUMENT, FELLAS. WE'RE **MOVING** THE CAPITAL TO PHILADELPHIA. STAY THERE OR GO WHERE?
WHO CARES?
VIRGINIA!
WELL, HAMILTON? WHAT DID YOU TWO DECIDE AT DINNER?
I GET TO BUILD THE SUPER-POWERFUL AMERICAN FINANCIAL SYSTEM.
I GOT THE U.S. CAPITAL MOVED TO VIRGINIA.
15 MILES FROM MOUNT VERNON, BABY!
NORTH OF MOUNT VERNON? IN THAT SWAMP?
NOT OUR PROBLEM. WE'LL BE OLD AND... OUCH!
SOMETHING WAS WRONG.
May 1790
GEORGE GOT **VERRRRY** SICK. CLOSE TO DEATH.
OOOHH...
THE PRESIDENT MUST REST. THE HAY QUIETS YOUR CARRIAGE WHEELS.
THE RIVALS COULD AGREE ON **THIS.**
WITHOUT GEORGE, THE NEW NATION MIGHT **FAIL.**
PRESIDENT VERRRRY SICK
U.S.A. VERRRRY WORRIED
BUT GEORGE BEING GEORGE, HE GOT BETTER IN A FEW WEEKS.

1791
Philadelphia

PHILADELPHIA WANTED THE GOVERNMENT TO STAY FOREVER.

PHILADELPHIA?
A Capital Idea!

WE'VE DONE THIS BEFORE. STAY!

PLEEEEZ? WE'LL BUILD YOU A **MANSION**!

YOU DON'T WANT TO LIVE IN A SWAMP!

THE **NEXT** GUY WILL LIVE IN A SWAMP.

LOOK AT **THIS** EXECUTIVE MANSION I'VE BEEN WORKING ON WITH PIERRE.

I'M THINKING WHITE.

PIERRE L'ENFANT, THE FRENCH ENGINEER DESIGNING THE NEW FEDERAL **CITY OF WASHINGTON**.

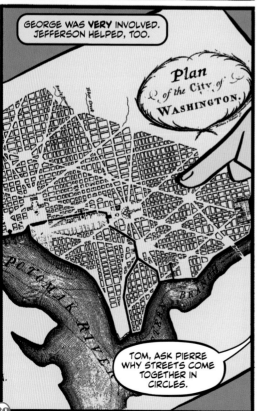

GEORGE WAS **VERY** INVOLVED. JEFFERSON HELPED, TOO.

Plan
of the City of
WASHINGTON.

TOM, ASK PIERRE WHY STREETS COME TOGETHER IN CIRCLES.

IF AN ARMY ATTACKS, THE SOLDIERS CAN DEFEND FROM EACH CIRCLE.

EXCELLENT!

WHY CALL IT **DISTRICT OF COLUMBIA**?

A DISTRICT ISN'T PART OF ANY STATE. IT WAS NAMED AFTER CHRISTOPHER COLUMBUS.

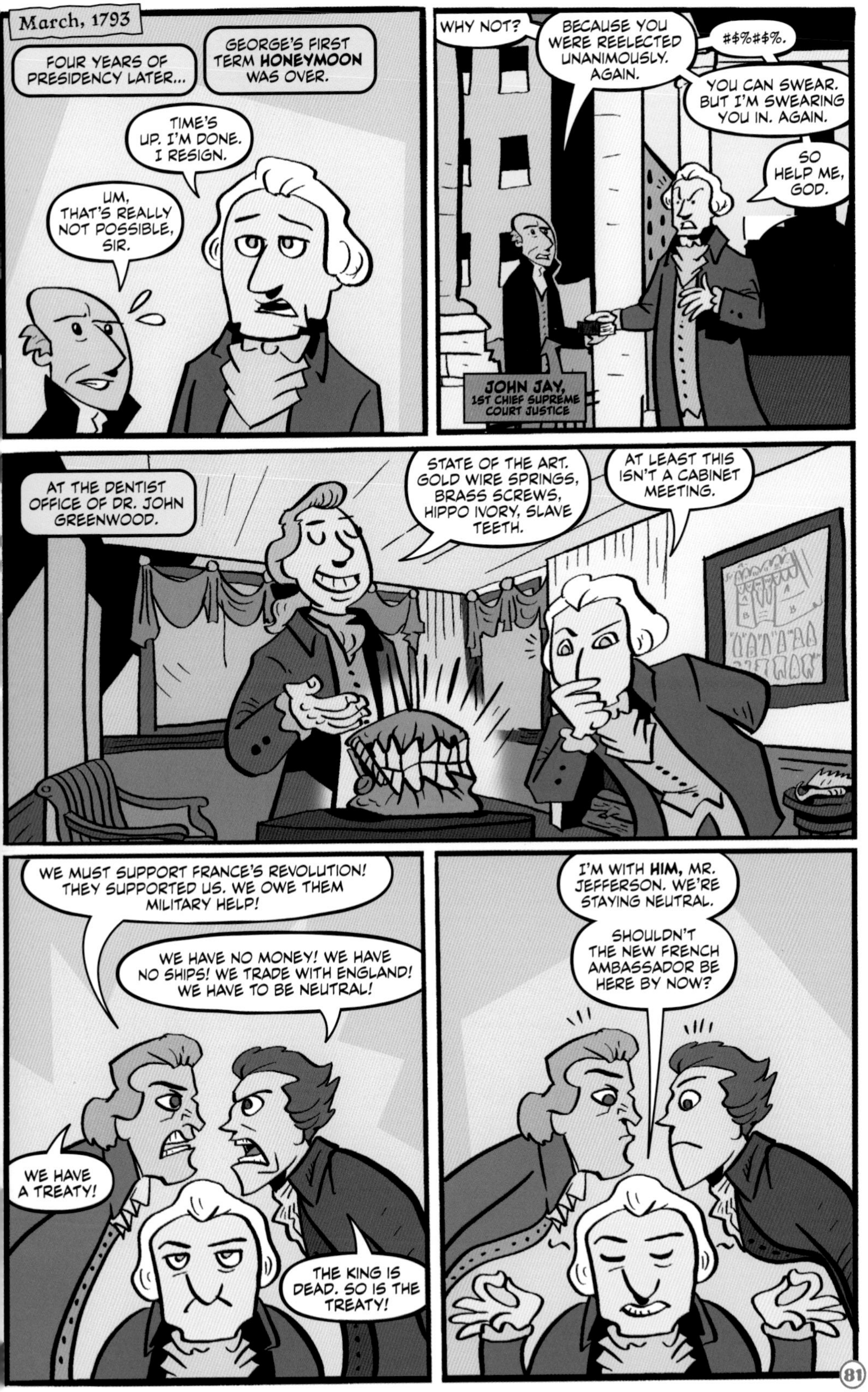
March, 1793
FOUR YEARS OF PRESIDENCY LATER...
GEORGE'S FIRST TERM HONEYMOON WAS OVER.
TIME'S UP. I'M DONE. I RESIGN.
UM, THAT'S REALLY NOT POSSIBLE, SIR.
WHY NOT?
BECAUSE YOU WERE REELECTED UNANIMOUSLY. AGAIN.
#$%#$%.
YOU CAN SWEAR. BUT I'M SWEARING YOU IN. AGAIN.
SO HELP ME, GOD.
JOHN JAY, 1ST CHIEF SUPREME COURT JUSTICE
AT THE DENTIST OFFICE OF DR. JOHN GREENWOOD.
STATE OF THE ART. GOLD WIRE SPRINGS, BRASS SCREWS, HIPPO IVORY, SLAVE TEETH.
AT LEAST THIS ISN'T A CABINET MEETING.
WE MUST SUPPORT FRANCE'S REVOLUTION! THEY SUPPORTED US. WE OWE THEM MILITARY HELP!
WE HAVE NO MONEY! WE HAVE NO SHIPS! WE TRADE WITH ENGLAND! WE HAVE TO BE NEUTRAL!
WE HAVE A TREATY!
THE KING IS DEAD. SO IS THE TREATY!
I'M WITH HIM, MR. JEFFERSON. WE'RE STAYING NEUTRAL.
SHOULDN'T THE NEW FRENCH AMBASSADOR BE HERE BY NOW?

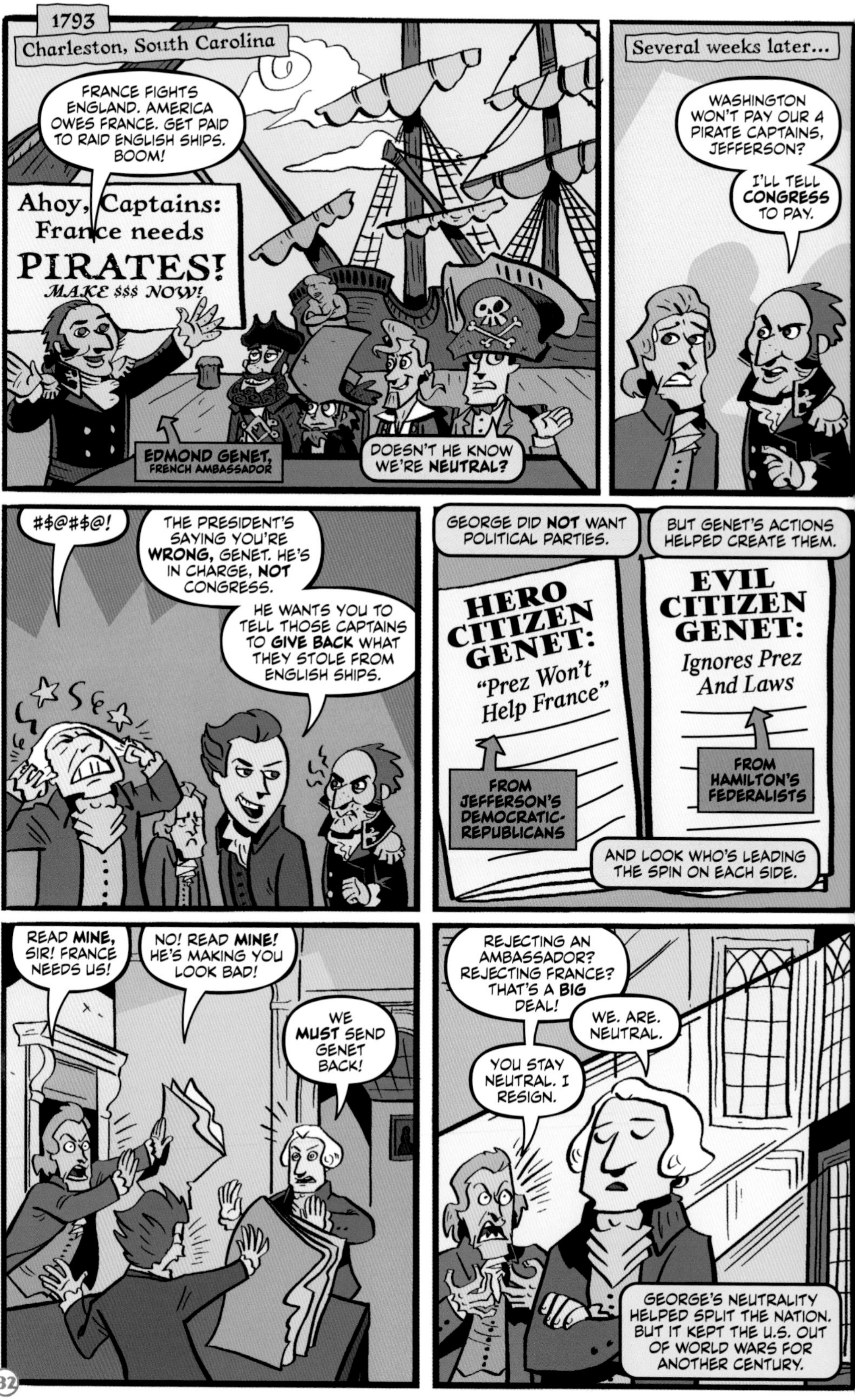
1793
Charleston, South Carolina
FRANCE FIGHTS ENGLAND. AMERICA OWES FRANCE. GET PAID TO RAID ENGLISH SHIPS. BOOM!
Ahoy, Captains: France needs PIRATES! MAKE $$$ NOW!
EDMOND GENET, FRENCH AMBASSADOR
DOESN'T HE KNOW WE'RE NEUTRAL?
Several weeks later...
WASHINGTON WON'T PAY OUR 4 PIRATE CAPTAINS, JEFFERSON?
I'LL TELL CONGRESS TO PAY.
#$@#$@!
THE PRESIDENT'S SAYING YOU'RE WRONG, GENET. HE'S IN CHARGE, NOT CONGRESS.
HE WANTS YOU TO TELL THOSE CAPTAINS TO GIVE BACK WHAT THEY STOLE FROM ENGLISH SHIPS.
GEORGE DID NOT WANT POLITICAL PARTIES.
BUT GENET'S ACTIONS HELPED CREATE THEM.
HERO CITIZEN GENET: "Prez Won't Help France"
FROM JEFFERSON'S DEMOCRATIC-REPUBLICANS
EVIL CITIZEN GENET: Ignores Prez And Laws
FROM HAMILTON'S FEDERALISTS
AND LOOK WHO'S LEADING THE SPIN ON EACH SIDE.
READ MINE, SIR! FRANCE NEEDS US!
NO! READ MINE! HE'S MAKING YOU LOOK BAD!
WE MUST SEND GENET BACK!
REJECTING AN AMBASSADOR? REJECTING FRANCE? THAT'S A BIG DEAL!
WE. ARE. NEUTRAL.
YOU STAY NEUTRAL. I RESIGN.
GEORGE'S NEUTRALITY HELPED SPLIT THE NATION. BUT IT KEPT THE U.S. OUT OF WORLD WARS FOR ANOTHER CENTURY.

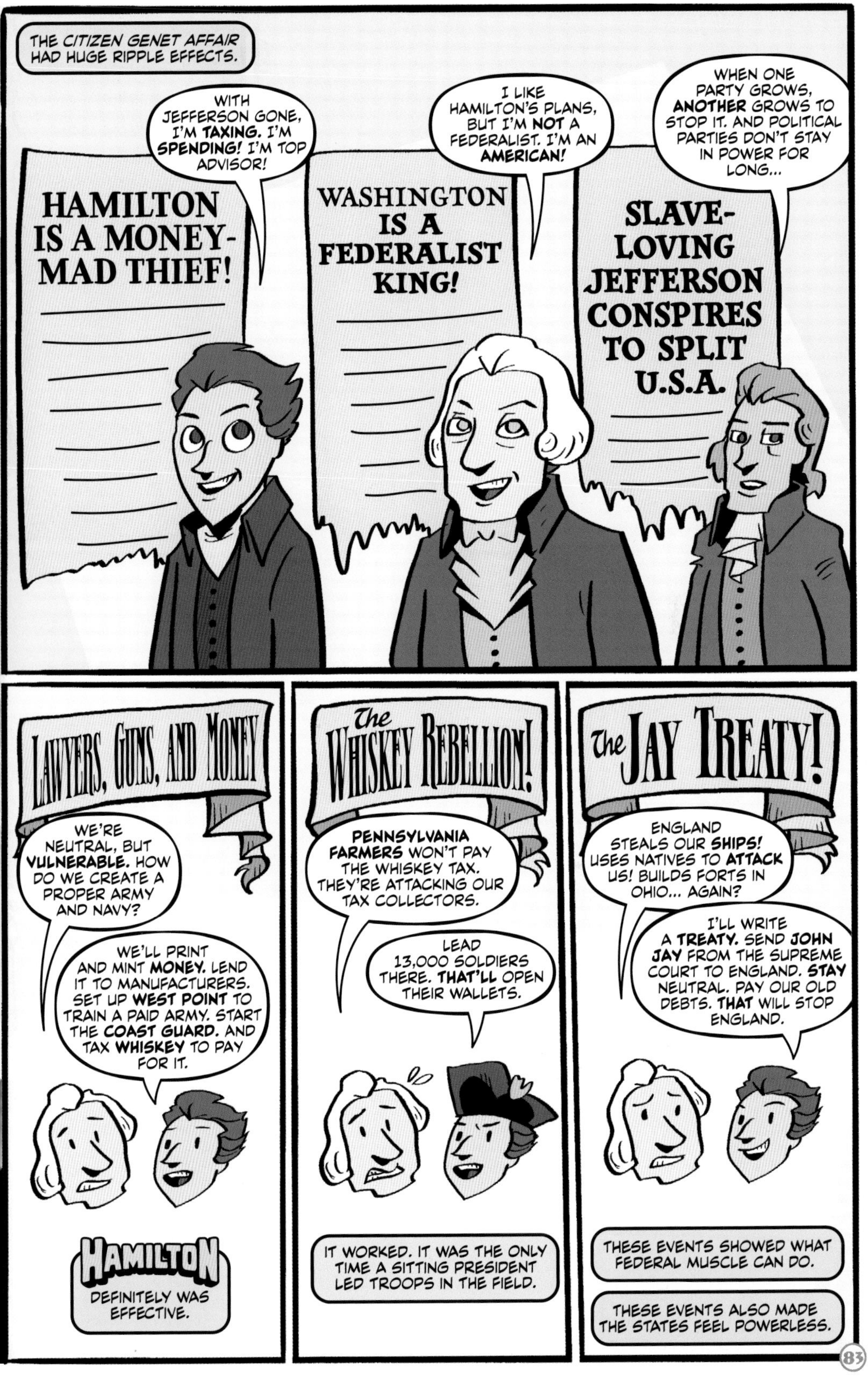
THE CITIZEN GENET AFFAIR HAD HUGE RIPPLE EFFECTS.
WITH JEFFERSON GONE, I'M TAXING. I'M SPENDING! I'M TOP ADVISOR!
HAMILTON IS A MONEY-MAD THIEF!
I LIKE HAMILTON'S PLANS, BUT I'M NOT A FEDERALIST. I'M AN AMERICAN!
WASHINGTON IS A FEDERALIST KING!
WHEN ONE PARTY GROWS, ANOTHER GROWS TO STOP IT. AND POLITICAL PARTIES DON'T STAY IN POWER FOR LONG...
SLAVE-LOVING JEFFERSON CONSPIRES TO SPLIT U.S.A.
LAWYERS, GUNS, AND MONEY
WE'RE NEUTRAL, BUT VULNERABLE. HOW DO WE CREATE A PROPER ARMY AND NAVY?
WE'LL PRINT AND MINT MONEY. LEND IT TO MANUFACTURERS. SET UP WEST POINT TO TRAIN A PAID ARMY. START THE COAST GUARD. AND TAX WHISKEY TO PAY FOR IT.
HAMILTON
DEFINITELY WAS EFFECTIVE.
The WHISKEY REBELLION!
PENNSYLVANIA FARMERS WON'T PAY THE WHISKEY TAX. THEY'RE ATTACKING OUR TAX COLLECTORS.
LEAD 13,000 SOLDIERS THERE. THAT'LL OPEN THEIR WALLETS.
IT WORKED. IT WAS THE ONLY TIME A SITTING PRESIDENT LED TROOPS IN THE FIELD.
The JAY TREATY!
ENGLAND STEALS OUR SHIPS! USES NATIVES TO ATTACK US! BUILDS FORTS IN OHIO... AGAIN?
I'LL WRITE A TREATY. SEND JOHN JAY FROM THE SUPREME COURT TO ENGLAND. STAY NEUTRAL. PAY OUR OLD DEBTS. THAT WILL STOP ENGLAND.
THESE EVENTS SHOWED WHAT FEDERAL MUSCLE CAN DO.
THESE EVENTS ALSO MADE THE STATES FEEL POWERLESS.

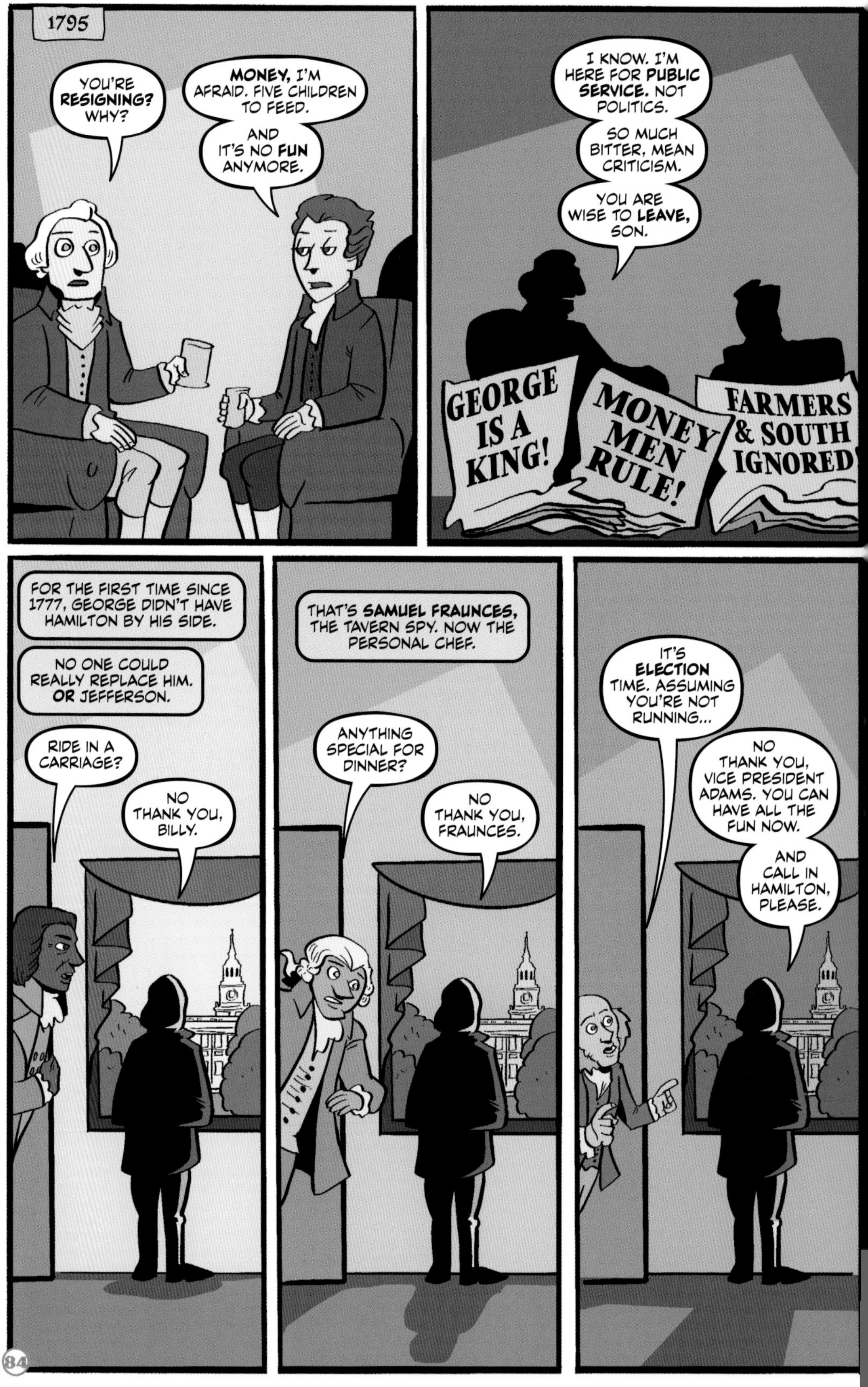
1795
YOU'RE RESIGNING? WHY?
MONEY, I'M AFRAID. FIVE CHILDREN TO FEED.
AND IT'S NO FUN ANYMORE.
I KNOW. I'M HERE FOR PUBLIC SERVICE. NOT POLITICS.
SO MUCH BITTER, MEAN CRITICISM.
YOU ARE WISE TO LEAVE, SON.
GEORGE IS A KING!
MONEY MEN RULE!
FARMERS & SOUTH IGNORED
FOR THE FIRST TIME SINCE 1777, GEORGE DIDN'T HAVE HAMILTON BY HIS SIDE.
NO ONE COULD REALLY REPLACE HIM. OR JEFFERSON.
RIDE IN A CARRIAGE?
NO THANK YOU, BILLY.
THAT'S SAMUEL FRAUNCES, THE TAVERN SPY. NOW THE PERSONAL CHEF.
ANYTHING SPECIAL FOR DINNER?
NO THANK YOU, FRAUNCES.
IT'S ELECTION TIME. ASSUMING YOU'RE NOT RUNNING...
NO THANK YOU, VICE PRESIDENT ADAMS. YOU CAN HAVE ALL THE FUN NOW.
AND CALL IN HAMILTON, PLEASE.

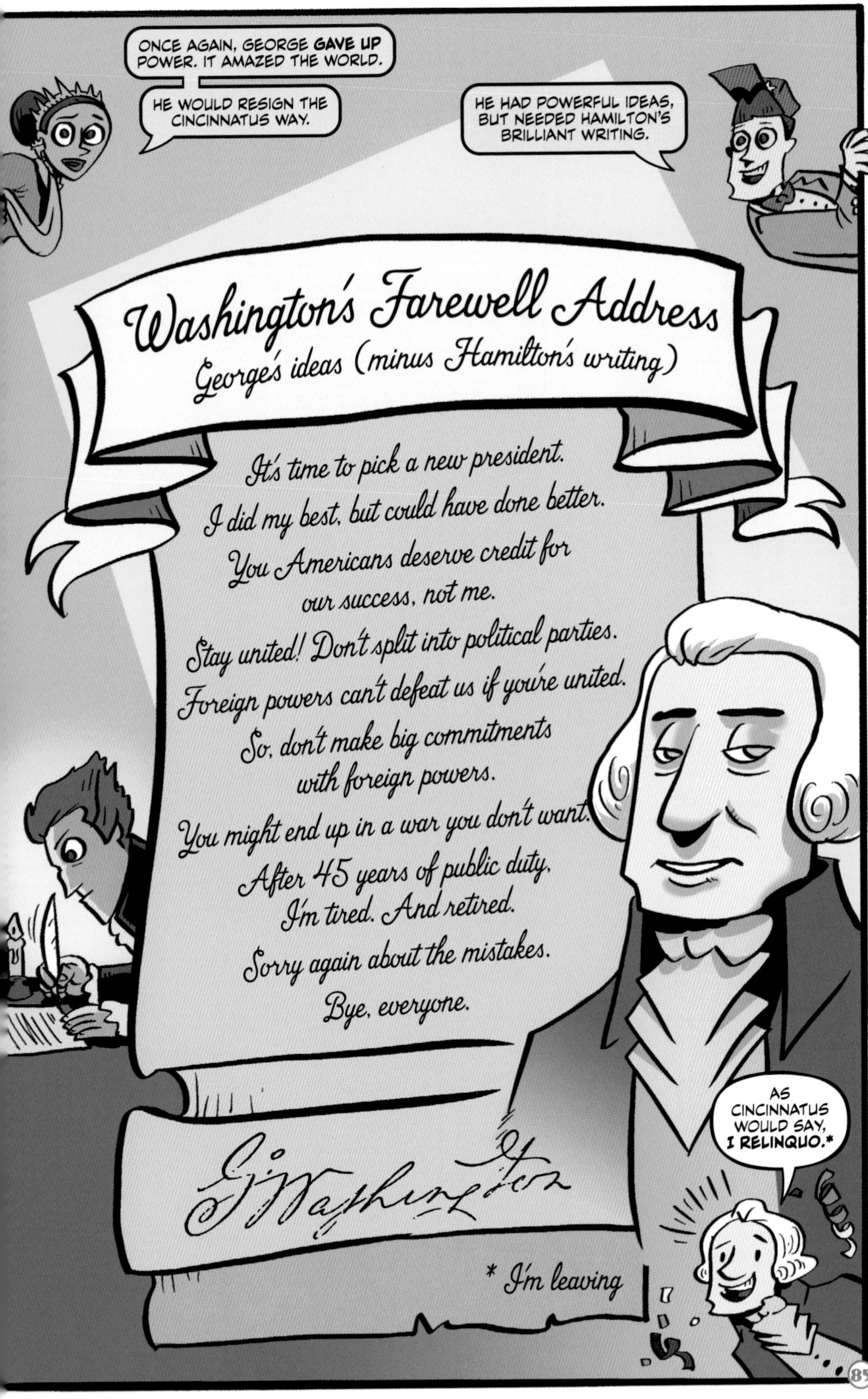

ONCE AGAIN, GEORGE GAVE UP POWER. IT AMAZED THE WORLD.
HE WOULD RESIGN THE CINCINNATUS WAY.
HE HAD POWERFUL IDEAS, BUT NEEDED HAMILTON'S BRILLIANT WRITING.
Washington's Farewell Address
George's ideas (minus Hamilton's writing)
It's time to pick a new president.
I did my best, but could have done better.
You Americans deserve credit for our success, not me.
Stay united! Don't split into political parties.
Foreign powers can't defeat us if you're united.
So, don't make big commitments with foreign powers.
You might end up in a war you don't want.
After 45 years of public duty, I'm tired. And retired.
Sorry again about the mistakes.
Bye, everyone.
G. Washington
* I'm leaving
AS CINCINNATUS WOULD SAY, I RELINQUO.*

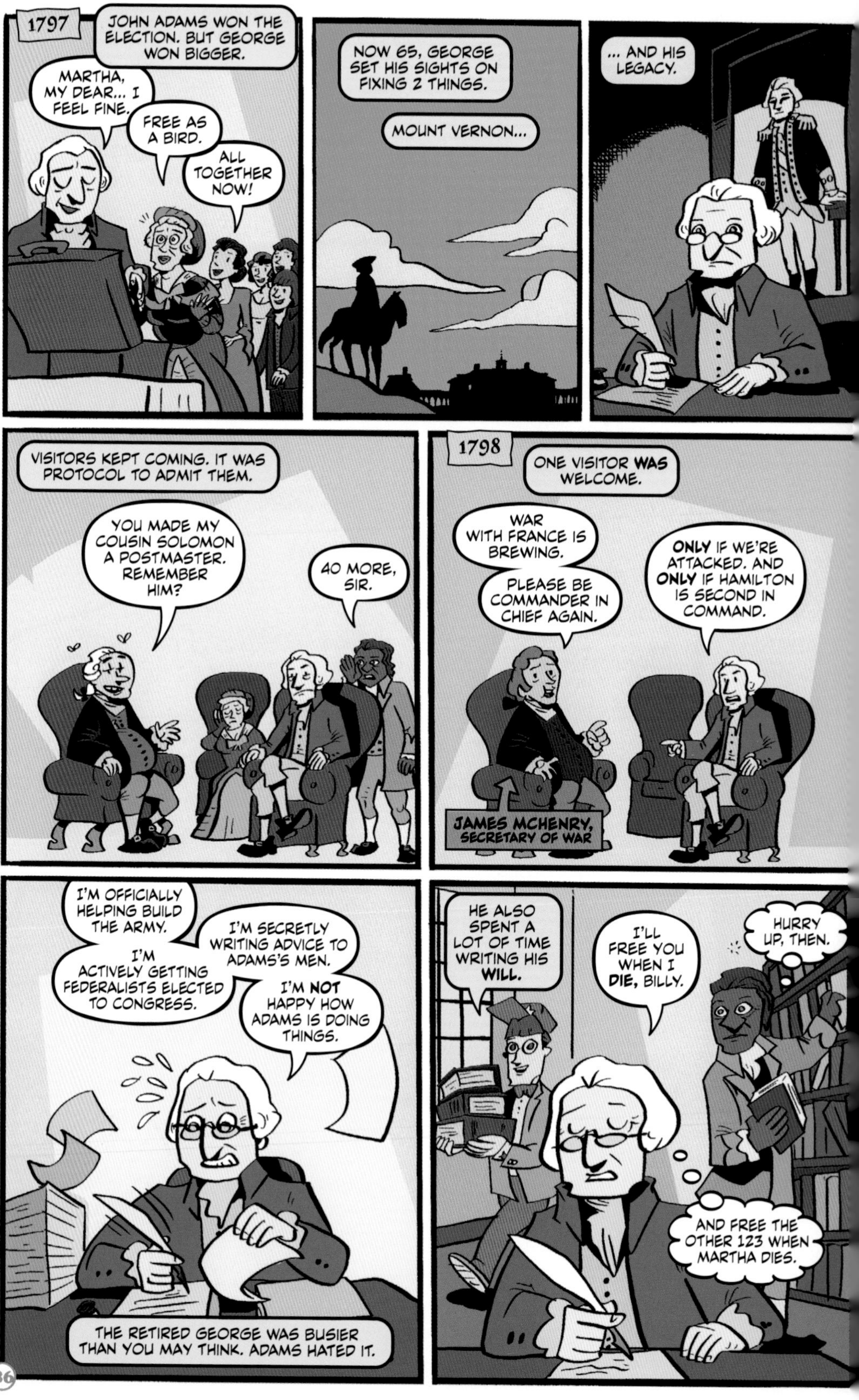
1797
JOHN ADAMS WON THE ELECTION. BUT GEORGE WON BIGGER.
MARTHA, MY DEAR... I FEEL FINE.
FREE AS A BIRD.
ALL TOGETHER NOW!
NOW 65, GEORGE SET HIS SIGHTS ON FIXING 2 THINGS.
MOUNT VERNON...
... AND HIS LEGACY.
VISITORS KEPT COMING. IT WAS PROTOCOL TO ADMIT THEM.
YOU MADE MY COUSIN SOLOMON A POSTMASTER. REMEMBER HIM?
40 MORE, SIR.
1798
ONE VISITOR **WAS** WELCOME.
WAR WITH FRANCE IS BREWING.
PLEASE BE COMMANDER IN CHIEF AGAIN.
ONLY IF WE'RE ATTACKED. AND **ONLY** IF HAMILTON IS SECOND IN COMMAND.
JAMES MCHENRY, SECRETARY OF WAR
I'M OFFICIALLY HELPING BUILD THE ARMY.
I'M SECRETLY WRITING ADVICE TO ADAMS'S MEN.
I'M ACTIVELY GETTING FEDERALISTS ELECTED TO CONGRESS.
I'M **NOT** HAPPY HOW ADAMS IS DOING THINGS.
THE RETIRED GEORGE WAS BUSIER THAN YOU MAY THINK. ADAMS HATED IT.
HE ALSO SPENT A LOT OF TIME WRITING HIS **WILL.**
I'LL FREE YOU WHEN I **DIE,** BILLY.
HURRY UP, THEN.
AND FREE THE OTHER 123 WHEN MARTHA DIES.

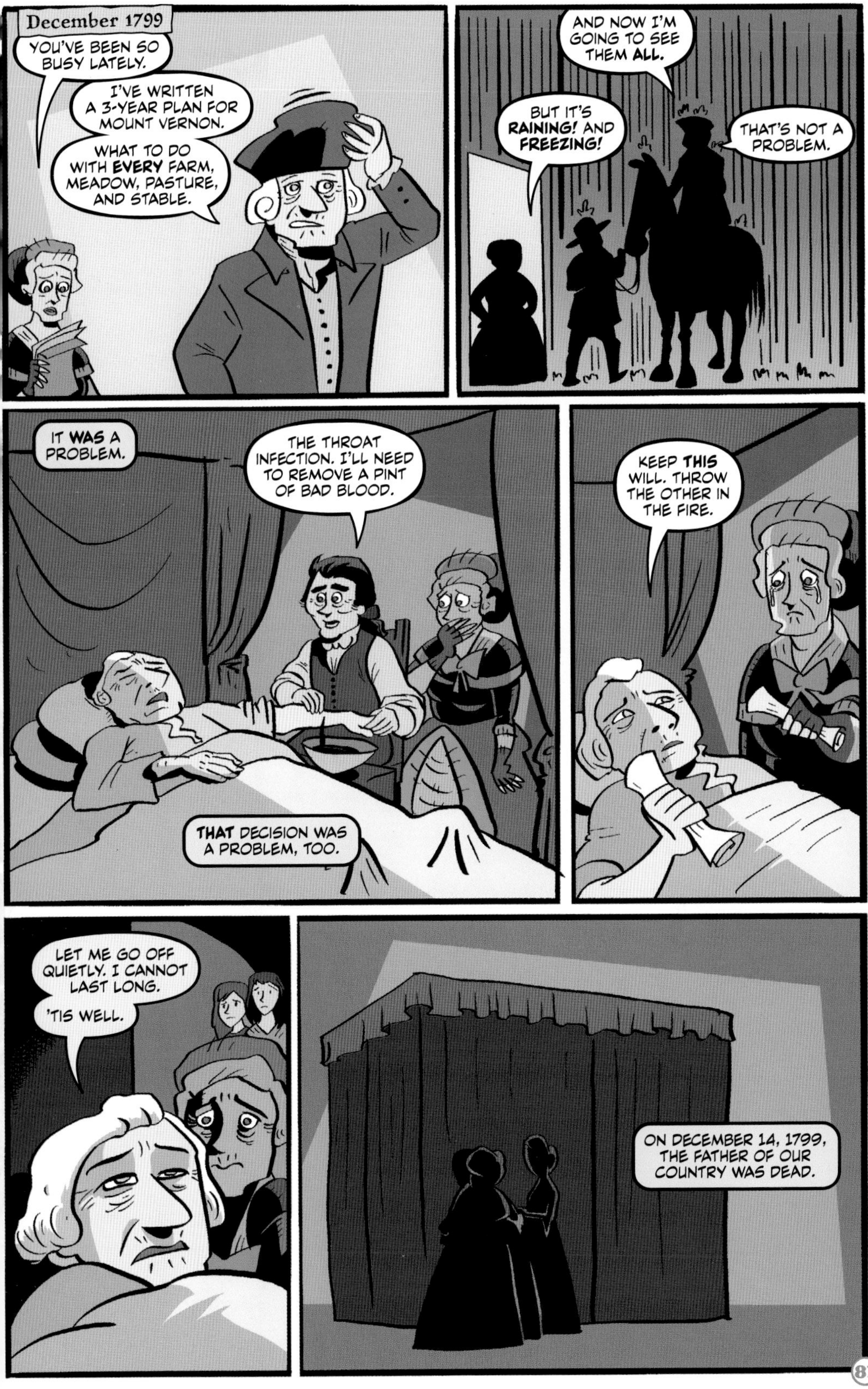
December 1799
YOU'VE BEEN SO BUSY LATELY.
I'VE WRITTEN A 3-YEAR PLAN FOR MOUNT VERNON.
WHAT TO DO WITH EVERY FARM, MEADOW, PASTURE, AND STABLE.
AND NOW I'M GOING TO SEE THEM ALL.
BUT IT'S RAINING! AND FREEZING!
THAT'S NOT A PROBLEM.
IT WAS A PROBLEM.
THE THROAT INFECTION. I'LL NEED TO REMOVE A PINT OF BAD BLOOD.
THAT DECISION WAS A PROBLEM, TOO.
KEEP THIS WILL. THROW THE OTHER IN THE FIRE.
LET ME GO OFF QUIETLY. I CANNOT LAST LONG.
'TIS WELL.
ON DECEMBER 14, 1799, THE FATHER OF OUR COUNTRY WAS DEAD.

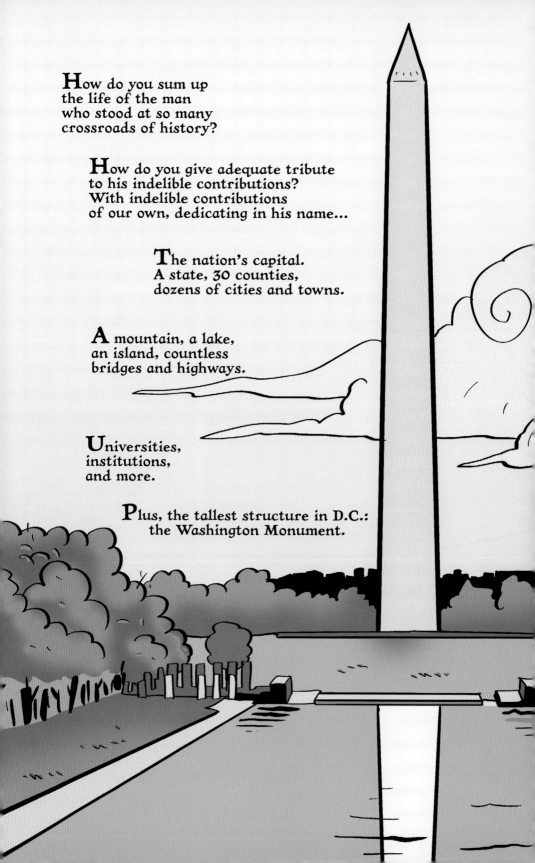

How do you sum up
the life of the man
who stood at so many
crossroads of history?

How do you give adequate tribute
to his indelible contributions?
With indelible contributions
of our own, dedicating in his name...

The nation's capital.
A state, 30 counties,
dozens of cities and towns.

A mountain, a lake,
an island, countless
bridges and highways.

Universities,
institutions,
and more.

Plus, the tallest structure in D.C.:
the Washington Monument.

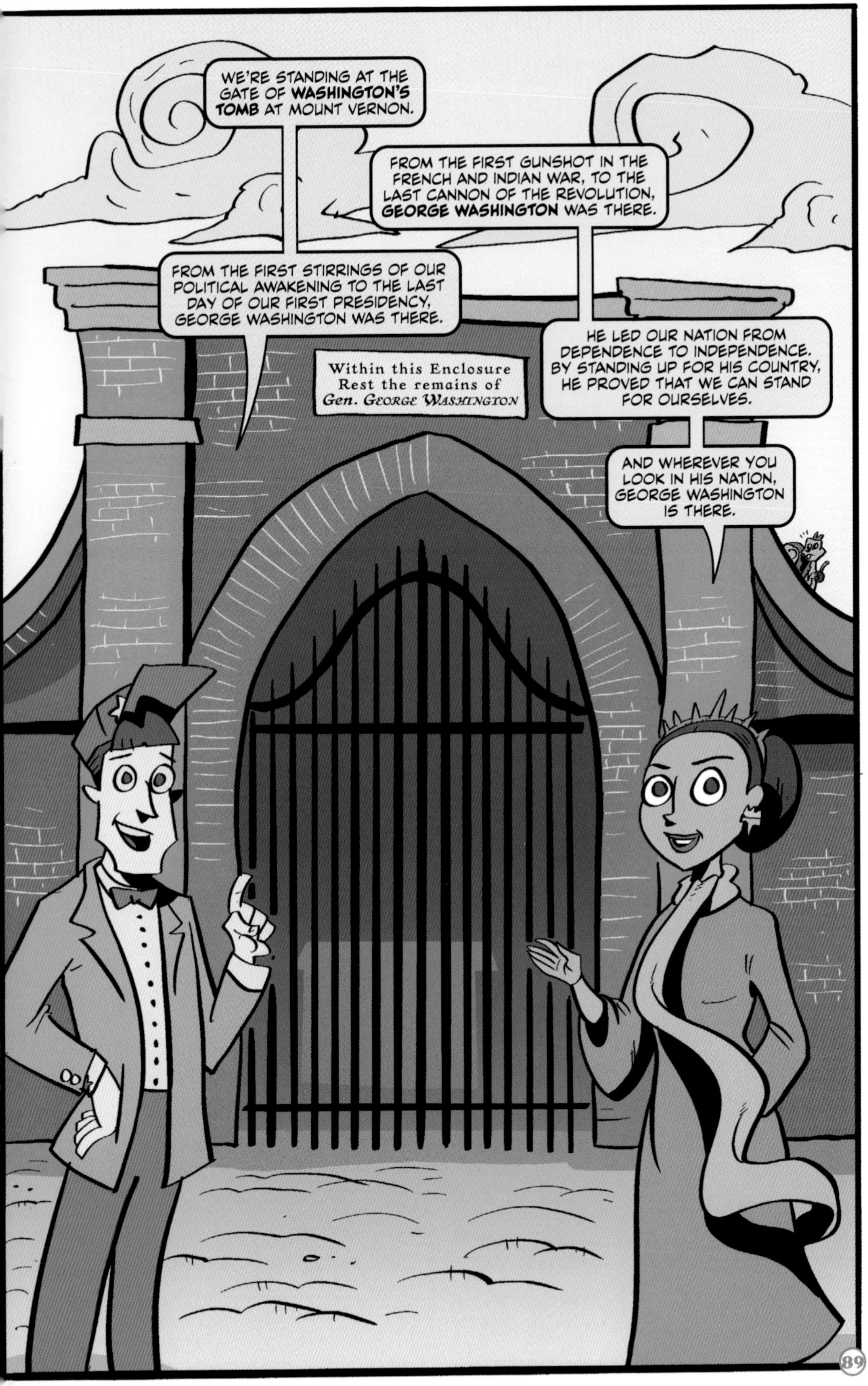
WE'RE STANDING AT THE GATE OF WASHINGTON'S TOMB AT MOUNT VERNON.
FROM THE FIRST STIRRINGS OF OUR POLITICAL AWAKENING TO THE LAST DAY OF OUR FIRST PRESIDENCY, GEORGE WASHINGTON WAS THERE.
FROM THE FIRST GUNSHOT IN THE FRENCH AND INDIAN WAR, TO THE LAST CANNON OF THE REVOLUTION, GEORGE WASHINGTON WAS THERE.
Within this Enclosure Rest the remains of Gen. George Washington
HE LED OUR NATION FROM DEPENDENCE TO INDEPENDENCE. BY STANDING UP FOR HIS COUNTRY, HE PROVED THAT WE CAN STAND FOR OURSELVES.
AND WHEREVER YOU LOOK IN HIS NATION, GEORGE WASHINGTON IS THERE.

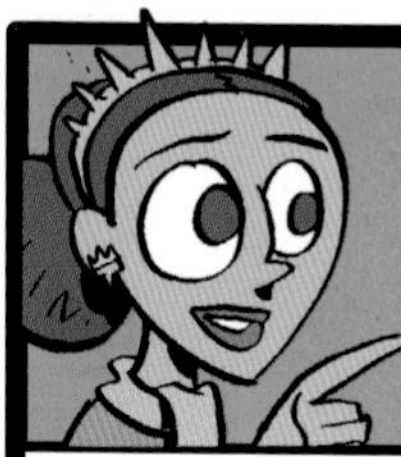

DID YOU KNOW??

MISTER MYTH GOES TO WASHINGTON

If there were an award for Most Myths Told (About), the winner would be George. Here are a few you may have heard. None are true.

GEORGE CHOPPED DOWN A CHERRY TREE AND SAID **"I CAN'T TELL A LIE, I DID IT."**

This supposedly happened the day he got a hatchet, at six. Even if his father asked which very short person cut down a tree near the house, the evidence was huge. Don't give George too much credit for confessing.

GEORGE HAD WOODEN TEETH.

No, but he sure had dentures. His fake teeth were made from metal, hippo ivory, animal teeth, and slave teeth. George liked wine, which stains old teeth, giving an appearance of wood.

GEORGE ASKED BETSY ROSS TO SEW THE FIRST FLAG.

There's no evidence that George commissioned a flag, and if he had, it wasn't with Betsy. This story was started a hundred years later… by her descendants.

GEORGE ONCE SKIPPED A SILVER DOLLAR ACROSS THE POTOMAC RIVER.

1. The Potomac is a mile wide.
2. There were no silver dollars until he was 62.
3. He once threw a piece of slate across a much, much, much narrower river. Was that what they meant?

GEORGE WAS A VICTORIOUS GENERAL.

Nope. He lost many more battles than he won.

GEORGE WAS BORN AT MOUNT VERNON, LIVED IN THE WHITE HOUSE, AND IS BURIED UNDER THE CAPITOL.

He was born on a tobacco farm in Virginia. The White House wasn't finished until he died. And his tomb is above ground at Mount Vernon.

Source: MountVernon.org

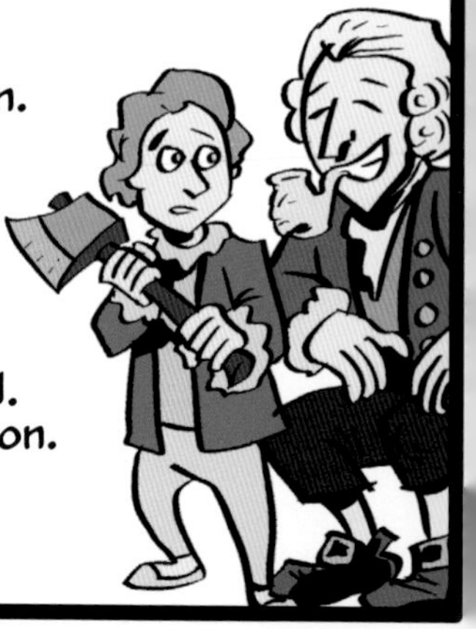

GEORGE WASHINGTON TIMELINE

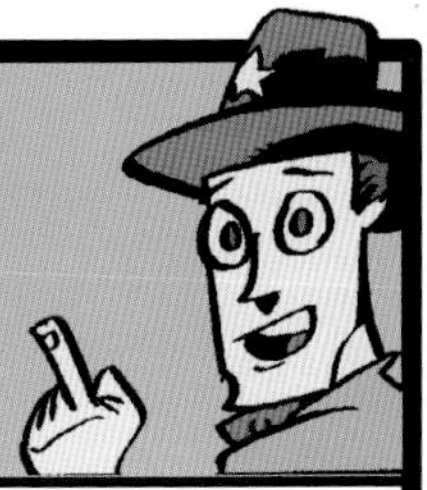

1732 George is born to Augustine and Mary Washington, on a tobacco farm in Virginia.

1738 The Washingtons move to nearby Ferry Farm.

1743 Augustine dies. George's formal education ends. His older brother Lawrence becomes a mentor.

1749 Appointed county surveyor of Culpeper County, VA.

1751-1752 Travels to Barbados with Lawrence, who is ill. George gets smallpox. After Lawrence dies, moves to Mount Vernon.

1753 As a Major in the Virginia militia, sent to Ohio Valley, demands the French leave. Fails.

1754 Returns with 150 soldiers, fails even worse. Accidentally starts French and Indian War.

1755 Returns with 1,300 soldiers, recognized for bravery in battle, given command of entire Virginia military force.

1759 Marries wealthy widow, Martha Dandridge Custis, mother of Jacky and Patsy. They move to Mount Vernon. Joins Virginia legislature.

1775 Appointed commander of the Continental Army. Revolutionary War begins.

1781 With much French help, captures 5,000 British troops at Yorktown, VA. British surrender, war ends.

1783 Resigns command of U.S. military, a remarkable act that makes him a hero. Returns to plantation life.

1787 Unanimously elected president of the Constitutional Convention.

1789 Unanimously elected President of the United States.

1793 Unanimously re-elected President of the United States. There's a pattern here.

1797 Returns to Mount Vernon, and mostly avoids politics.

1799 Dies on December 14 from a throat infection.

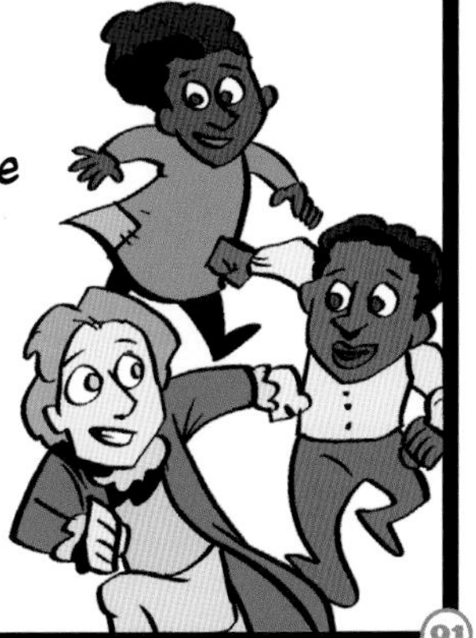

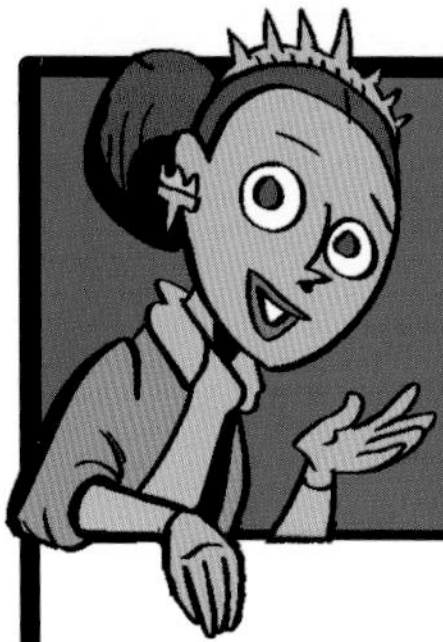

GLOSSARY

AMEND: To alter or add. Amendments are additions to the U.S. Constitution.

BOYCOTT: An organized plan to force change by not buying or using a product or service.

BURGESS: An old term for a member of a legislature. The House of Burgesses was Virginia's colonial congress.

CINCINNATUS / CINCINNATI: Related to Lucius Cincinnatus, the Roman general and leader who surrendered power to return to farming.

PROTOCOLS: Customs or formalities that a society follows.

RATIFY: To vote to approve or confirm a formal agreement, like the Constitution.

SCUTTLE: To sink a ship intentionally, often to keep an enemy from capturing it.

SURROGATE: Someone who takes the role that another would have. Lawrence was a surrogate father to George.

SURVEY/SURVEYOR: To survey is to study and create a detailed view of something, specifically land. A person doing this is a surveyor.

UNANIMOUS: Accepted with complete agreement by everyone involved.

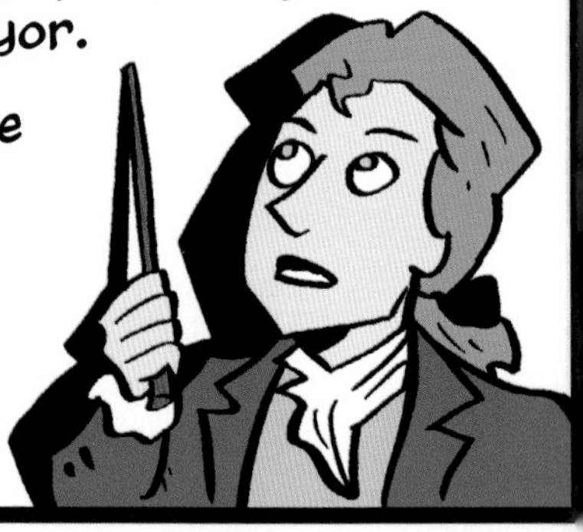

FURTHER INFO

BOOKS

Allen, Thomas B. *George Washington, Spymaster: How the Americans Outspied the British and Won the Revolutionary War.* Washington, D.C.: National Geographic Children's Books, 2004

Chernow, Ron. *Washington: A Life.* New York: Penguin Press, 2010

Edwards, Roberta. *Who Was George Washington?* Who Was? series. New York: Penguin Group, 2009

Foster, Genevieve, and Joanna Foster. *George Washington's World.* Massachusetts: Beautiful Feet Books, 1997

January, Brendan. *George Washington: America's 1st President (Encyclopedia of Presidents Second Series).* New York: Scholastic, 2003

WEBSITES

Mount Vernon: www.mountvernon.org

History.com: www.history.com/topics/us-presidents/george-washington

The Washington Monument: www.nps.gov/wamo

I'M THE FATHER OF MY COUNTRY. SO THAT MAKES THIS POP-CORN!

SHOW ME HISTORY!

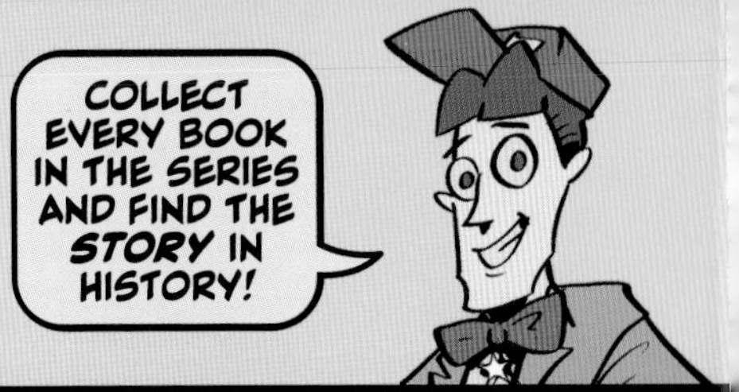

COLLECT EVERY BOOK IN THE SERIES AND FIND THE STORY IN HISTORY!

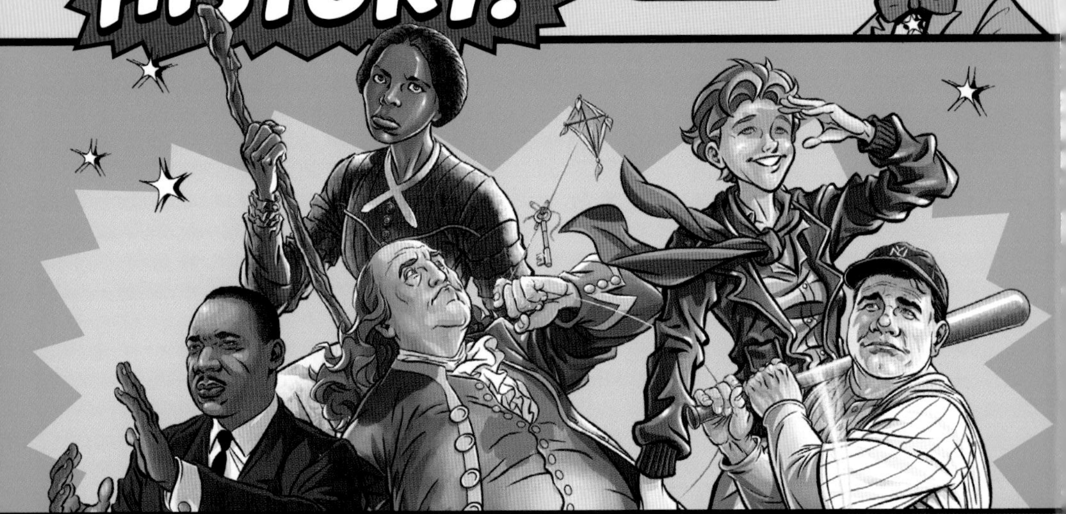

ABRAHAM LINCOLN
DEFENDER OF THE UNION!

ALEXANDER HAMILTON
THE FIGHTING FOUNDING FATHER!

AMELIA EARHART
PIONEER OF THE SKY!

BABE RUTH
BASEBALL'S ALL-TIME BEST!

BENJAMIN FRANKLIN
INVENTOR OF THE NATION!

GEORGE WASHINGTON
SOLDIER AND STATESMAN!

HARRIET TUBMAN
FIGHTER FOR FREEDOM!

JESUS
MESSENGER OF PEACE!

MARTIN LUTHER KING JR.
VOICE FOR EQUALITY!

MUHAMMAD ALI
THE GREATEST OF ALL TIME!

SACAGAWEA
COURAGEOUS TRAILBLAZER!

SUSAN B. ANTHONY
CHAMPION FOR VOTING RIGHTS!

WALT DISNEY
THE MAGICAL INNOVATOR!

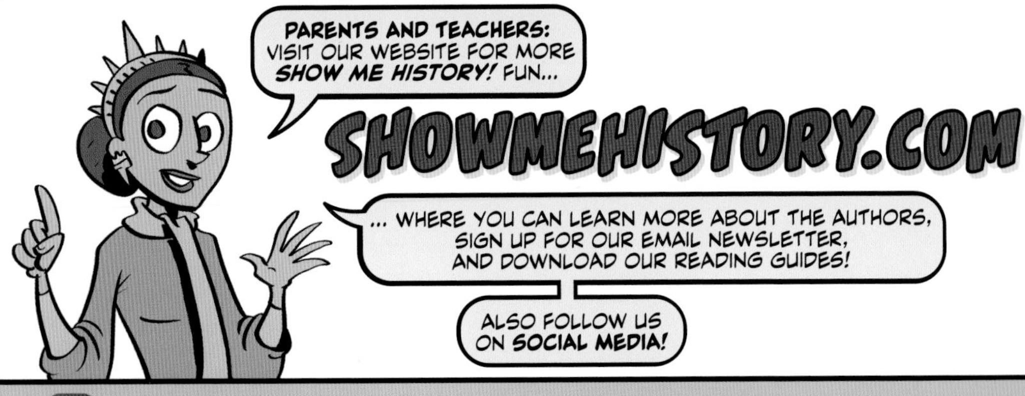

PARENTS AND TEACHERS: VISIT OUR WEBSITE FOR MORE SHOW ME HISTORY! FUN...
SHOWMEHISTORY.COM
... WHERE YOU CAN LEARN MORE ABOUT THE AUTHORS, SIGN UP FOR OUR EMAIL NEWSLETTER, AND DOWNLOAD OUR READING GUIDES!
ALSO FOLLOW US ON SOCIAL MEDIA!

@showmehistorybooks | www.facebook.com/portablepress | www.pinterest.com/portablepress | @portablepress

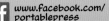

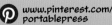

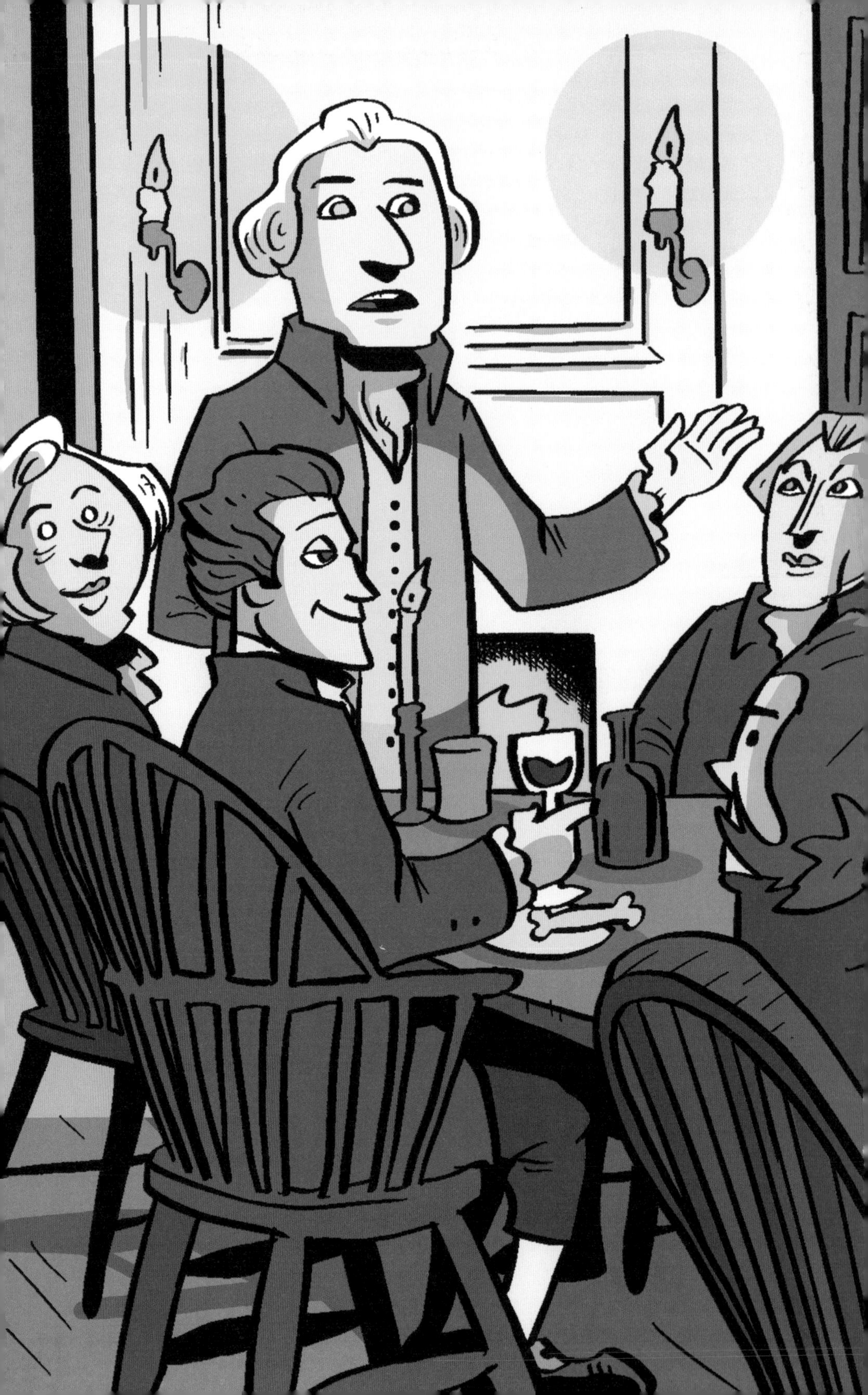